# SPYCRAFT SECRETS

## AN ESPIONAGE A-Z

# NIGEL WEST

The History Press

First published 2016

Paperback edition first published 2017

The History Press
The Mill, Brimscombe Port
Stroud, Gloucestershire, GL5 2QG
www.thehistorypress.co.uk

British Library Cataloguing in Publication Data.
A catalogue record for this book is available from the British
Library.

ISBN 978 0 7509 8375 4

Typeset in 10/13pt Sabon by The History Press
Printed and bound in India by Replika Press Pvt. Ltd.

# CONTENTS

Foreword by David Petraeus, Former Director of the CIA    6

Acknowledgements    9

Acronyms and Abbreviations    10

Introduction    13

Chronology    17

The A to Z of Spycraft    29

# FOREWORD

Good intelligence is rarely stumbled upon by accident. More typically, it is the result of what Nigel West describes in this book as great *spycraft*.

As West explains, good intelligence is, in fact, the product of operations by dedicated, highly trained intelligence professionals with extensive experience, employing solid tradecraft, with exceptional technical support and reliable, secure communications, all after having undertaken thorough planning *and* after carefully weighed the potential risks and rewards. The overall effort is typically overseen by the station chiefs in respective countries, together with their individual operators and chiefs of operations, in consultation with leaders above them, depending on the sensitivity of the operation. They develop and 'wargame' specific plans, striving to ensure preparation for every possible contingency – all while recognising that even the best of plans may not survive contact with an adversary.

Such operations can yield extraordinary insights on the thinking, activities, capabilities, and limitations of a country's adversaries. To be sure, that is not always the case. And some observers of intelligence organisations, unaware of many extraordinary but never revealed achievements, tend to characterise the intelligence agencies' performance by compiling a catalogue of incidents that have gone awry. In part, this is because the most significant intelligence successes are typically not made public for at least a number of decades, as it is important to protect sensitive sources and methods. By contrast, intelligence failures are often immediately evident and remain in newspaper archives forever, ready for use by commentators recalling such failures, often without full appreciation of what may have been accomplished even in those endeavors deemed missteps, much less in those that have gone well.

At the forefront of the intelligence collection architecture is the case officer, the so-called 'core collector' or HUMINT (human intelligence) collector – a highly trained individual who identifies, cultivates, recruits and then handles a human source or carries out a sensitive technical operation in the quest for information that will support pursuit of the foreign policy goals of one's government. Each of the stages of recruitment and handling of human sources entails an element of risk; but, however hazardous, the rewards, in terms of insights and information for policy-makers, can be considerable.

Case officers rarely act on their own and they seldom operate as portrayed in the movies. The lone, intuitive, multi-lingual, Ironman triathlete maverick with bulging muscles is a rarity. More typically, painstaking research, careful relationship building, imaginative initiatives and ingenious choreography – employed by individuals who look like average citizens (though they are not) working together as a team – are the components of a project that, upon fruition, will be so carefully protected that the sources recruited and the methods employed are highly restricted even within the overall organisation, not to mention the rest of government.

The men and women who carry out such operations may, again, *seem* to be typical citizens, but they are not. And the teams they comprise are nothing short of exceptional. I was privileged to be sworn in as the director of the CIA in early September 2011 after some thirty-seven years in uniform. Based on considerable interaction as a military commander with many Agency officers, particularly in the decade after 9/11, I knew the men and women of the Agency were extraordinary. But, on taking the reins as D/CIA, I was struck by just *how* extraordinary the talented, quiet professionals of the Agency really were. Indeed, the skills, commitment, patriotism, expertise, creativity and spirit of camaraderie of the men and women who inhabit that *sub rosa* world were often truly breathtaking as they planned and carried out complex missions in some of the most challenging environments in the world.

Of course, human intelligence involves much more than persuading individuals to act against their natural instincts – or to act on other motivations. In any case, there is a very important human dimension in the conduct of source recruitment, as the case officer builds a bond of mutual trust with a potential high-value asset. Throughout that process, good tradecraft is absolutely essential, as it is what the case officer employs to minimise the danger of compromise while performing particularly sensitive tasks.

The CIA has a proud record, dating back to 1947, of initiating and running to a successful conclusion some truly remarkable enterprises. Occasionally news of such a venture, such as the salvage of a Soviet submarine from the ocean floor, the capture of a notorious terrorist in international waters off Cyprus, the establishment of a backchannel to a pariah, the resettlement of a defector or the rescue of US diplomats from a hostile regime, will seize the headlines and maybe attract the attention of Hollywood. The common denominator in those well-known endeavours, and in many more tightly held operations, is the tradecraft that enabled such operations to be executed while minimising the potential for harm to the participants and political blowback for the governments involved.

The continuing development of the tradecraft employed by intelligence operatives is essential to the conduct of their operations. The reservoir of tradecraft comprises the knowledge and techniques accumulated over many years, in many different territories and cultures, that have been required for professionals in the field to carry out potentially perilous assignments with confidence. And that is *spycraft*, the focus of this book – each episode of which is publicly known, but the compilation of which makes for an enthralling, thrilling read!

General (Ret.) David Petraeus
Former director of the CIA
Arlington, Virginia

# ACKNOWLEDGEMENTS

The author is grateful for the generosity of numerous intelligence professionals, among them Gervase Cowell, Brian Latell, Ray Batvinis, Michael Fox, Keith Melton, Tony and Jonna Mendez, Patrick Magee, Martin McGartland, Oleg Kalugin, Oleg Gordievsky, Dan Mulvenna, Hayden Peake, Mark Williams, Brian Stewart and the late Harry Williamson, Juan Pujol, Tommy Robertson, Ed Wilson, Harry Verlander, Oleg Tsarev and Arthur Martin.

# ACRONYMS AND ABBREVIATIONS

AA        Anti-Aircraft
AVH       Államvédelmi Hatóság (former Hungarian intelligence
          agency)
BfV       Bundesamt für Verfassungsschutz (Federal German
          security service)
BND       Bundesnachrichtendienst (Federal German intelligence
          service)
BRUSA     British–US Communication Intelligence Treaty
BSC       British Security Coordination
CIA       Central Intelligence Agency
CPUSA     Communist Party of the United States of America
DCI       Director of Central Intelligence
DGI       Dirección General de Inteligencia (Cuban intelligence
          service)
DGSE      Direction Générale de la Sécurité Extérieure (French
          intelligence service)
DIA       Defense Intelligence Agency
DIE       Departamentul de Informatii Externe
DO        Directorate of Operations
DS        Darzhavna Sigurnost (former Bulgarian intelligence
          service)
DST       Direction de la Surveillance du Territoire (French security
          service)

| | |
|---|---|
| EOKA | Ethniki Organosis Kyprion Agoniston |
| FBI | Federal Bureau of Investigation |
| FCC | Federal Communications Commission |
| FSB | Federalnaya Sluzhba Bezopasnosti (Russian counterintelligence agency) |
| G-2 | Irish intelligence service |
| G-2 | Cuban intelligence service |
| GCHQ | Government Communications Headquarters |
| GRU | Glavnoye razvedyvatel'noye upravleniye (Russian military intelligence service) |
| HOW | Home Office Warrant |
| HVA | Hauptverwaltung Aufklärung (former intelligence service for the German Democratic Republic) |
| INLA | Irish National Liberation Army |
| IRA | Irish Republican Army |
| IRB | Bureau of Intelligence and Research |
| IS9 | Intelligence School 9, RAF Highgate |
| ISK | Intelligence Source Knox |
| ISOS | Intelligence Source Olive Strachey |
| JIC | Joint Intelligence Committee |
| KaPo | Kaitsepolitseiamet (national security service of Estonia) |
| KGB | Soviet intelligence service |
| MI5 | British Security Service |
| MI6 | British Secret Intelligence Service |
| MI 11 | Field Security Police |
| MoD | Ministry of Defence |
| NIS | Naval Investigative Service |
| NKVD | Narodny Komissariat Vnutrennikh Del (former Soviet intelligence service) |
| NOC | Non-Official Cover |
| NSA | National Security Agency |
| NVA | National Peoples' Army |
| OGPU | Obyedinyonnoye gosudarstvennoye politicheskoye upravleniye (former Soviet intelligence service) |
| OSS | Office of Strategic Services |
| OTP | One-Time Pad |
| PCO | Passport Control Officer |
| PIRA | Provisional Irish Republican Army |

| | |
|---|---|
| PUS | Permanent Under-Secretary |
| RATS | Remote Administration Tool |
| RHSA | Reichssicherheitshauptamt (Reich security agency) |
| RID | Radio Intelligence Division |
| RUC | Royal Ulster Constabulary |
| SAPO | Säkerhetspolisen (Swedish security police) |
| SAVAK | Sazeman-e Ettela'at va Amniyat-e Keshvar (former Iranian intelligence service) |
| SB | Służba Bezpieczeństwa (former Polish intelligence service) |
| SCI | Special Counterintelligence |
| SDECE | Service de documentation extérieure et de contre-espionnage (former French intelligence agency) |
| SHAEF | Supreme Headquarters Allied Expeditionary Force |
| SIFE | Security Intelligence Far East |
| SIME | Security Intelligence Middle East |
| SIS | Secret Intelligence Service |
| SRAC | Short-Range Agent Communication |
| Stasi | Staatssicherheit (former East German security apparatus) |
| StB | Státní bezpečnost (former Czech intelligence agency) |
| SVR | Sluzhba vneshney razvedki (Russian foreign intelligence service) |
| TSD | Technical Services Division of the CIA |
| UAV | Unmanned Aerial Vehicle |
| UB | Urząd Bezpieczeństwa (former Polish intelligence agency) |
| UCN | Unidentified Cover Name |
| UKUSA | United Kingdom–United States Signals Intelligence Agreement |
| UNSUB | Unidentified Subject |
| UpDK | Main Administration for Service to the Diplomatic Corps |
| UPI | United Press International |
| UVF | Ulster Volunteer Force |
| VCO | Visiting Case Officer |
| V-Mann | Vertrauensmann |
| WIN | Wolność i Niezawisłość (Polish Freedom and Independence movement) |
| X-2 | Counterintelligence branch of OSS |
| Y | Signal interception |

# INTRODUCTION

Like most other professions, the espionage business has developed its own lexicon. For example, a 'rolling car meet' refers to a very specific method for a case officer to hold a rendezvous with an agent while on the move in a vehicle. It should not be confused with a Treff, the German word for a planned encounter that has been adopted by the intelligence community to mean a clandestine rendezvous with a sensitive source.

The public's interest in this alternative argot was captured most memorably by the novelist John le Carré, who began to write spy thrillers while still serving as a member of the British Secret Intelligence Service station in Hamburg. Fully aware of the tendency for his organisation's staff to speak in something approaching a private patois he invented an entirely new glossary that included 'lamp-lighters' (for the Watcher Service), 'scalphunters', 'pavement artists', 'wranglers' and 'janitors', many of whom were alleged to inhabit the dingy headquarters building, known as 'the Circus'.

All these terms were fictional, and SIS was never based in Cambridge Circus, although each had its own authentic equivalent, which the author, perhaps for reasons of discretion, had not disclosed. In the real, sub rosa world of intelligence-gathering, each of these epithets acts as a veil of secrecy over particular types of activity, and the purpose of this book is to explain, and give examples of, how these operations happened, drawing on the first-hand experience of defectors to and from the Soviet Union; surveillance 'operators' who kept terrorist suspects under observation in Northern Ireland; case officers who have put their lives at risk by 'pitching' a target in a 'denied territory'; and the NOCs who lived under alias, carrying 'black documentation' to spy abroad.

It was not until the successful decryption of the VENONA intercepts that Western analysts fully understood the extent to which the Soviets had created for themselves their own private intelligence language, a code within a sophisticated cipher system, that added an extra layer of secrecy, so that even if an adversary succeeded in decrypting a message and transforming it into plain-text, much of the content would remain opaque because commonly used words, such as New York, Washington and Britain were known as TYRE, CARTHAGE and the ISLAND, respectively. The United States was the COUNTRY and SIDON was London.

The true identities of individual agents were concealed behind semi-transparent cryptonyms, with Julius Rosenberg referred to as ANTENNA, for example. To insiders who knew that he had served in the US Army's Signal Corps as a radio technician, the connection was obvious. Any local, hostile security apparatus was called the GREENS, with members of the Communist Party being COMPATRIOTS, members of the Young Communist League GYMNASTS, and agents PROBATIONERS. Whereas analysts found the repetition in this code increasingly easy to understand, the cipher, based on supposedly randomly generated five-figure groups, was intended to be absolutely unbreakable through the application of conventional cryptanalysis.

The delicate business of handling what are sometimes termed Covert Human Intelligence Sources became especially fraught during the thirty-two years of 'the Troubles' in Ulster. Several different British security agencies ran competing and overlapping intelligence organisations across the province in an environment that was particularly challenging. External penetration of the target paramilitary groups was almost impossible as the Republicans came from the same families, schools and neighbourhoods, and had been known to each other for generations. This mitigated against the deployment of an imposter or someone from outside the closely knit largely (but not exclusively) Roman Catholic community. Physical surveillance was next to impossible in streets where strangers and their vehicles were likely to come under close scrutiny by gangs of youths engaged on look-out duties to give early warning of raids, and the establishment of static observation posts was problematic in the extreme.

In these circumstances the authorities came up with ingenious solutions, such as recruiting military personnel with family backgrounds in the six counties to 'retire' and return to their homes to make themselves available to the local paramilitaries. This strategy, adopted by the British Army's Force Research Unit, produced around a dozen good inside informants. There was considerable investment in long-distance observation from sites on top of tower blocks, and overhead reconnaissance from helicopters. Technology was also adapted to assist in the task of monitoring telephone conversations, disrupt the signals from remote-controlled devices employed to detonate explosives, and rescue agents in jeopardy.

Agents considered especially vulnerable were sometimes issued with ostensibly ordinary household items, such as domestic radios, that had been converted to transmit an emergency signal in the event of imminent compromise. Some agents also carried 'sick-pills', which when ingested would trigger violent retching and vomiting, thus providing a good excuse not to participate in some planned crime.

As in so many fields, a shooting war will create a climate in which many technological and other developments will be accelerated because of immediate necessity, and the same is true for espionage. It was the requirement to collect accurate information about enemy troop movements that in the First World War led to the creation of the train-watchers, a network of Allied agents taught to recognise particular types of railway rolling stock and associate them with the deployment of German infantry, cavalry and artillery.

In the Second World War the Axis occupation of much of central and western Europe provoked resistance movements and German responses with their own particular vocabulary, with *passeurs*, mouse-traps, reseaux and Funkspiel. This was a concentrated period of technical research which produced sabotage equipment, concealment devices, miniaturised transmitters and mobile direction-finding apparatus in support of what amounted to the first truly global espionage conflict.

Many of the lessons learned in the Second World War, ranging from strategic deception through the management of double agents to the exploitation of signals intelligence, were applied, often by the very same participants, during the Cold War. Ideological commitments made during the fascist era formed the foundation for post-war espionage, and the molehunters of the 1960s often found themselves delving into the university politics of the depression to track changed allegiances.

Forty-five years of superpower confrontation gave plenty of scope for the exponents of covert action, special political action and active measures to engage in a life-and-death struggle to promote their own interests. These manifested themselves in proxy wars fought in the developing world, sometimes colonial brush fires fuelled by Soviet or Chinese-sponsored nationalists, full-scale counter-insurgency emergencies, or minor police actions.

The conflicts, of varying scale, in Aden, Algeria, Borneo, Cyprus, Hong Kong, Indo-China, Kenya, Malaya, Oman, Palestine and Vietnam have all been accompanied by their own intelligence problems, and experience gained in one theatre has often found a useful application in another. Nowhere was this more true than in Northern Ireland where, for the longest period, four intelligence agencies took on an unprecedented challenge and ultimately prevailed. No wonder then that many of the personalities in today's efforts to isolate Islamic terrorism cut their teeth during a lengthy commitment against rather different political extremists.

The purpose of *Spycraft Secrets* is to assemble the nomenclature from as many sources as practicable to present a reasonably comprehensive window into a fascinating, arcane world that, for most outsiders, is as intriguing as it is forbidden.

Nigel West

# CHRONOLOGY

1909 The British Secret Service Bureau is established.

1910 Captain Hubert von Rebeur-Paschwitz is placed under surveillance during a visit to London. MI5 creates the Watcher Service.

1911 The mail of Karl Gustav Ernst, a German hairdresser in London's Caledonian Road, is intercepted on a Home Office warrant. The 1883 Official Secrets Act is amended.

1912 A German spy, George Parrott, formerly HMS *Agamemnon*'s chief gunner, is arrested at home in Battersea. Three spies, Walter Rimann, Adolph Schroeder and Armgaard Graves, receive questionnaires.

1913 The Secret Intelligence Service opens its first overseas bureau in Brussels. Wilhelm Croner commits suicide.

1914 A large number of German espionage suspects, including Marie Kronauer and Carl Gustav Ernst, are arrested upon the outbreak of hostilities.

1915 German spies equipped with the ingredients for secret writing are arrested in London.

1916 The Reuters news agency is bought secretly by the British government.

1917 The US Congress passes the Espionage Act. The Bolsheviks seize power in Russia.

| | |
|---|---|
| 1918 | The Soviet military intelligence service, the Third Department of the Red Army's General Staff, is established. |
| 1919 | The Third International in Moscow declares world revolution. |
| 1920 | Vladimir Orlov is sent to western Europe to organise an espionage network. |
| 1921 | The British government signs a trade agreement with the Soviet Union as a prelude to formal diplomatic relations. |
| 1922 | White Russian forgers produce fake Soviet documents in Turkey. |
| 1923 | Nikolai Kroshko, code-named A/3, reports on the White Guards from their headquarters at Strenski Karlowtzy. |
| 1924 | The forger Vladimir Orlov fabricates the Zinoviev Letter. |
| 1925 | Under interrogation in Berlin, Druzhelovsky implicates Vladimir Orlov. |
| 1926 | Ukrainian General Simon Petlura is murdered in Paris. |
| 1927 | Nikolai Kroshko reports to Moscow on Orlov's activities. |
| 1928 | The Abwehr is established in Germany. |
| 1929 | Vladimir Orlov is prosecuted in Berlin for forgery. |
| 1930 | Russian General Aleksandr P. Kutepov is abducted in Paris. Arkady Petrovich Kerr arrives in Berlin to penetrate the Brotherhood of Russian Truth. |
| 1931 | Leopold Trepper travels to Belgium to establish a GRU illegal network. |
| 1932 | Gaik B. Ovakimian arrives in New York supposedly to work as an engineer for Amtorg, but actually to run a network of NKVD illegals. |
| 1933 | Christopher Draper is recruited as a German spy but acts as a double agent for MI5. A group of Metropolitan-Vickers engineers is arrested in the Soviet Union and charged with espionage. |
| 1934 | Rudolf von Scheliha is recruited as a Soviet spy while serving at the German embassy in Warsaw. The US Congress passes the Federal Communications Act. |
| 1935 | The *Völkischer Beobachter* correspondent, Dr Hans Thost, is expelled from London. Henry Landau publishes *Secrets of the White Lady*. |

1936     Arnold Deutsch and Theodore Maly run the NKVD's illegal *rezidentura* in London. The British Joint Intelligence Committee is established.

1937     The FBI arrests Sergeant Gunther Rumrich. General Eugene Miller is abducted by the NKVD in Paris. Claude Dansey creates the Z Organisation.

1938     Jenifer Hart handles telephone intercept warrants at the Home Office. Karl Zeiss patents the microdot. Jessie Jordan is arrested in Dundee.

1939     A German spy, Ensign Jean Aubert, is executed by a firing squad in Toulon. Two SIS officers, Sigismund Payne Best and Richard Stevens, are abducted by German agents at Venlo.

1940     Peter Fleming creates the Auxiliary Units stay-behind organisation. Leon Trotsky is assassinated in Mexico City. Clarence Hince and Hugh Clegg of the FBI are indoctrinated into the Radio Security Service's cryptographic breakthroughs.

1941     Based in Cairo, SIME double agent CHEESE creates the concept of strategic deception. Abwehr D/F apparatus detects the Red Orchestra in Brussels. TRIPLEX exposes a Portuguese diplomat in London, Rogeiro de Menezes, as a spy. Gustave Jones is appointed the FBI legal attaché in Mexico City.

1942     The Office of Strategic Services establishes liaison personnel with MI5 and SIS. Lavrenti Beria introduces XY *rezidenturas*. The Abwehr's radio network in Brazil is closed down. The *Liverpool Evening Post* announces the death of William Gerbers.

1943     The first ferret mission is flown against a Japanese radar site on Kiska in the Aleutians. An SIS officer, David Russell, is murdered in Romania for his gold sovereigns. Lydia Altschuler acts as a courier for the NKVD in New York. Escapees Pieter Dourlein and Johan Ubbink reveal that SOE's Dutch network is in German hands.

1944     GARBO's network of notional agents participate in the Allies' D-Day deception campaign. Harry Gold meets David Greenglass in Albuquerque. SCI units enter Paris and take control of the Abwehr's stay-behind network.

| | |
|---|---|
| 1945 | TICOM 6 seizes the BalkanArchiv at Burgscheidungen. Igor Gouzenko defects in Ottawa. A Special Counterintelligence unit attempts to entrap Friedrich Kaulen. Elizabeth Bentley makes a statement to the FBI implicating dozens of NKVD spies. |
| 1946 | Great Britain and the United States sign the BRUSA communications intelligence agreement. Smersh is wound up. Judith Coplon is charged with espionage. The XX Committee is reestablished in London. |
| 1947 | MI5 investigates Klaus Fuchs for a security clearance. The National Security Act establishes the CIA. Roy Farran is charged with the murder of Alexander Rubowitz in Palestine. |
| 1948 | Jan Masaryk is the victim of a defenestration in Prague. The CIA introduces the polygraph. The CIA influences the Italian general election to ensure a Christian Democrat victory. |
| 1949 | Klaus Fuchs is identified as a Soviet spy. CBS's George Polk is shot dead in Salonika. The British government begins to check the backgrounds of civil servants. |
| 1950 | Harry Gold leads the FBI to David Greenglass. Emil Goldfus rents an apartment in New York. |
| 1951 | Reino Hayhanen is issued with a passport by the US embassy in Helsinki. Kim Philby is dismissed from the Secret Intelligence Service. |
| 1952 | Harry Houghton offers to spy for the UB while working at the British embassy in Warsaw. William Marshall is arrested for espionage. Two CIA officers, John T. Downey and Richard G. Fecteau, are imprisoned in China. |
| 1953 | The UKUSA communications intelligence agreement is signed. The CIA begins MK/ULTRA experiments with hallucinogenic drugs. A hollow nickel containing a Soviet message is found in Brooklyn and handed to the FBI. The *Sverdlovsk*'s hull is surveyed during the Coronation review at Spithead. *Encounter* magazine is founded by the CIA. |
| 1954 | Vladimir and Evdokia Petrov defect in Australia. Manfred Rotsch leaves East Germany as a KGB agent. Paddy |

Costello gives New Zealand passports to Lona and
Morris Cohen.

1955    The Berlin tunnel goes operational. John Vassall is caught
in a homosexual honeytrap in Moscow and blackmailed
by the KGB. A GRU illegal, Aleksei Chisov, approaches
the CIA in Paris. Mossad runs a false-flag operation in
Germany against missile scientists working for Egypt.

1956    Buster Crabb disappears under the *Ordzhonikdze*
in Portsmouth. The CIA's Edward Ellis Smith is
compromised by his maid Valya in Moscow. SIS's network
in Egypt is arrested.

1957    Lev Rebet is assassinated in Munich. Mieczyslaw
Reluga defects in London. Nikolai Khokhlov survives
an assassination attempt in Frankfurt. Reino Hayhanen
defects to the CIA in Paris.

1958    Otto Georgi is betrayed by George Blake and imprisoned.
CIA pilot Allen Pope is imprisoned in Indonesia.

1959    Stepan Bandera is assassinated in Munich. Frantisek Tisler
defects from the Czech embassy in Washington.

1960    Three CIA technicians are imprisoned in Cuba after being
caught in the act of installing bugs in the New China
News Agency. The first CORONA satellite is placed in
orbit. An Israeli spy, Wolfgang Lotz, is established in
Cairo. A Soviet spy, Willie Hirsch is arrested in Chicago.

1961    Two USAF fliers, John B. McKone and Freeman B.
Olmstead, are released in a spy swap. Konon Molody,
the KGB illegal *rezident* in London, is arrested. Bogdan
Stashinsky defects to the CIA. MI5 recruits Stephen Ward.
SIS Colin Figures runs a UB spy, code-named NODDY, in
Warsaw. Anatoli Golitsyn defects to the CIA in Helsinki.

1962    Douglas Britten is recruited by the KGB. John Vassall is
arrested in London. KGB illegal *rezident* Willie Fisher is
exchanged for CIA pilot F. Gary Powers.

1963    A CIA agent, Rolando Cubela Secades, is given a poison-
pen device in Paris to assassinate Fidel Castro. Stephen
Ward commits suicide. Yuri Krotkov defects in London.

1964    Anthony Blunt receives an immunity from prosecution in
return for his confession. Yuri Noseko defects and reveals

KGB surveillance techniques. Greville Wynne is released in exchange for Konon Molody.

1965    CIC Sergeant Glen Rohrer defects to Czechoslovakia with a polygraph machine. Mossad spy Eli Cohen is arrested in Damascus. Robert G. Thompson is sentenced to thirty-five years' imprisonment.

1966    The FBI ceases all black-bag operations. Oleg Timanov defects in Libya. Gerda Osterreider is appointed a cipher clerk at the German foreign ministry.

1967    The NSA Special Collection Service is established. Leonard Safford is sentenced to twenty-five years' imprisonment. John Walker begins spying for the KGB. The first CAZAB conference is held.

1968    Cartha DeLoach reviews the FBI's black bag operations. Philip Agee resigns from the CIA. British ambassador Sir Geoffrey Harrison is compromised by his chambermaid in Moscow.

1969    Ashraf Marwan offers to supply information to Mossad. Yuri Loginov is returned to the Soviet Union in a spy swap.

1970    MK/NAOMI is terminated by the CIA. Alexander de Marenches is appointed the DGSE's director.

1971    Denis Donaldson is recruited by the RUC Special Branch. The PHOENIX programme is terminated in Vietnam. SIS's Frank Steele opens secret talks with the Provisional IRA.

1972    A covert Automatic Number-Plate Recognition system is introduced in Northern Ireland. Black September massacres Israeli athletes at the Munich Olympics. Oleg Lyalin defects in London. The CORONA satellite project is terminated.

1973    DCI James Schlesinger orders a review of the CIA's domestic activities. Jim Bryson and Patrick Mulvenna are shot dead in Ballymurphy. Standa Kaplan defects from the Czech StB. Vladimir Vetrov recruits Pierre Bourdiol.

1974    Otis Pike and Frank Church commence hearings in Congress on allegations of CIA misconduct. A group of Mossad *katsas* are arrested in Lillehammer, Norway. Oleg Gordievsky is recruited by SIS in Copenhagen.

1975    An RUC informant, Eamon Molloy, is abducted in Belfast and murdered. Vaclav Jelinek arrives in London as an StB illegal alias Erwin van Haarlem. Bill Colby shows Congress a poison-dart gun.

1976    The KH-11, the first digital imagery satellite, is placed in orbit. Toxic spy-dust is detected in Moscow. Senator Frank Church reveals that fifty American newsmen are on the CIA's payroll.

1977    Martha Peterson is arrested by the KGB as she services a dead drop in Moscow. David Holden of *The Sunday Times* is murdered in Cairo.

1978    Robert G. Thompson is released in a spy swap. Raymond Gilmour is recruited by the RUC Special Branch. Georgi Markov is killed with a ricin pellet in London. UN diplomat Arkadi Shevchenko defects in New York. The Foreign Intelligence Surveillance Act is passed. Ion Paceta defects in Bonn.

1979    The US embassy in Tehran is seized and occupied by Iranian students. Stanislas Levchenko defects in Tokyo. Robert Hanssen passes FBI secrets to the GRU in New York.

1980    Ronald Pelton visits the Soviet embassy in Washington and offers to spy. The CIA's David Barnett is arrested. The CIA successfully exfiltrates six American diplomats from Tehran. Congress passes the Classified Information Procedures Act. Frank Terpil flees to Havana. Victor Sheymov is exfiltrated from the Soviet Union by car.

1981    Christopher Black becomes the first supergrass. A grocery bag containing false British passports is found in a London telephone kiosk. Vladimir Potashov is recruited by the CIA.

1982    Raymond Gilmour is resettled. A clandestine RAF radar station is established at Balmaceda in Chile. Vladimir Vetrov is arrested in Moscow. BND agent Dietrich Nistroy is sentenced to life imprisonment. Gerry Tuite is convicted in Dublin of terrorist offences committed in London.

1983    MI5 officer Michael Bettaney offers to spy for the KGB. Pierre Bourdiol is arrested after he is betrayed by his KGB recruiter, Vladimir Vetrov. An East German physicist, Alfred Zehe, is arrested in Boston.

1984    Two major PIRA arms caches are found in England. The Grand Hotel in Brighton is bombed in a bid to assassinate Margaret Thatcher. Detlef Scharfenorth is arrested in Cologne. Vladimir Vorontsov of the KGB's Second Chief Directorate is recruited by the CIA. Soviet spy Manfred Rotsch is arrested in Germany.

1985    Vitali Yurchenko defects to the CIA in Rome. Oleg Gordievsky is exfiltrated from Moscow. Edward Howard escapes FBI surveillance in Santa Fe. A Polish UB officer, Jerzy Kaczmarek, is arrested in Bremen.

1986    Gerard McDonnell is sentenced to life imprisonment. Parliament passes the Interception of Communications Act. *Spycatcher* is publishēd. Jerzy Kaczmarek is released in a spy swap. Ronald Pelton is imprisoned in a plea bargain.

1987    Eight PIRA gunmen are shot dead in an SAS ambush at Loughgall. Secretary of Defense Caspar Weinberger offers a damage assessment at Jonathan Pollard's sentencing.

1988    The DGI's Carlos Medina Perez, shoots an MI5 officer in a London street. A KGB officer, Alexander Zhomov, approaches the CIA's Jack Downing on a train to Leningrad.

1989    The Security Service Act is passed to legitimise MI5. Vaclav Jelinek is sentenced to ten years' imprisonment in London. Philip Agee participates in a false-flag operation for the Cuban DGI.

1990    PIRA bomb-maker Dessie Ellis is extradited to face trial in London. Gerald Bull is murdered at his apartment in Brussels. *Observer* journalist Farzad Bazoft is executed in Baghdad.

1991    Martin McGartland is abducted in Belfast. Aldrich Ames is recalled for a second polygraph. The DGSE is caught engaging in industrial espionage in Houston.

1992    Three touts are murdered in South Armagh. The Matrix Churchill prosecution collapses and the Scott Inquiry is established, Aleksandr Kouzminov defects and describes the truth serum SP-117.

1993      KGB defector Victor Sheymov publishes *Tower of Secrets*.
          The CIA's Valerie Plame spends a year at the London
          School of Economics. A French list of industrial espionage
          targets is leaked.

1994      Aldrich Ames is arrested. The Intelligence Services Act is
          passed. PIRA prisoners break out of Whitemoor prison.
          The StB's Vaclav Jelinek is released from prison and
          deported to Prague.

1995      A CIA mole in the DGI, Rolando Sarraff Trujillo, is
          arrested in Havana. DCI John Deutsch briefs Congress on
          the Aldrich Ames damage assessment. The CIA terminates
          research into remote viewing.

1996      The CIA's Jim Nicholson is arrested at Dulles Airport.
          MI5 begins Operation AIRLINES to defeat PIRA's South
          Armagh Brigade. PIRA's Edward O'Brien is killed by his
          own bomb in London.

1997      David Shayler leaves MI5. Mossad attempts to assassinate
          Hamas leader Sheikh Khaled Mashal in Amman. The
          SAS's B Squadron arrests four Crossmaglen snipers. The
          FBI suspects CIA officer Brian Kelley is a Soviet mole
          code-named KARAT. Princess Diana is killed in a car
          accident in Paris

1998      Sinn Féin discovers a listening device in Gerry Adams's
          car. Igor Sutyagin is recruited by SIS at a conference in
          Birmingham. The RED WASP spy-ring is indicted in
          Florida.

1999      Two PIRA gunmen, Jim Errington and Patrick Sheehy, are
          murdered in Nenagh. Rafid Ahmed Alwan, later code-
          named CURVEBALL, leaves Iraq and settles in Munich.
          The first Predator is deployed operationally over Kosovo.

2000      Colonel Alexander Zaporozshky is resettled in Virginia
          by the FBI. Al-Qaida attacks the French oil supertanker
          *Limburg*.

2001      Al-Qaida attacks targets in New York and Washington,
          DC. The DIA analyst Ana Montes is arrested as a DGI
          spy. Al-Qaida's military commander in Afghanistan,
          Mohammed Atef, is killed by a CIA operated UAV.

| | |
|---|---|
| 2002 | Donald Rumsfeld remarks about 'known unknowns'. Al-Qaida leader Qued Salim Sinan al-Haethi is killed by a UAV in Yemen. The Belgian government acknowledges responsibility for the murder of Patrice Lumumba in 1961. |
| 2003 | The Coalition invades and occupies Iraq. Michael McKevitt, the Real IRA leader, is imprisoned in Dublin. A Canadian terrorist suspect, Maher Arar, is released from detention in Syria. |
| 2004 | Charges are dropped against the GCHQ linguist Katharine Gun. Two Mossad officers, Elia Cara and Uriel Zoshe Kelman, are arrested while tombstoning in New Zealand. |
| 2005 | Denis Donaldson admits that he has been an RUC Special Branch source for the past twenty years. Details of the CIA's black sites are leaked to the *Washington Post*. |
| 2006 | Denis Donaldson is shot dead at his home in Donegal. Alexander Litvinenko dies after ingesting polonium-210. Valerie Plame resigns from the CIA. |
| 2007 | Ashraf Marwan is defenestrated at his flat in London. Kendall Myers retires from the US State Department Bureau of Intelligence and Research. |
| 2008 | A PIRA bodyguard, Roy McShane, is identified as an MI5 asset and withdrawn from Belfast. The JIC ceases to distribute the weekly Red Book. |
| 2009 | Kendall Myers and his wife Gwendolyn are arrested and convicted of spying for Cuba. |
| 2010 | Ten SVR illegals are arrested in the United States and exchanged in a spy swap. Hamas military commander Mahmoud al-Mabhouh is murdered by Mossad in Dubai. |
| 2011 | A North Korean assassin is interdicted in Seoul. Osama bin Laden is killed in Abbottabad. |
| 2012 | Mark Haddock is acquitted on murder charges in Northern Ireland. The Jonathan Pollard damage assessment is declassified and released. |
| 2013 | PIRA bomber John Downey is arrested at Gatwick Airport. Rogue contractor Edward Snowden begins to |

leak NSA secrets. Victor Sheymov complains about his handling by the CIA in *Tiebreaker*.

2014    Rolando Sarraff Trujillo is released from prison in Havana in exchange for three Cuban spies.

2015    Frederick Forsyth acknowledges having worked for SIS. Jonathan Pollard is released on parole from a federal prison at Banner, North Carolina.

# THE A TO Z OF SPYCRAFT

## A

## ABDUCTION

The abduction of opponents of the Bolshevik regime became almost commonplace in Paris before the Second World War, the known victims being mainly White Russians, and some supporters of Leon Trotsky.

The Soviets also employed the technique on an almost industrial scale in post-war Austria and Germany when numerous scientists, technicians and other targets were routinely seized off the street and forced to work in Soviet labour camps. A GRU **defector**, Grigori Tokaev, was prompted to seek political asylum from the British in 1947 precisely because of the disagreeable nature of his duties, which included instructions to abduct Focke-Wulf's chief designer, Dr Kurt Tank. Typical was the abduction of Dr Walter Linse who had fled East Germany in 1947 and later became the anti-Communist leader of the Society of Free Jurists. He was taken from West Berlin in July 1952 and died in a Soviet prison camp in December 1953. Similarly, Bohumil Lausman, a prominent Czech anti-Communist who fled to the west in 1949, disappeared from Vienna in 1953 and was driven to Prague where he was imprisoned. Ukrainian nationalists were also targeted, with Dr Alexander Trushnovich seized in West Berlin in April 1954 and Valeri P. Tremmel taken from Linz in June 1954.

In February 1964 a CIA assessment of Soviet kidnappings, drawn
up for the Warren Commission, referred to incidents in Calcutta in
January 1958 when Aleksandr F. Zelenovskiy tried to defect, and in
Rangoon in May 1959 when Mikhail I. Strygin was physically prevented from seeking asylum at the US embassy. Such interventions
were not unusual, as was demonstrated by the removal of Konstantin
Volkov and his wife from Istanbul in September 1945, days after he
had offered to defect to the British.

In the modern era such abductions are relatively rare; **rendition**, as
the process is now often known, is not recognised by international
law as a legitimate alternative to extradition proceedings. In July
1984 a former Nigerian minister, Umaru Dikko, was grabbed off a
London street by Mossad agents working on behalf of the Nigerian
government in an abortive attempt to fly him back to Lagos from
Stansted Airport. Similarly, in September 1986 an Israeli technician, Mordechai Vanunu, responsible for newspaper leaks about his
country's stockpile of nuclear weapons, was lured from London to
Rome where he was bundled aboard a ship, eventually to face trial
in Tel Aviv.

## ACCESS AGENT

An intermediary who is employed by an intelligence agency for the
specific purpose of introducing a case officer to a potential recruit
is known as an access agent. The scenario created for the meeting,
known as 'the **bump**' may range from a small dinner party, to a major
academic conference.

## ACTIVE CONCEALMENT

A **concealment device** that fulfils two functions, to provide a hiding
place and to work as intended, is referred to as an active concealment. Classic examples include cigarette lighters that really work,
but contain a cavity in which microfilms can be stored, hand-held
torches in which one of the battery cells has a hollow space, or tubes
of branded toothpaste that have been repackaged to conceal something incriminating.

## ACTIVE MEASURES

A Soviet term for an aggressive operation or propaganda campaign, often involving **disinformation**, and roughly equivalent to the CIA definition of **covert action**, active measures embrace every component of aggressive operations.

## AGENT AUDIT

Introduced to the CIA by DCI Admiral Stansfield Turner who had expressed doubt about the performance of sources run by the DO, Agent Audit was a mandatory assessment of individual agents intended to weed out those considered unproductive.

Turner, a teetotal Christian Scientist who headed the CIA between March 1977 and January 1981 and never disguised his preference for technical intelligence, undertook an unprecedented review of the DO's staff in 1977 which became known as the Halloween Massacre and resulted in the premature retirement of 820 staff, some of whom were the most experienced case officers of the era. The CIA lost two Deputy Directors of Operations (DDI), William E. Nelson in May 1976 and William W. Wells in December 1977. In addition Turner transferred Jack McMahon from the Directorate of Science and Technology in January 1978 and Bill Wells, a Mandarin-speaking Far East expert who had been in the DO since 1962, and had served in Manila, Taipei, Tokyo and Hong Kong, was replaced.

Morale at the CIA plummeted as the Agency was cut to 14,000 personnel and the annual budget reduced to $6 billion. Bob Gates, who was Turner's executive assistant, recalled that, 'with the people fired, driven out or lured into retirement, half our **analysts** had less than five years' experience. And our analysis wasn't all that sharp, forward-looking or relevant. Our paramilitary capability was clinically dead. What covert action we did carry out was super-cautious and lacked any imagination.'

The problem with Agent Audit was that sometimes a human source would lose access to the required information, but experienced **handlers** knew that such individuals often regained access, or could find a replacement, and in any event were always grateful for continued support during a difficult period. Any loyalty demonstrated was often repaid with dividends, while termination, though a short-term expedient, would create resentment.

When, in November 1979, sixty-six Americans, among them the CIA station chief Tom Ahern and three of his subordinates, were taken hostage at the US embassy in Tehran, the DO was left with virtually no agent network in Iran, and not a single DO officer fluent in Farsi. As a consequence, the CIA was obliged to rehire a retiree to head its Iranian Task Force.

## AGENT OF INFLUENCE

Such an individual, usually associated with **fellow travellers** and sometimes a **confidential contact** of a local foreign embassy, is not a conventional intelligence source, but is usually ideologically motivated. During the Cold War such agents often occupied posts that enabled them to exercise influence on behalf of Moscow.

Following the defections of Oleg Gordievsky in 1985 and Vasili Mitrokhin in 1992 evidence emerged that several well-known British left-wing journalists had allegedly received undeclared financial support from the KGB, among them the *Guardian*'s literary editor Richard Gott, and the long-serving editor of *Tribune*, Dick Clements.

Not all agents of influence are necessarily conscious, although Michael Foot, one of *Tribune*'s editors, who would become leader of the Labour Party, would be criticised for apparently not noticing a large subsidy from the Soviet embassy for what purported to be a volume subscription to the weekly journal.

One Soviet channel was Pierre Charles Pathé, son of the movie magnate and one of the leading French journalists of his era. He was arrested in July 1979 and convicted of having accepted undeclared payments over the previous twenty years from two KGB officers, Yuri Borisov and Igor Kuznetsov, and for having inserted pro-Soviet articles into his magazine, *Synthesis*. Pathé was sentenced to five years' imprisonment but was released in 1981. In the same category was François Saar-Demichel, a French businessman who had fought in the resistance during the Second World War and until 1947 served in the DGSE, but was **honeytrapped** in Moscow in 1961. Later he became close to the Elysée Palace and acted as an informal foreign policy adviser to President Charles de Gaulle on East–West relations until his activities were investigated by the DST in 1970, which effectively terminated his access.

## AGENT PROVOCATEUR

Defined as a person conducting themselves in a manner to entrap others, the classic *agent provocateur* will lead a target to incriminate themselves, and then warn the appropriate authorities so action can be taken.

During the Second World War one of the longest and most sophisticated *agent provocateur* operations was run by MI5's F3 section to identify Nazi sympathisers and fifth columnists in Britain, and to determine the scale of the threat they posed. An MI5 officer fluent in German, John Bingham, adopted the **alias** of Jack Roberts, code-named JACK KING, and posed as Gestapo officer in London on a mission to verify the credentials of potential supporters who could be relied upon to assist a Fascist government after a successful invasion.

The first victim was Irma Stapleton, a factory worker and ardent Nazi. Her case was referred to by MI5's director of counter-espionage, Guy Liddell, as explained in his diary entry for 18 November 1941:

> We had a Directors' meeting and I raised the question of Irma Stapleton. From the transcript notes taken by mike [sic] of her last interview with John Bingham posing as a representative of the German secret service there seemed no doubt that she was prepared to go to any lengths and that she could quite easily bring out a whole shell from the factory where she works. She has swallowed our bait hook, line and sinker. If we went on with the case there seemed little doubt that we could get her seven years' at the Old Bailey. We were to some extent forced to adopt these methods because if we interned people under 18(b) because we felt they were a potential danger, they were almost invariably released. I rather wondered how far it would be worth the expense and trouble of trying to get a woman of this type sentenced to seven years, particularly since the case could not be held in an open court. The Director-General said he would give this matter his consideration.

On 19 November Stapleton was arrested, and Liddell observed the following day:

Irma Stapleton was arrested last night. She had brought an empty shell out of the factory, and a note in her own hand-writing giving the position of Wade's garages. She also gave John Bingham full production figures for Wade's garage. Her reaction was immediately to denounce Bingham as a Gestapo agent who she was intending to hand over to the police at the earliest opportunity. She insisted on making a statement which is said to be a tissue of lies. Bingham was arrested at the same time and carried away struggling and handcuffed. This morning she was remanded at Bow Street for fourteen days.

Stapleton subsequently was convicted under the Defence of the Realm Act and sentenced to ten years' imprisonment, although the full role played by MI5 in the case was not disclosed in court.

For three years from November 1941 Bingham presented himself as working for the Gestapo, and cultivated Marita Perigoe, a woman known to have expressed disloyal, strongly anti-Semitic views, whose husband Bernard had been detained in Brixton prison. Through her, KING was introduced to Hans Kohout, a former member of the British Union who wanted to spy for Germany, but was persuaded he could undertake more valuable tasks than espionage. KING was also able to gather information about internees held in the Isle of Man and their attempts to maintain contact with Germany. An MI5 summary dated July 1942 set out what KING had accomplished:

All disloyal persons are extremely suspicious of so-called members of the German Secret Service or Gestapo as they are well aware that this technique is used by all Security Services to find out who is loyal and who is not. It would not be an exaggeration to say that during thirty percent of Jack's time with the fifth column, members firmly believe that he is in MI5; it is only owing to his outstanding ability that this idea has been dispelled and he has been able to continuehis work. Mrs Bray, to whom reference will be made later, recently stated to another member of the organisation that it was obvious that Jack was a member of MI5. If the Germans had another good organisation in this country as one might think from what Jack said, why should they bother to send spies over here by parachute or disguised as patriotic escapees from occupied countries? Furthermore, she was aware that all espionage within this country was now done through the Spanish Embassy, and she proposed to send a piece of important information which her husband had recently acquired to that embassy. Jack dissuaded her from taking this course and the information is now in MI5 … It is difficult to indicate how delicate and lengthy a process it is to gain the confidence of these disloyal persons. This case started two years ago and it is doubtful if it will have reached a point when a prosecution would be possible or worthwhile for at least another year, it is only in the last few weeks that Jack has persuaded Marita to accept payment ('expenses') for her work. She is paid £2 a week, the money being sent in a double envelope, the inside one being blank, in pound notes. Letters are posted from different parts of London every Thursday evening. Although Marita is fully aware that the British authorities impose HOWs, she was persuaded by Jack to accept payment through the post. She feels secure because the money is sent in a double envelope so that 'if any curious person at the GPO were to hold the letter up to the light, he would not see the pound notes inside. Photostats of the banknotes are obtained from the HOW on Marita's correspondence and the legal implications of the matter have been discussed with Major Edward Cussen. Marita has provided this office with the names of disloyal persons with whom she, or her sub-agents, are in contact.

Jack's role with the employees of Siemens Schuckert (GB) Ltd was that of a disloyal Englishman anxious to help the enemy but not knowing how. It was hoped that he would be talent-spotted by someone in Siemens Schuckert, and this would lead to profitable results. Marita, as mentioned above, was found to be a different proposition and it was decided that Jack would have to change his role. Bearing in mind the general dangers of provocation techniques and the bad psychological effects that certain unfortunate episodes in other cases have had on MI5 agents who are now nervous of being accused of being agents provocateurs, it was decided at the start to obviate any possibility of this accusation by the following method. Jack, after weeks of cautious preparation, stated that he was an English representative of the Gestapo. He said he was not a representative of the German Secret Service, which is concerned with the acquisition of intelligence, and he was not interested in espionage nor sabotage. His job in this country was to check up on persons who might be loyal to the Fatherland. On instructions from Head Office, he has carefully avoided any suggestion that Marita or the other persons with whom she is in touch should engage in espionage, as it was not his job: all he required was the names of persons who were believed to be one hundred percent loyal to the Fatherland; he would relay these names to Germany for use in time of invasion, particularly from the point of view of giving food, lodging and hiding to invading forces. Although this was satisfactory for MI5 in that we could never be accused of provocation, it had disadvantages. One person in touch with the Duke of Bedford's group pointed out to Marita that the technique employed by Jack, as if he was a Gestapo agent, was exactly the technique that an MI5 agent would use. An MI5 agent would dissuade persons who were loyal to the Fatherland from committing any act which might endanger the security of this country, though at the same time such an agent would attempt to find out who was disloyal, with a view to view to interning them in time of emergency.

Another disadvantage that the decision to discourage all forms of espionage has incurred is that Marita and certain of her friends are so anxious to take a more positive role than the mere acquisition of information about sympathisers all over the country that it has been found impossible to control her. On more than one occasion she has spontaneously committed acts of espionage involving considerable ingenuity, against our instructions. Whenever such acts have occurred, we consulted Major Cussen with a view to proceedings at a later date.

It is inevitable, as our head agent is a woman, that there should be a tendency for women to come to notice first; but Jack's organisation now includes an almost equal number of men. It is proposed at a later stage to provide all members of the organisation with badges, which will probably take the form of some innocuous object like the Union Jack, which they will be instructed to hide until orders are given from headquarters.

From then onwards they will wear them. The object of this plan is to enable the police easily to identify members of this fifth column organisation in time of emergency. It is also hoped to arrange for them to go to specific addresses in time of invasion.

The introduction of Jack Bingham was achieved by intercepting the mail of a Siemens employee, Walter Wegener, who was interned, but not before his letters had identified his sister Dorothy Wegener, a lonely neurotic, as a likely target. She was a member of a correspondence club which Bingham joined to cultivate her, and after they had met, and exchanged suitably pro-Nazi sentiments, 'Jack King' confided to Dorothy that he worked at the Kryn & Lahy metal factory in Letchworth, and had stolen a blueprint for the Vickers tank which he wanted to pass to Germany.

Dorothy arranged for Jack King to meet Marita, and thereafter MI5 effectively took control of her network of fifth columnists. However, none of the membership was ever prosecuted because of the danger that MI5 would be accused of having entrapped them.

MI5's sensitivity about the use of *agents provocateurs* dated back to 1940 when a prominent Quaker, Ben Greene, was denounced by an MI5 agent, Harald Kurtz, and detained under the Defence of the Realm regulations. Greene was exceptionally well connected and eventually proved that Kurtz was a wholly unreliable informant who had given false information to MI5 in the hope of financial reward. The case became a major embarrassment when Greene's appeal reached the House of Lords, where Kurtz was identified by name as MI5's source, and Greene was freed. Thereafter the Security Service exercised great caution in any investigation involving *agents provocateurs*, and legal advice was taken from such eminent authorities as (Sir) Edward Cussen, QC.

## AGENTSUMPF

During the Cold War Berlin was often called the *Agentsumpf*, meaning spy swamp, as the city was infested by spies, with all the major agencies represented. Intelligence services sometimes acted with impunity, confident that in their own zones of occupation there would be minimal **blowback** if a particularly aggressive operation went awry. In addition to conventional, human intelligence activities, there was a major Anglo-American signals intelligence facility atop the Teufelsberg in the British sector which intercepted Warsaw Pact radio traffic from deep into Poland and Czechoslovakia, and thereby became a priority target for Eastern Bloc espionage.

The local CIA base (subordinate to the CIA station in Bonn) developed an extensive organisation into Eastern Europe and, through the recruitment of Piotr Popov, managed a major **penetration** into the GRU *rezidentura* at Karlshorst. A tunnel, code-named Operation GOLD, built under the border at Rudlow into the Soviet zone, intercepted a cable duct beside the Schönefelder Chaussee, which carried traffic from the Soviet military headquarters in Zossen-Wünsdorf. This provided access to high-grade Red Army landline communications from May 1955 for a period of eleven months until it was betrayed by one of the project's SIS planners, George Blake.

British and American intelligence operations in Berlin were severely compromised by Blake who served at the SIS station, located at the Olympic stadium, between January 1955 and the summer of 1959. Almost as soon as Blake had been posted back to London, the East German Stasi, directed by the KGB, began a comprehensive **roll-up** of SIS's **assets**.

## ALIAS

Intelligence officers often adopt an alias to undertake missions, depending on passports that have been forged for the purpose, or on genuine passports issued for the purpose, or authentic foreign passports applied for under a false identity. It is unusual for a foreign passport to be fabricated, although several agencies possess the capability, because detection would compromise the holder. More likely the sponsoring state will arrange for a genuine passport to be issued. The third option, often a necessity when a true nationality is to be concealed, requires a technique known as **tombstoning**, a procedure disclosed publicly by the author Frederick Forsyth in his novel *The Day of the Jackal*. In 2015 Forsyth acknowledged in his memoir *The Outsider: My Life of Intrigue* that when he had worked for the Reuters news agency he had been an SIS **asset**.

Foreign travel on alias documentation may require supporting **pocket litter,** such as a driving licence and credit card, and a claimed occupation may involve complicated **backstopping** in anticipation of a challenge.

Many intelligence professionals operate under a light alias to protect their true identity, for example when handling an agent, and invariably use their own given name, and probably a surname beginning with the same letter of the alphabet as their true identity, so as to explain initials or monograms.

Eastern Bloc intelligence agencies have occasionally turned to **impersonation** as a method of enhancing an alias identity, but this procedure has inherent hazards, as demonstrated by the cases of Jerzy Kaczmarek in 1985 and Erwin van Haarlem in 1988.

## ANALYST

Non-operations intelligence personnel who assess intelligence and draft **finished intelligence** reports are known as analysts. Some intelligence agencies, especially in the United States, employ their own analytical branch, such as the CIA's Directorate of Intelligence, staffed by experts in their field who may have, or be undergoing a temporary secondment from, an academic institution. In the British model the intelligence agencies submit their reporting for independent scrutiny by the Joint Intelligence Staff which prepares assessments for the Joint Intelligence Committee.

During the Cold War the Western intelligence community regarded the KGB's lack of an analytic capability as a fundamental weakness which engendered a lack of intellectual rigour. Although a huge organisation, the KGB never employed analysts because, it was argued, Central Committee policy-makers in the Kremlin were in a better position to make what were perceived to be mainly political judgments. As the 'sword and the shield' of the Communist Party of the Soviet Union (CPSU), the KGB's principal objective was to support the CPSU and the politburo, and to refrain from expressing opinion that could amount to political dissent. In contrast, the West's analytic principle, as espoused by Sherman Kent, was 'to speak truth unto power' however unpopular that advice might be.

## ASSASSINATION

As instruments of political power, intelligence agencies are occasionally instructed to kill an adversary, and there have been circumstances in which the capability has been institutionalised, as happened with the NKVD's creation of Smersh in April 1943 for the liquidation of counter-revolutionaries, opponents of the regime and Nazi collaborators. This ostensibly wartime Soviet expedient was perpetuated into the Cold War by the First Chief Directorate's notorious Thirteenth Department, which employed the **defectors** Nikolai Khokhlov and Bogdan Stashinsky who both gave detailed accounts of the organisation in 1954 and 1961 respectively. The department had been headed by Nikolai Rodin, **alias** Korovin, formerly the NKVD *rezident* in London, and had employed about sixty specialists, some of them deployed to the Soviet zones in Germany and Austria. One failed attempt was on the life of Lisa Stein, a radio broadcaster in West Germany, who, in March 1955, only narrowly survived a dose of the lethal toxin scopolamine concealed in a box of chocolates. In June 1962 a defector from the Hungarian AVH, Lieutenant Bela Lapusnyik, died from a mysterious bacteriological infection while in protective custody in the maximum security wing of Rossauerlande prison in Vienna. Four years later another AVH defector, Laszlo Szabo, who applied for political asylum in London, revealed that an Austrian official had been bribed to gain access to the victim. Similarly, in April 1982 a Bulgarian DIE illegal, Matei Haiducu, defected and claimed that he was assigned to murder two expatriate writers, Paul Goma and Virgil Tanase.

The origins of the Thirteenth Department lay in the creation in 1936 of the Department for Special Tasks, headed by Pavel Sudoplatov, which had been responsible for the assassination of the NKVD **illegal** Ignace Reiss, who was shot in Lausanne in September 1937, and the death of Leon Trotsky in Mexico in August 1940. Reiss's widow, Elizabeth Poretsky, was also a target, but was saved when her intended assassin, Gertrude Schildbach, had at the last moment lost her nerve and snatched back a box of chocolates laced with strychnine.

Several of Trotsky's supporters met mysterious deaths, including his son Leon Sedov who died in February 1938 in a Paris clinic run by White Russians. One of Sedov's assistants, Rudolf Klement, was a young German who disappeared while en route to Brussels carrying important papers, and his headless body was found in the Seine. When Trotsky had taken refuge in Prinkipo, in Turkey, he had been visited by Jacob Blumkin, a veteran revolutionary who had been implicated in the murder in 1918 of Count Mirbach, the German ambassador to Moscow, and later had joined the OGPU. When Stalin was informed that Blumkin was in touch with Trotsky, he was sentenced to death, and he was lured back over the Soviet border by his former lover, Lisa Zarubina, and shot.

The KGB was also implicated in the murder in Paris in 1960 of the Polish illegal Wladyslaw Mroz who had defected to the DST and was shot dead in Paris. The full details only emerged following the defection of the UB officer Janusz Kochanski, to the CIA in February 1967. However, although the KGB learned the resettlement details of the defectors Igor Gouzenko in Canada and Vladimir Petrov in Australia, no action was taken against either.

During the KGB's reorganisation in 1968/9 the Thirteenth Department was abolished and its staff of around fifty officers transferred to Department V, a new section created with a broader role, encompassing sabotage, and placed within Directorate S under the personal authority of chairman Yuri V. Andropov. Its principal function was to plan disruption in target countries so that in the event of hostilities a fifth column of agents could be mobilised by radio to strike at the heart of government and create chaos.

The West's knowledge of Department V was to be enhanced in 1972 by a Canadian-born Czech, Anton Sabotka, who had been placed under surveillance by the RCMP several years earlier, and the defector Oleg Lyalin, the Department V representative in the London *rezidentura*. His defection in August 1972 in London embarrassed the Kremlin, and as part of a programme of counter-measures to mitigate the damage all Department V personnel were withdrawn from the field. Created in its place was the Eighth Department of Directorate S, which was henceforth restricted to a planning and training role, with the officers with operational experience dispersed between the Directorate's four geographical departments.

According to Lyalin, the KGB had closed down the Thirteenth Department after Stashinsky's embarrassing disclosures, but had retained a combined sabotage and assassination capability. He also revealed a wartime contingency plan prepared by his *rezidentura* to infiltrate agents disguised as official messengers into Whitehall's system of underground tunnels to distribute poison gas capsules.

SIS sought to accommodate Prime Minister Sir Anthony Eden's instruction to kill Egypt's Gamal Abdel Nasser in 1955, and the EOKA leader George Grivas in 1956, but failed on both occasions. President Nasser proved too difficult a target, although some plans were drafted, and the sanction for a sniper, Stephen Hastings, a former wartime SAS officer, to shoot Grivas was withdrawn at the last moment. A further request, by Foreign Secretary Dr David Owen, to eliminate Uganda's President Idi Amin, was received with a shocked refusal by the rather saintly SIS Chief, Maurice Oldfield.

The French SDECE's Action Service has had few qualms in employing assassins recruited from the Marseilles underworld and the Unione Corse, as was demonstrated by the campaign conducted by *les barbouzes,* a deniable group of hitmen, against the Organisation Armée Secrète during the Algerian dirty war. Among their victims was Camille Petitjean, a suspected OAS leader, abducted and shot in February 1962.

Although allegations of the CIA's involvement in the assassination of foreign leaders were investigated by Congress in 1974, prior to the ban imposed by President Gerald Ford in February 1976 when he issued his Executive Order 11905, none was substantiated. That prohibition remained in force, confirmed by Jimmy Carter in January 1978 (Executive Order 12036) and by Ronald Reagan in December 1982 (Executive Order 12333).

One of the assassinations attributed to the CIA, that of Patrice Lumumba in January 1961, was later discovered to have been the handiwork of the Belgian Sûreté d'État. The Belgian government formally acknowledged this in 2002. The plot, code-named Operation-L, had been formulated in 1960 when a journalist, allegedly named Bogaerts, was sent to the Congo to prepare for the assassination by replacing Lumumba's medicine with poison, and was followed in November by a hitman, 'George the Greek' who had been hired by the Belgian historian Jo Gerard. This first scheme failed, apparently through fraud, so a second was directed by Colonel Louis Marliére and Major Jules Loos who were based in Elizabethville under **diplomatic cover** provided by the minister, Harold d'Aspremont Lynden, at the Belgian Technical Mission.

Lumumba, regarded as pro-Communist, had been arrested at the Elizabethville airport in December 1960 and imprisoned at an army camp outside Leopoldville before being moved, allegedly for his own safety, to Belgian-controlled Katanga. Also murdered were two companions, the Youth Minister Maurice Mpolo and the former Senate Vice-President Joseph Okito.

'George the Greek' was most probably the American gangster Donald Frankos who committed numerous contract killings for the Luccese mafia family in New Jersey. Born in Hackensack, New Jersey, Frankos became a US prosecution witness and died in March 2011, having collaborated with William Hoffman on a 1993 biography entitled *Contract Killer*.

## ASSASSINATION EQUIPMENT

Specialist devices designed and built for the purpose of **assassination** are often quiet, or deliberately suppressed, and a few examples have been publicly revealed. During the Second World War the British Special Operations Executive (SOE) contracted Birmingham Small Arms to create the Welrod, a silenced 9mm bolt-action handgun with a magazine in the grip containing six rounds. Some 3,000 examples of the pistol were manufactured, and a 22 Special Air Service trooper armed himself with one while participating in a mission to Argentina during the 1982 Falklands conflict. The Welrod acquired its name because the original concept was created at SOE's Station IX, an establishment located at a residential hotel, The Frythe, near Welwyn in Hertfordshire. As well as the Welrod, Station IX also developed another assassination weapon, the sleeve gun, a concealed breech and barrel which included a noise suppressor and was intended to be fired on contact with the victim. There are no records of the use of either weapon.

In 1961 an KGB assassin, Bogdan Stashinsky defected to the CIA in Berlin and revealed that he had been entrusted with a cyanide gas gun to kill certain Ukrainian nationalists, among them Lev Rebet in October 1957 and Stefan Bandera in October 1959; both had been singled out for assassination in Munich. On each occasion Stashinsky had discarded the weapon, a seven-inch steel tube containing a glass ampoule of prussic acid, immediately after the attack, so the CIA had to rely on Stashinsky's description. He said it consisted of three sections screwed together, and included a firing-pin ignited by a small powder charge which activated a lever that crushed the ampoule, thus releasing the vapour which was lethal almost instantly if inhaled from a distance of about eighteen inches. No trace would be left.

In training, Stashinsky had been taught to swallow an antidote, a pill of thiosulphate, immediately before using the weapon, and then to sniff a dose of amyl nitrate straight afterwards.

When debriefed, Stashinsky revealed that in February 1957 another KGB killer had assassinated Danylo Skoropadsky, the son and heir of Hetman Pavlo Skoropadsky, the leader of the Ukrainian monarchist movement, in London with an experimental version of the poison air gun he had been given.

At the Church and Pike hearings in the US Congress in 1974 the CIA disclosed various items of equipment designed for assassination, among them a silenced weapon, but it had never been used. The testimony revealed that Dr Sidney Gottlieb of the TSD had supervised research into various methods of assassination as part of ZR/RIFLE, an operation authorised by President Jack Kennedy and his brother Attorney General Robert Kennedy. One scheme involved some of Fidel Castro's favourite brand of cigars contaminated with a deadly quantity of botulin. These were passed to an agent in February 1961, but he failed to follow through with the plan.

In November 1963, immediately after the death of President Kennedy, a CIA officer in Paris gave a poison pen to an agent, Rolando Cubela Secades, code-named AM/LASH, then the senior Cuban delegate to UNESCO, who was instructed to hand it to Castro. The ballpoint pen built by the TSD concealed a hypodermic needle dosed with a commercial toxin Black Leaf 40. AM/LASH smuggled the pen back to Cuba but failed in his mission so he was also supplied with a silenced pistol and a silenced FAL rifle before contact was abandoned finally in June 1965.

Gottlieb studied numerous toxins and collaborated with the US Army Chemical Corps' Special Operations Division at Fort Detrick, Maryland, to produce saxitoxin, a compound that naturally occurs in contaminated shellfish, which was issued to U-2 pilots as a method of suicide. Experiments were also conducted with LSD and numerous other drugs and gases, but the problem of administering the material without arousing suspicion proved insurmountable.

In 1978 Georgi Markov, an émigré Bulgarian journalist working for the BBC, became a target for assassination after he had attracted the ire of Bulgaria's dictator, Todor Zhivkov. On 7 September, Markov was injected with a pellet containing the deadly toxin ricin and died in the hospital four days later.

According to the KGB counterintelligence chief Oleg Kalugin, the pellet gun had been developed in Moscow by the KGB and then delivered to the Bulgarians on the direct orders of the chief of the KGB's First Chief Directorate, Vladimir Kryuchkov. Kalugin asserted that 'by the late 1970s, the KGB had virtually stopped pulling off **"wet jobs"**', but had retained the services of Sergei M. Golubev of the Operational and Technical Directorate, who ran the *Kamera,* also known as Laboratory 12, which had been created by Stalin to devise methods of eliminating enemies. Golubev's unit 'invented new ways of killing people, from poisons that could be slipped into drinks to jellies that could be rubbed on a person to induce a heart attack'. Allegedly one such toxin was used against Alexander Solzhenitsyn 'in a store in Russia in the early 1970s, making him violently ill but not killing him'. It had been Golubev, assisted by Yuri Surov, the officer in charge of tracking down KGB **defectors**, who had gone to Sofia to assist in the DS effort to trace and eliminate Markov in London, where he broadcast on the BBC's World Service. Initially this had proved unsuccessful. They opted against treating the handle of his car door with the toxin for fear of killing his girlfriend, and thereby alerting him to the threat; they were unable to smear the poison jelly on Markov while he was at a beach resort in Italy; and they failed to tamper with his food during a trip to Germany. They finally selected a novel method, of shooting Markov with a tiny platinum pellet containing a lethal quantity of ricin, and this was achieved in September 1978 as the Bulgarian dissident was walking across Waterloo Bridge, not far from the BBC's headquarters at Bush House. He was shot in the leg by an assassin using a gun disguised as an American-manufactured umbrella, and he succumbed in hospital a few days later, his doctors baffled by his symptoms. By the time the microscopic pellet had been recovered from Markov's thigh, and the ricin discovered, it was too late.

A subsequent investigation linked the Markov incident to an attempt on the life of a Bulgarian defector, Vladimir Kostov, who had survived an identical attack while he was travelling on the Paris Metro ten days earlier.

Only Kalugin has acknowledged the KGB's complicity in the Markov assassination, although when General Ivan T. Savchenko, who was the KGB *rezident* in Sofia between 1969 and 1980, was asked about the Markov case, and the subsequent disappearance of Markov's DS file, he replied that its destruction 'would be a completely unprofessional action'. The principal suspect remains Francesco Guillino, a Dane of Italian parentage and a reputed hired assassin, who is a fugitive.

When General Ion Pacepa, who had headed Romania's DIE, defected to the CIA in Bonn in July 1978 he revealed that his organisation had killed several journalists working for Radio Free Europe in Munich by depositing lethal quantities of plutonium in their desk drawers. When disturbed, the almost invisible toxin was ingested and created cancers in the victims' lungs. Further investigation confirmed that the DIE's targets, all smokers, had been diagnosed as having died of natural causes.

The Church and Pike Congressional committees investigated allegations of the CIA's involvement in plots to murder Fidel Castro; President Diem of Vietnam; the Congolese leader Patrice Lumumba; President Rafael Trujillo of the Dominican Republic; and General René Schneider, Chile's commander-in-chief, but concluded that none had died at the hands of CIA assassins. Nevertheless, during testimony presented to the Church Committee, which later published the *US Senate Select Committee to Study Governmental Operations with Respect to Intelligence Activities*, it emerged that the CIA had developed a capability to administer lethal poisons. As Frank Church explained, the hearings demonstrated 'the illegal possession of deadly biological poisons which were retained within the CIA for five years after their destruction was ordered by the President, and for five years after the United States had entered into a solemn international commitment not to maintain stocks of these poisons except for very limited research purposes'. Although the Agency had admitted having found a vault containing just 11 grams of the shellfish toxin, a CIA chemist, Carl Duckett, stated that if administered orally (which was the most inefficient method) this quantity was enough to kill 40,000 people.

In evidence given to the Church Committee on 16 September 1975 the director of Central Intelligence, Bill Colby, accompanied by Sayre Stevens, assistant deputy director of the CIA's Science and Technology Division, and Nathan Gordon, a chemist and former chief of the Chemistry Branch, Technical Services Division, produced an electric poison-dart gun resembling a .45 calibre automatic. Colby testified that this had been developed by the CIA to fire an undetectable, lethal cobra venom in the form of a frozen 5mm flechette, and leave the target temporarily paralysed or dead, ostensibly the victim of a heart attack, depending upon the load. The gun, part of a project code-named MK/NAOMI which ran from 1952 to 1970, had a range of about 100 metres and was powered by a battery housed in the handgrip. In subsequent evidence given two days later, on 18 September, by the designer Charles A. Senseney, it was explained that the device had never been used against a human target, but a compound designated 46-40 had been developed for tranquilising guard dogs at premises where an illicit entry was intended, or for use by Special Forces in Vietnam. However, Senseney acknowledged that the device had been tested against a mannequin to determine whether the 25mm-long flechette could penetrate clothing, and that the firing mechanism, the M-1, could be disguised as an umbrella, cane or pen.

In his testimony Dr Gordon explained that the shellfish toxin had been distilled at the Edgewood Arsenal in Maryland where a poly-toxin from the sea anemone had been identified as being particularly insidious, and was then isolated and its protein chemistry analysed. It was manufactured, albeit in a minute quantity, at the Northeast Shellfish Sanitation Research Center, a US Public Health Service facility at Narragansett, Rhode Island.

According to the former British Secret Intelligence Service officer Richard Tomlinson, he witnessed a discussion at headquarters over the possibility of assassinating the Serb leader Slobodan Milošević using a powerful light source to blind his driver temporarily, causing his car to crash. As a disaffected SIS officer, who also alleged SIS's involvement in the death of Princess Diana in Paris in 1997, he was somewhat discredited.

In September 2011 a North Korean assassin was intercepted in Seoul, armed with a gun and a poisoned needle, both disguised as Parker ball-point pens, and a third gun loaded with three bullets which appeared to be a torch, apparently on his way to murder Park Sang-hak, a defector and political activist who had fled the regime in 1999. Named only as Ahn, he had made an appointment to visit Park, on the pretext of funding his anti-Pyongyang propaganda campaign. He was sentenced in April 2012 to four years' imprisonment. Under interrogation, Ahn, who had defected from North Korea in 1995, claimed to have served in North Korea's special forces, and to have been recruited during a visit to Mongolia in 2005, after which he was offered £6,500 to kill Park.

## ASSET
A generic term for agent, an asset describes an individual who may perform a variety of quite different roles for an employer.

## ASYMMETRIC
The challenge to conventional British military doctrine by the Boers in the two South African wars, and later by the Irish Republican Army, is recognised by the term asymmetric warfare which reflects a scenario in which a hugely disproportionate number of uniformed troops are tied down by hit-and-run tactics. This unconventional warfare gives an advantage to the small groups of fighters who commit sabotage, mount ambushes and indulge in general harassment while being indistinguishable from the civilian population. The principle is to avoid pitched battles and major confrontations by melting away in the face of overwhelming force, reliant on a degree of support among the local community. Strategies adopted to counter these insurgencies, such as internment, secure villages, tight movement control, the introduction of identity documents and other measures may be so draconian as to alienate the local communities and prove counterproductive. Other solutions include **penetration**, the **cultivation** of informers and **defectors**, and **counter-gangs**.

Examples of asymmetric warfare may be seen in the operations of the Maquis in the Second World War, so named because of the dense scrub vegetation characteristic of the terrain in southern France, and the Vietcong in south-east Asia.

During the post-war colonial era British Intelligence gained significant experience in such operations while countering the Irgun in Palestine, Mau Mau in Kenya, Chinese Communists in Malaya, EOKA in Cyprus and other skirmishes in Aden, Oman and Borneo. All these localised campaigns were characterised by significant levels of intelligence support from the relevant security apparatus, usually directed from London through a regional organisation such as Security Intelligence Middle East (SIME) or Security Intelligence Far East (SIFE).

Other colonial powers, including the French, Dutch and Portuguese, found themselves being drawn into expensive, escalating conflicts with nationalist and independence movements which enjoyed Soviet or Chinese sponsorship. These brush-fire wars were unpopular among their domestic constituencies, and the conflicts in Algeria, Indonesia and Angola became such a drain on limited economic and military resources that the stability of the home governments was imperilled.

## AUTOMATIC NUMBER PLATE RECOGNITION (ANPR)

Originally developed as a counter-terrorism technique in Northern Ireland in 1972, ANPR was conceived as a method of monitoring the movements of vehicles used by suspected paramilitaries. The classified contract specified a system, code-named GLUTTON, capable of covertly capturing the registration number of a vehicle moving at seventy miles an hour in the dark, without a tell-tale camera flash, and converting the data into a digital form for computer processing compatible with an existing database code-named CRUCIBLE. Furthermore, the sensors would have to be sufficiently small to be concealed among other traffic management equipment on existing motorway gantries. The original work on GLUTTON was undertaken at the Home Office's Scientific Development Branch at Sandridge in Hertfordshire.

GLUTTON proved highly successful and was installed at a few selected **choke-points** in Ulster, managed by the British Army, before the technology became more widely available and is now the standard for congestion-charge cameras and on-board police patrol car computers.

In July 1984 SIS uncovered a plot to abduct the former Nigerian transport minister Umaru Dikko and send him back to Lagos in a packing case, accompanied by a Mossad doctor. The scheme was thwarted at Stansted Airport as the Israeli agents tried to place their illicit cargo aboard an aircraft as part of a diplomatic consignment from the Nigerian High Commission. Dikko was to be charged with corruption, but was freed by SIS's covert intervention.

## B

## BACKSTOP

The support of what is sometimes termed a **legend**, the false background adopted by an agent or intelligence officer operating under **alias**, is known as a backstop, and may range from a permanently manned office to nothing more sophisticated than a telephone answering machine. The object is to provide immediate confirmation of a detail in an individual's fabricated curriculum vitae. During the CIA's operation to **exfiltrate** American hostages from Tehran in 1980 a Hollywood movie production company was established in Los Angeles to give credence to the **narrative** that some of the film crew had travelled to Iran to scout locations.

**Illegals**, being especially vulnerable, require comprehensive backstopping, as illustrated by Wolfgang Lotz, a German-born Israeli **agent**. A Jewish refugee to Palestine from Mannheim in 1933 who then had served as an interrogator in the British Army, Lotz undertook the difficult task of masquerading as a veteran of the Second World War Afrika Korps. Lotz spent a year in Germany preparing his **legend** as a former Wehrmacht officer and Nazi Party member, before he arrived in Cairo in 1960 to open an equestrian centre, claiming to have spent the previous eleven years in Australia.

Lotz collected military intelligence on the Egyptian armed forces until his arrest in 1965 when he admitted under interrogation to having been working for the Bundesnachrichtendienst, and on that basis he was sentenced in August 1965 to life imprisonment. He was released to Israel in a prisoner exchange in February 1968.

Lotz's supporting background documentation was sufficiently robust to survive much more than superficial scrutiny and ensure that his true role would not be revealed, even after his arrest. Similarly, another Israeli agent, Eliahu Cohen, adopted the **alias** of Kamel Amin Thaabet, supposedly a businessman born in Beirut who had made his fortune in textiles in Argentina, where he had emigrated in 1947, and had then returned to Damascus in December 1961, via a ship sailing from Genoa to Alexandria and then Beirut. Cohen, who had been born to Syrian parents in Alexandria and had spent a year in Argentina to build up his **cover story**, posed as a high-living wealthy

Arab merchant trading in furniture and tapestries. He set out to cultivate members of the regime, but in January 1965 was arrested in the act of transmitting a radio signal, having been detected by Soviet **direction-finding** equipment. Cohen was publicly hanged in Marjeh Square in May 1965.

Both Lotz and Cohen exploited their natural language skills to fulfil their missions, and even though Lotz operated under an authentic name, the investment required to backstop the details in both cover **stories** was immense.

## BANDIT COUNTRY

The border area of South Armagh in Northern Ireland was known to the security forces as bandit country because of the hostility of the generally republican local communities, and the severe danger involved in mounting regular patrols. During 'the Troubles' all marked police vehicles would be accompanied by a military escort, and routes to and from the heavily fortified police stations and military garrisons were occasionally planted with culvert mines or became the scenes for ambushes, often involving explosives detonated by a command wire or radio signal transmitted from across the largely unmarked border with Eire. The risk at some establishments from attack by snipers and home-made mortars was assessed to be so high that deliveries of personnel and supplies were restricted to helicopter flights.

Part of the challenge for the civil authorities was the existence of numerous properties which straddled the border, making raids problematic unless coordinated with the Garda, thereby increasing the risk of leaks and compromise. Notoriously, Tom 'Slab' Murphy, a former commander of the South Armagh PIRA brigade, and then from 1997 to 2005 PIRA chief of staff and member of the seven-man Army Council, owned a farm at Ballybinaby, near Hackballscross, on both sides of the border, and lived in a building on the County Louth side of the international frontier. Such locations provided opportunities for smuggling, and PIRA funded some of its activities by moving cattle, pigs and grain over the border to claim European Union subsidies, and contraband fuel oil and cigarettes to take advantage of price differentials. Having denied his PIRA role, Murphy lost a libel action brought in Dublin in 1998 when evidence was given by two

PIRA **penetration agents,** Sean O'Callaghan, formerly PIRA's director of research, and Eamon Collins.

PIRA's South Armagh brigade effectively laid siege to the garrisons in Newry and Crossmaglen, and committed numerous sectarian atrocities. It was also responsible for the deployment of Active Service Units to the mainland to carry out bombings, usually in London. However, in 1996 an MI5 operation code-named AIRLINES concentrated on the South Armagh Brigade when Donal Gannon, a bomb-maker code-named PARADISE NEWS, was placed under surveillance. His fingerprints had been recovered from a bomb factory found in Clapham in December 1988, and he was spotted in Battersea public library looking at a reference book detailing the electricity grid in southern England.

Gannon had been linked to Nicholas Mullen, a PIRA quartermaster, who had fled to Zimbabwe in December 1988 when his rented flat was raided by police following reports of a shooting in which a putative car thief had been shot by the sleeping occupant of a parked Renault. A cache of detonators and 106 pounds of **Semtex** explosive had been found in the empty flat, but a forensic examination identified the other recent occupants as Mullen's girlfriend and daughter, a plasterer from Limerick named Patrick Sheehy, and another PIRA gunman, Jim Errington. Sheehy would later be found shot dead, in January 1999, in Nenagh, County Tipperary.

Gannon was under MI5 observation when he visited a house in Lugard Road, Tooting, to meet a former US Marine, John Crawley, code-named ANOTHER TOMORROW, and Gerard Hanratty, code-named TULIP STEM. The following day a fourth member of the ASU, Eoin Morrow, code-named BREAD BOARD, was identified, and then RAVE DOWN arrived to stay with Hanratty at his flat, also in Tooting. Three days later Gannon was followed to Birmingham where he was under observation as he met Clive Brampton, code-named GALLERY PICTURE.

Meanwhile Patrick Martin, code-named CRAFT FAIR and someone unknown to MI5, Francis Rafferty, code-named EXCESS MONEY were under observation as they moved into the Lugard Road address. In total, eight members of the South Armagh ASU were identified, and then watched as they conducted a reconnaissance of electricity substations across London. All but Rafferty had criminal records, and two were known expert bomb-makers.

On 15 July all three addresses were raided and components for forty-seven individual bombs recovered. A lock-up in Wimbledon was also searched and found to contain bomb-making paraphernalia, including seventy-three timing and power devices in wooden boxes, although no cache of explosives was recovered. The eight were charged with terrorist offenses and later each was convicted and sentenced to thirty-five years' imprisonment.

The same ASU was suspected of having been responsible for the massive truck bomb which had detonated in Corporation Street, Manchester on 15 June, and although the vehicle had been bought in Peterborough and loaded with ammonium nitrate explosives in London before being driven to its target, no charges were brought against any of the eight men already in prison. The explosives detonated in Manchester were subsequently traced to Slab Murphy's farm.

In April 1997 troopers of 22 Special Air Service's B Squadron raided a haybarn at Freeduff, near Crossmaglen and after a brief scuffle arrested four PIRA members, James McArdle, Michael Caraher, Bernard McGinn and Martin Minnes. Also seized was a high-powered .50-inch Barrett M-90 sniper rifle, concealed in the roof of a horsebox, which was linked forensically to the murder in February 1997 of Lance Bombardier Stephen Restarick, shot in the back at a vehicle checkpoint in Bessbrook. The four gunmen had been preparing a Mazda 626, which had been converted into an armoured sniper's platform, for an operation, unaware that 14 Intelligence Company technicians had fitted it with a **tracker**, and covered the site with covert cameras.

Under interrogation by RUC detectives at Gough Barracks, Armagh, McGinn, the man credited with having built the Canary Wharf truck bomb, and the brother-in-law of Caoimhghín Ó Caoláin, later a Sinn Féin member of the Irish Dáil, identified the South Armagh Brigade commander as Frank McCabe, recently released from Portlaoise prison, and named twenty of his subordinates. McGinn claimed that the brigade had been responsible for the home-made bomb packed into a Transit van which detonated outside the Baltic Exchange in the City of London in April 1992, killing three people and destroying the ancient building. In March 1999 McGinn was convicted of twenty-three offences, including the murder of three soldiers, and sentenced to three terms of life imprisonment, but in

July 2000 was released from the Maze prison. Aged 56, he was found dead, apparently of natural causes, at his home in Killyconnigan in December 2013.

Between 1970 and 1997 forty-two RUC police officers were murdered in the South Armagh area, together with 123 soldiers and seventy-five civilians. According to the RUC's statistics, there were 1,255 bombings and 1,158 shootings in the area during the same period. In 1986 a chain of ten observation towers was built to improve intelligence-gathering, and in 1994 PIRA suffered a series of significant defeats, including the arrest of the local brigade's entire sniper team. Then, following the 1997 peace process, the brigade was split by the formation of a hard-line splinter faction, the Real IRA, by PIRA's quartermaster general, Michael McKevitt. In August 2003 McKevitt was sentenced in Dublin to twenty years' imprisonment on terrorism charges, largely on the evidence of an FBI **asset**, David Rupert, who cooperated with MI5 to penetrate the Real IRA.

Thus, following MI5's Operation AIRLINES, and McGinn's cooperation with the RUC, the PIRA organisation in South Armagh was neutralised, and in later years the brigade's membership disintegrated into bitter recriminations and bloody feuding. As recently as February 2015 Frank McCabe's son was injured by a Real IRA bomb as he attempted to remove a booby-trapped poster outside Crossmaglen denouncing his father as a **tout**.

## BARIUM MEAL

The technique of providing an item of traceable information to a suspect for the purpose of monitoring its progress takes its name from the medical procedure designed to illuminate specific parts of the body on an X-ray. In an intelligence context the barium meal may be plausible and intended to provoke a specific reaction which, when observed, will provide evidence of the route of a leak.

## BEACON

An electronic device that transmits a signal to identify its location, a beacon can be invaluable where covert surveillance is required. Such apparatus may be miniaturised to reduce the risk of discovery and will be limited only by output and the nature of the power source.

## BIGOT

During the planning for D-Day in the months before 6 June 1944 personnel who had been indoctrinated into the invasion secrets were known as bigots. To be 'bigoted' meant that a particular individual had been entrusted with the most sensitive aspects of the plan. As so much of the success of the undertaking would depend on the element of surprise, the circle of those allowed to learn the highly classified information was strictly limited.

## BLACK

A clandestine, deniable operation, most likely one that has a high political or diplomatic embarrassment factor, is known almost universally as 'black', although the term does not imply that it has in-built deniability or is unauthorised. **Exfiltrations** are invariably 'black' because they are, by their nature, necessarily covert, although in the event of exposure there would be bound to be considerable **blowback** for the participants. When, following 9/11, the CIA was authorised to establish a network of unacknowledged interrogation facilities across the globe, they were referred to euphemistically as 'black sites', but details of them were leaked to the *Washington Post* in November 2005.

## BLACK BAG JOB

Clandestine entries are often known as 'black bag jobs', conducted by **'second-storey men'** who are specialists in gaining access to protected premises. In the United States a team of FBI burglars operated between 1942 and 1967, and their role was taken over by a joint CIA/NSA unit, the Special Collection Service.

In Britain the Security Service occasionally undertook illicit entries, although they were not known by the same nickname, and employed a skilled locksmith, Leslie Jagger, to facilitate burglaries that, until the Security Service Act 1989, were authorised under the legally dubi-ous Royal Prerogative. Thereafter the euphemism 'interference with property' was employed and could be sanctioned by a warrant signed by one of several Cabinet ministers. The annual report of the chief surveillance commissioner for 2011/12, Sir Hugh Rose, observed:

Excluding renewals, property interference authorisations were granted on 2,646 occasions; a decrease of 55 on last year. Five authorisations were quashed by Commissioners. The overall trend is flat but a decrease in activity involving residential premises is countered by an increase in the use of vehicle tracking devices. Providing that the necessity test has been satisfied, the use of a tracking device is often more proportionate, more accurate and safer than using scarce surveillance personnel.

## BLACK DOCUMENTATION
Travel papers and other material forged or fabricated to support an **alias** identity is known as black documentation.

## BLACK JUMBO
Since before the Second World War summaries of diplomatic intercepts have been circulated in Whitehall under the designation 'BJ', sometimes referred to as 'blue jackets' but actually the initials of the **code name** BLACK JUMBO.

## BLOWBACK
Adverse political consequences following a miscarried intelligence operation is known as blowback. In Great Britain there was serious political embarrassment when in April 1956 an SIS **asset**, Commander Lionel ('Buster') Crabb disappeared in Portsmouth Harbour while undertaking Operation CLARET, an underwater survey of the Soviet cruiser *Ordzhonikdze* while it was on a goodwill visit to Britain. The operation had been authorised inadvertently by SIS's Foreign Office adviser, Michael Williams, who had given his consent during a brief telephone conversation while distracted by the news of his father's death.

Crabb's mission ended not just in disaster for himself, but led to a major domestic political scandal, an internal enquiry into SIS's activities headed by a former Cabinet secretary, Sir Edward Bridges, and an international crisis because the cruiser had been carrying Soviet premier Nikita Khrushchev and Marshal Bulganin to Britain on an official visit. The prime minister, Sir Anthony Eden, thought he had banned any potentially embarrassing operations for the duration of the visit, but the head of SIS's London station, Nicholas Elliott, agreed to conduct a mission requested by the admiralty and assigned the task to a subordinate, Ted Davies. The admiralty often requested such assistance, and it was not unusual for a ban to be placed on potentially embarrassing operations at moments of diplomatic sensitivity. For example, in June 1953, when the *Sverdlovsk* had participated in the Coronation fleet review at Spithead, a photographic reconnaissance mission to be undertaken by the RAF had been vetoed on the grounds that such a venture would be a breach of the monarch's hospitality.

Davies had escorted the 46-year-old Crabb to Portsmouth the day before the target ships arrived, and they both checked into the Sallyport Hotel, registering under their own names. During the course of the next day, however, Crabb suffered a minor heart attack, but insisted on being allowed to continue with his mission, and Davies appears to have acquiesced. Early on the morning of 19 April they took Crabb's equipment to the Gosport ferry slip and the experienced diver donned his gear and swam towards the cruiser and one of its escorts, the destroyer *Smotriashchin*. A few minutes later he returned to adjust the weights on his belt, and then disappeared from view, not to be seen again until a headless, handless body dressed in the frogman's distinctive, Italian-made two-part rubber drysuit was recovered from the entrance to Chichester Harbour twelve miles away, in June the following year. The Soviets registered a formal diplomatic protest, supposedly after a sentry spotted a diver on the surface between the two Soviet warships, and this had made the matter public, forcing the admiralty to acknowledge that Crabb had gone missing, allegedly three miles away in Stokes Bay while testing classified equipment. Sir Anthony Eden admitted to the House of Commons on 9 May that 'what was done was done without the authority or the knowledge of Her Majesty's Ministers. Appropriate disciplinary steps are being taken.' He declined to make any further statement, insisting it was not in the national interest to do so, thus fuelling a frenzy of speculation. Behind the scenes, Eden was furious, not least because the relatively new foreign secretary, Selwyn Lloyd, had not been informed of what had happened until 3 May when the First Lord of the Admiralty, Viscount Cilcennin (the former James Thomas, MP), had told the Foreign Office, and the Cabinet Office had not learned of the incident until the following morning when Cilcennin had walked over to speak to the Cabinet secretary, Sir Norman Brook.

Shocked by Cilcennin's news, Eden asked Bridges 'to prepare a short report' which took just four days for him to draw up, and was presented to a Cabinet sub-committee consisting of the prime minister, Cilcennin, Defence Secretary Walter Monckton and Selwyn Lloyd. Having read Bridge's conclusions, and his recommendation for disciplinary action, the committee asked him 'to look further into the question of ministerial responsibility, and inter-departmental coordination of certain types of covert operation'. None of this, however, was the fault of the SIS Chief, Sir John ('Alec') Sinclair but as he was anyway ready to retire, having only committed himself to SIS for ten years, when he was originally persuaded to join, he announced his departure, leading many to conclude that Eden had sacked him, which was not true.

The other principal victims of the Bridges Inquiry were Michael Williams, Sinclair's Foreign Office adviser who was promoted to the post of minister at the embassy in Bonn, and Ted Davies who was sacked by SIS, leaving him to complain that he had been made a scapegoat.

The principal post-war embarrassment for MI5 was the **recruitment** in June 1961 by the D Branch **case officer** Keith Wagstaffe of an **access agent**, Stephen Ward, who was a society osteopath known to be in contact with a possible candidate for **defection**, Lieutenant Commander Eugene Ivanov, a GRU officer under assistant naval attaché **cover** at the Soviet embassy in London.

The planned **entrapment** operation went awry a month later when Ward reported to Wagstaffe that he had just spent the day with Ivanov at Cliveden, the country home of Lord Astor who had been entertaining a weekend house-party that had included the secretary of State for War, John Profumo. MI5 then approached the Cabinet secretary, Sir Norman Brook, to obtain the politician's cooperation, but Profumo misunderstood Brook's request and believed that he was being warned about an unwise friendship with Ward, and by implication his affair with Ward's flatmate, Christine Keeler. In reality, MI5 would not learn of their affair for a further seven months.

Profumo's relationship with Keeler lasted just six weeks, but it would create a major scandal, prompt a judicial inquiry headed by Lord Denning, and undermine the Conservative government, which would be defeated in the general election held in October 1964.

In December 1974 *The New York Times* published a series of articles written by the journalist Seymour Hersh about allegations of misconduct by the CIA, based on disclosures made to him by director of Central Intelligence Bill Colby. Hersh revealed that the CIA had engaged in numerous domestic operations far outside the terms of the 1947 National Security Act, and consequently both the US Senate and House of Representatives established committees, under the chairmanship of Frank Church and Otis Pike, respectively, to investigate the allegations of illegal **wiretaps**, break-ins, surveillance and the **penetration** of political groups.

Ironically, so many French governments have experienced major political scandals that the president is usually relatively immune from what the Americans sometimes call 'flap potential'. Opinion polls indicate that the French public expects their intelligence agencies to conduct questionable operations and occasionally get caught, as happened in 1985 when the DGSE sank the Greenpeace ship *Rainbow Warrior* in Auckland Harbour to prevent it from leading a protect against nuclear tests in Polynesia. Two DGSE officers, Alain Mafart and Dominique Prieure, were arrested and imprisoned, and the DGSE, Chief Admiral Pierre Lacoste and Defence Minister Charles Hernu resigned.

## BLUE BADGE
On CIA premises staff holding a blue badge are identified as employees who are permitted to be unescorted. Personnel carrying green badges are contractors whose movements will be subject to restrictions.

## BRA CAMERA
Among the more ingenious items of surveillance equipment created during the Cold War was a silent, miniature camera concealed inside a specially designed East German brassiere, and used by Stasi personnel to take clandestine photographs. The bra contained a Soviet-made F-21 Ammer spring-driven camera that was cradled in the bottom of the bra while the lens was positioned centrally, between the cups. Almost completely undetectable, the device could take up to twenty pictures and be worn with a summer dress with the shutter controlled by a remote release held in a pocket. Codenamed WEISE ('meadow'), the bra was perfected by a group of four Stasi women in the province of Suhl, fabricated by some of the Stasi's disguise experts at the Operativ-Technischer Sektor, and then distributed to other surveillance units.

## BRUSH CONTACT

When a **case officer** and **agent** pass each other silently, without apparent recognition, and exchange a package, perhaps containing information, money or a **questionnaire**, the encounter is known as a brush contact. The manoeuvre is intended to defeat any hostile surveillance, and can be effective in crowded environments, such as busy public transport, even in **denied territory**. In 1961 a future SIS Chief, Colin Figures, perfected the art of the brush-past when handling NODDY, a UB colonel who had been one of three **walk-ins** recruited by his predecessor at the Warsaw station.

## BUMP

The moment of introduction, between a **case officer** and a potential recruit, is known as the bump. The target will have been the subject of attention from a **talent spotter**, and maybe will have been **cultivated** to ensure suitability. The bump is the carefully choreographed encounter between the two, which will be planned to appear accidental or coincidental, but offer an opportunity for a conversation, during which the intelligence professional may not necessarily describe himself or herself as such.

## BURN NOTICE

When a particular source, often an agent, has been thoroughly compromised, or has been identified as a **fabricator**, a burn notice will be circulated to warn others of the dangers of continued contact or reliance. Once a fabricator has been confirmed, past intelligence emanating from that source, deemed to be contaminated, will be withdrawn and the appropriate cautions will be added to the files.

The KGB defector Oleg Gordievsky allegedly exposed the *Guardian* journalist Richard Gott as a long-term agent of influence. The author and former foreign correspondent in Latin America denied this but admitted having attended undeclared meetings with senior KGB officers in Austria, Greece and Cyprus, and resigned from the newspaper in September 2011.

# C

## CAR TOSS

The car toss is a method of receiving or delivering a package or message instead of resorting to a **dead drop**. Typically it will involve two drivers who draw up close enough to throw an item through the open windows, or perhaps a pedestrian who drops the package into a vehicle.

## CASE OFFICER

The intelligence professional who is responsible for handing a human source is known as a **handler** or case officer. Invariably a case officer will adopt an **alias** so as to prevent the **agent** from learning their contact's true identity. This procedure offers a measure of protection to both parties, and can allow a case officer to **disconnect** a source without the fear of **blowback.** When Paul Henderson, a director of the Midlands engineering firm Matrix Churchill, was prosecuted by HM Customs & Excise in November 1992, he tried to establish his SIS case officer's true name so he could be called as a defence witness, but he was untraceable. Later, during the Scott Inquiry the officer, identified only by the alias John Balsom and wearing a wig and large spectacles, recounted that he had told his agent so many lies to reassure him that, in a reference to Pinocchio, he had 'felt his nose grow longer and longer'.

Case officers will be routinely circulated to avoid the danger of one 'falling in love with an agent', a term applied to a relationship between the two individuals where the case officer deliberately overlooks flaws or contradictions in a source's reporting. During the Second World War, when Abwehr officers often conducted the **recruitment,** and then management of an **asset,** it became apparent that they occasionally ignored indications of compromise, probably because their own future was inextricably linked to their agents' performance. If demotion or a transfer from a comfortable billet in a neutral country would be the consequences of expressing professional doubts about an asset's continued integrity, there was little incentive to articulate those concerns.

Routine changes in case officers also prevents the dishonest from fabricating an expensive source and pocketing their purported expenses, as happened to Peter Middleton, an SIS officer in Paris who invented an agent who was alleged to be a senior official in a French Communist trade union. When, in 1983, the time came to pass on the source, the case officer was exposed and dismissed.

## CAZAB

A highly classified forum in which selected counterintelligence personnel from Canada, Australia, New Zealand, Great Britain and the United States met periodically to exchange information relating to KGB and GRU operations. Created in 1967 by James Angleton, then the CIA's Chief of Counterintelligence, and the FBI's Bill Sullivan, the CAZAB conference met periodically in different secure locations sponsored by the participating sponsoring agency with the first hosted by the Australian Security Intelligence Organisation in Melbourne. A two-tier membership of this exclusive group was governed by strict rules which excluded a candidate with a single blackball and required a personal recommendation from the head of the sponsoring service for full access.

CAZAB's existence was revealed publicly for the first time by Peter Wright in 1986 in *SpyCatcher*, and when more was revealed by Stella Rimington in her memoir *Open Secret*, its name was changed.

## CELL STRUCTURE

Experience has demonstrated that the most expedient architecture for any clandestine organisation is a cell structure in which **compartmentalisation** will mitigate, if not prevent, compromise through cross-contamination. Conventional vertical command-and-control structures are vulnerable to decapitation – a senior figure may be in possession of information that, in the hands of an adversary, may neutralise or even destroy the organisation. If the objective is to build an organisation where the loss of any individual component will not lead to a domino-type disaster, the cell system is infinitely more preferable than the *reseaux* relied upon in German-occupied France during the Second World War when the loss of a key individual could spell disaster.

Whereas MI5 had always depended on single **case officers** to manage **agents**, SIS had preferred to employ intermediaries, or **cutouts**, to insulate station staff from direct contact with members of a network. Shortly before the outbreak of the Second World War the SIS station in The Hague experienced almost complete **penetration** when a pair of Dutch agent-runners, Folkert van Koutrick and Harry Hendricks, both entirely trusted by the Passport Control Office, sold out to the Abwehr and betrayed the entire organisation and its **assets.** After he was withdrawn to England, van Koutrick, code-named WALBACH, was transferred from SIS to MI5 and worked as an interrogator.

In August 1956 SIS suffered a similar debacle in Egypt when the SIS network was managed under journalistic **cover** by James Swinburn who headed the Arab News Agency bureau in Cairo. A search of his apartment by the Mukhabarat revealed enough incriminating material for the entire organisation to be **rolled up.**

The Provisional IRA was obliged to adopt a cell system in 1973 when the organisation was imperilled by violent internal divisions, conflict with the Official IRA and the breakaway Irish National Liberation Army, and by some notable successes inflicted by the British Army. At the time the Belfast Battalion's commander was Gerry Adams, but the death of Jim Bryson and Adams's brother-in-law Patrick Mulvenna in a British ambush in Ballymurphy forced Ivor Bell, PIRA's adjutant in Belfast, to restructure the entire organisation and divide the membership into thirty-two four-man cells under his direct control. Bell, a Protestant, was interned in February 1974 after having been denounced by a tout, Eamon Molloy, but later escaped briefly. A hardliner, opposed to the peace process, Bell would be expelled from the PIRA.

Under Bell's guidance PIRA recovered from its near defeat in 1973, which prompted a ceasefire, and his new cell system ensured a high degree of internal security, allowing the Active Service Units to regroup and renew the armed conflict.

## THE CENTRE

During and after the Soviet era the headquarters of the foreign intelligence service (the OGPU, then NKVD, KGB and now the SVR) has always been referred to internally, and in communications, simply as 'the Centre' or 'Moscow Centre'. In the VENONA traffic the Centre is called HOUSE.

## CHEKIST

The greatest compliment that could be paid to a Soviet, and later a Russian intelligence officer is that they are 'an old Chekist'. The attribute dates back to the era of 'the great illegals', when committed Communists, absolutely dedicated to the cause whatever the personal cost, operated across Europe to identify and recruit ideologically motivated spies. That period was marked by the establishment in London in the early 1930s of an **illegal** *rezidentura*, headed by a series of charismatic intelligence professionals, Arnold Deutsch, Theodore Maly (**alias** Paul Hardt and Peters) and Willi Brandes (alias Stevens). Together they have been credited with the **recruitment** and management of, among others, the Cambridge Five (Kim Philby, Guy Burgess, Anthony Blunt, Donald Maclean and John Cairncross) and the Woolwich Arsenal spyring (Percy Glading, George Whomack, Charles Munday and Albert Williams). The old Chekists, imbued with the spirit of *konspiratsia*, were efficient, successful and never caught, although paranoia in Moscow ultimately led to imprisonment and, for Maly, execution.

## CHICKEN-FEED

Information cleared for consumption by an adversary is known as chicken-feed, and the mechanics of developing such material, and obtaining the appropriate consent for its disclosure, often create dilemmas for those planning to deceive, or **case officers** managing **double agents**. If sources fail to gain access to the quality of information sought by their **handlers**, they risk being abandoned. Furthermore, any agent consistently found to be supplying false information may also suffer the same fate. However, there are bound to be strong political, moral and military objections to passing authentic data to an enemy, so plausible chicken-feed may need to be a combination of genuine information which may be relatively harmless, together with fabricated material which is harder to verify but has every appearance of being authentic.

## CHIS

The acronym for a Confidential Human Information Source, CHIS is one of several terms used by law enforcement agencies for confidential informants. The 2011/12 annual report of the chief surveillance commissioner, Sir Hugh Rose disclosed these statistics:

There were 3,361 CHIS recruited by law enforcement agencies during this reporting period. 3,656 authorised CHIS were cancelled in the same period (including some already authorised from the previous year); and 3,312 remained authorised at the end of this reporting period.

## CHOKE-POINT

Physical areas where potential targets for surveillance are likely to be concentrated are known as choke-points. In a maritime context these include the Straits of Gibraltar and the Greenland–Iceland–UK gap, where undersea acoustic arrays detect the transit of hostile submarines.

On land, choke-points for pedestrians tend to be at the entrances to diplomatic compounds, particularly in Moscow and Beijing, making it easier for the local security apparatus to monitor the movement of embassy staff. For vehicles they are likely to be bridges, and during the Cold War MI5 routinely positioned the **Watcher Service** on the south side of the Thames bridges in central London so as to spot cars driven by Eastern Bloc officers working under **diplomatic cover**. Similarly, the FBI installed electronic devices at strategic choke-points in Washington, DC, which remotely activated **trackers** and **beacons** already concealed in the target vehicles.

## CIRCUIT

In the Second World War parlance of Special Operations Executive a network was referred to as a circuit, the equivalent in English of a *reseau*. Implied in the term was radio contact with London.

## CLEAN SKIN

An individual who has absolutely no past links with a particular organisation, and no criminal record or association with political extremism, is known as a clean skin. In a Northern Ireland context the Provisional IRA rarely had the opportunity to employ such an **asset**, as most activists, supporters and sympathisers were likely to be known to the security authorities. However, occasionally a clean skin would slip through the net, such as Patricia Black, aged 19 from Lenadoon in West Belfast, and Frank Ryan, aged 25 and also from West Belfast but born in Isleworth, who were both killed outside a bank in St Albans in November 1991 by the bomb she was carrying. Such an incident, where inexpert terrorists are killed by their own bomb, is known within the intelligence community as an **own goal**. Ryan was suspected of having been responsible for a twenty-pound **Semtex** bomb, planted outside the Beck Theatre in Hayes five months earlier, on 28 June, which had failed to detonate. The common denominator was a performance by the band of the Blues and Royals in west London and in St Albans.

The PIRA quartermaster who supplied Ryan with the **Semtex** was later identified by MI5 as Jimmy Canning, born in Scotland but brought up in South Armagh, who was arrested on 14 April 1992 after more than eighty pounds of **Semtex** was found in his lock-up garage in Northolt, together with six Kalashnikov assault rifles, one of which was linked forensically to the weapon used to shoot and wound Air Marshal Sir Peter Terry and his wife at their home in Milford, Staffordshire, in September 1990. Canning had been placed under observation during Operation CATNIP but his Special Branch surveillance team had lost sight of him briefly on 6 April 1992 while he planted a bomb in Bridle Lane, Soho. Canning's fingerprints also linked him to the Beck Theatre device.

According to Audrey Lamb, the woman with whom he had lived for two years at her bungalow at 15 Islip Gardens, Canning had been responsible for a series of incendiaries and small bombs placed in the West End between August 1991 and their arrest eight months later. Aged 37, Canning had five children in Ireland, and served seven years of a thirty-year prison sentence.

In a similar case Edward O'Brien, from Gorey in County Wexford, was killed by his own bomb on a London bus on 18 February 1996 in the Aldwych. The device consisted of two kilograms of **Semtex**, and when his address was searched a further fifteen kilograms of the explosive, twenty timers, and four detonators were recovered. Also found was a quantity of ammunition for the Walther 9mm handgun he was carrying, and documents suggesting that he had arrived in London for his mission eighteen months earlier, in August 1994.

Previously unknown to the police, O'Brien, aged 22, had been responsible for placing another bomb in a telephone kiosk in Litchfield Street, in London's West End, three days earlier, which had been found by the police and defused.

## CLEARANCES

Security clearances reflect the degree to which an individual's background has been screened, and dictate the access allowed to certain categories of information. Background checks in the United Kingdom were introduced in 1949 following concern that civil servants with political sympathies deemed extreme, such as membership of the Communist Party of Great Britain, had infiltrated Whitehall. Initially the checks were limited to processes known as Negative Vetting, which was simply a review of MI5's indices and the Criminal Records Office, and Positive Vetting (PV), which required the completion of a questionnaire, a list of nominated references, and some field enquiries to confirm the suitability and status of the referee. When the PV process proved inadequate, Enhanced Positive Vetting was imposed.

Currently the STRAP classification procedure involves three levels of access, being Developed Vetting (DV) for anyone with routine or unsupervised access to top secret material, which is granted upon completion of a fifty-three-page assessment form, followed by an interview which can last up to three hours. The Security Check (SC) level allows routine access to secret material, but only occasional supervised access to top secret papers. Applicants complete a twenty-nine-page form and are subject to a standard credit reference agency check. The lowest clearance level is a Counter-Terrorism Check (CTC) which equates to the original PV procedure.

## COAT-TRAILER

The deployment of an individual who manifests the behaviour of someone who wishes to be **recruited** is known as a coat-trailing. In a counterintelligence scenario such an operation may be undertaken to determine whether a particular target is indeed an intelligence professional, based on the assumption that a genuine intelligence officer will not pass up the opportunity to exploit the contact.

## CODE NAME

A word chosen to conceal the identity of an individual **agent** whose true identity requires protection is a code name. For some of their wartime **double agents**, MI5 **handlers** chose BRONX for a woman who was fond of that cocktail, TATE for a Nazi spy who resembled the famous music-hall comedian, and GARBO 'because he was the best actor in the world'. However, in July 1941, an MI5 **case officer's** decision to assign Maria Macek the code name KISSMEQUICK was over-ruled. A Croatian domestic servant, she had been sent to England by the Abwehr to report on food prices, morale and bomb damage, and she was run by MI5 until 1943, but under the new code name of THE SNARK.

Analysis of the VENONA traffic suggested that names chosen by Soviet case officers were similarly vulnerable. A lawyer, Harry Dexter White, was dubbed JURIST; the Vassar graduate Elizabeth Bentley was CLEVER GIRL; the Swedish politician Georg Branting was SENATOR; Professor J.B.S. Haldane was INTELLIGENTSIA and Lord Swaythling's son, the Hon. Ivor Montagu, was NOBILITY. Remarkably, the Hollywood producer Boris Morros was MOROZ, the Russian word for frost.

Any codeword system that establishes a pattern may serve to undermine the security it was designed to enhance. The fact that MI5's pre-war agents supervised by the legendary Max Knight were given sequential numbers after his one initial, M-1, M-2, etc. helped the NKVD **mole** Anthony Blunt identify M-8 as a *Daily Express* journalist, Tom Driberg. Some types of code name can give clear indications of their origins, such as the **digraph** system employed by the CIA.

## CODEWORD

Beyond top secret, codeword classification restricts access to compartmented information. The highest categories usually relate to specific technical sources, such as imagery and signals intercepts.

Codewords assigned to human sources are especially sensitive, and security dictates that as far as possible such **code names** are randomly selected so no clue is given to the concealed identity. This measure was introduced generally during the Cold War when it became apparent that individual **case officers**, if given the discretion to make their own choices, would select a word too closely associated with the **agent** requiring protection.

## COLD PITCH

The potentially dangerous **recruitment** bid known as the cold pitch is invariably a last resort, and involves a **case officer** making an unexpected approach to an identified adversarial intelligence officer. Such ploys rarely succeed, but do make it clear to the target, who may be operating under diplomatic or other **cover**, that their true role has been exposed. The counterintelligence objective is to convey just such a message, and maybe present the target with a dilemma, now that their operational value had been compromised, of whether to cooperate, perhaps even defect, or to report the pitch and thereby reduce their career prospects.

## CONCEALMENT DEVICE

When an ostensibly innocent household item is converted to hide incriminating espionage paraphernalia, it is known as a concealment device. Often the device is an everyday object, such as a shaving brush, the base of which has been hollowed out to provide a receptacle for a cipher pad or microfilm.

In June 1953 the FBI was alerted to the existence of a Soviet spy in Brooklyn when a hollow nickel split apart in the hands of a newspaper delivery boy to reveal a tiny photograph containing an encrypted message consisting of 1,035 numbers arranged in ten columns of five-figure groups, printed on a foreign-manufactured typewriter. The boy told a friend, the daughter of a police officer, and the matter was reported to the Bureau's Louis Hahn, who took possession of the microfilm but failed to decrypt the cipher.

It was not until Reino Hayhanen defected in Paris four years later, and proved his credentials by offering a hollowed-out Finnish 5 markka coin, that the FBI acquired the key to the 1953 message. He revealed that his personal hand cipher was a substitution system combined with two transpositions, based on a grid using the Russian word for snowfall, *chetotia*. To transform the groups into cleartext the recipient also needed three additional pieces of information: the first twenty letters of a popular Russian song, the date of the Allied victory over Japan, and finally a personal identification number. Under Hayhanen's instructions, the New York message was solved:

1. WE CONGRATULATE YOU ON A SAFE ARRIVAL. WE CONFIRM THE RECEIPT OF YOUR LETTER TO THE ADDRESS 'V REPEAT V' AND THE READING OF LETTER NUMBER 1.

2. FOR ORGANIZATION OF COVER, WE GAVE INSTRUCTIONS TO TRANSMIT TO YOU THREE THOUSAND IN LOCAL [CURRENCY]. CONSULT WITH US PRIOR TO INVESTING IT IN ANY KIND OF BUSINESS, ADVISING THE CHARACTER OF THIS BUSINESS.

3. ACCORDING TO YOUR REQUEST, WE WILL TRANSMIT THE FORMULA FOR THE PREPARATION OF SOFT FILM AND NEWS SEPARATELY, TOGETHER WITH [YOUR] MOTHER'S LETTER.

4. IT IS TOO EARLY TO SEND YOU THE GAMMAS. ENCIPHER SHORT LETTERS, BUT THE LONGER ONES MAKE WITH INSERTIONS. ALL THE DATA ABOUT YOURSELF, PLACE OF WORK, ADDRESS, ETC., MUST NOT BE TRANSMITTED IN ONE CIPHER MESSAGE. TRANSMIT INSERTIONS SEPARATELY.

5. THE PACKAGE WAS DELIVERED TO YOUR WIFE PERSONALLY. EVERYTHING IS ALL RIGHT WITH THE FAMILY. WE WISH YOU SUCCESS. GREETINGS FROM THE COMRADES. NUMBER 1, 3RD OF DECEMBER.

Hayhanen was able to explain that GAMMA was the KGB's **code name** for a burst transmitter, and this message had been intended for him after his arrival in New York in October 1952, but he had never received it. Evidently it had been entrusted to the KGB's **illegal** *rezident* in New York, Willie Fisher, **alias** Mark Collins, who had not only failed to deliver it, but had misplaced its concealment device, thereby allowing it to reach the FBI.

## CONFIDENTIAL CONTACT

Within the KGB's unique lexicon was the term 'confidential contact', a slightly nebulous role that has no direct equivalent among its Western counterparts, but **agent of influence** probably came closest. The issue of definition became significant in 1985 when the KGB *rezident*-designate in London, Oleg Gordievsky, named three Labour Party politicians, Joan Lester, Jo Richardson, and Joan Maynard, as confidential contacts. All were known instinctively to parrot the Kremlin line on any topic, and maybe receive some guidance from Soviet diplomats, perhaps taking care not to have any direct contact with the *rezidentura.*

## CONTACT REPORT

British Intelligence personnel are required to complete a document known as a contact report as soon as is practical after any meeting with a source. These documents are considered extremely secret because they often contain more than enough information to identify a particular asset, and are therefore highly classified. The only SIS contact reports ever made public, albeit in a heavily redacted form, were released during the Scott Inquiry into the collapse of the Matrix Churchill trial in November 1992.

## COOPTEE

A non-professional who accepts some limited operational intelligence role, perhaps a regular diplomat, is known as a cooptee. As a resource they can be invaluable, especially in any attempt to confuse a hostile security apparatus about the true status of a diplomat. When the Soviet diplomat Arkady Shevchenko defected to the CIA in April 1978 in New York he explained during his debriefing that in his estimate at least half of the 700 Soviet personnel based in New York, either at the United Nations, the UN Permanent Mission or the consulate-general, were either full-time GRU or KGB officers, or their cooptees.

Cooptees can be especially useful as decoys, deployed deliberately to attract the attention of hostile surveillance and draw an adversary's attention away from wherever a sensitive operation is planned.

## COUNTER-CLANDESTINE

The task of identifying illicit signals traffic is termed counter-clandestine, and developed just before the Second World War in anticipation of enemy agents relying on radio for their clandestine communications. The British established the Radio Security Service in 1939 under the leadership of Colonel J.P.G. Worlledge, with a group of amateur licence holders approved by the Radio Society of Great Britain, to monitor particular frequencies and identify any illicit transmissions.

As it turned out, the Abwehr relied heavily on encrypted radio channels, but duplication of messages in vulnerable hand ciphers with identical traffic enciphered with an Enigma key gave RSS early access to the enemy's traffic, a breakthrough that would have a profound and lasting impact on the Allied prosecution of the war. In the absence of any uncontrolled signals from the United Kingdom, RSS's role shifted from surveillance of the domestic airwaves to the interception of Abwehr radio nets on the Continent, so the organisation was absorbed into SIS and renamed the Radio Intelligence Service under the direction of Kenneth Morton Evans. At the end of the war it was reassigned to GCHQ and reduced to a section headed by a former Bletchley Park cryptographer, James Blair-Cunynghame.

During the Cold War MI5, SIS and GCHQ created a Counter-Clandestine Committee to deal with the perceived threat of Soviet **illegals**. Although the opportunities to intercept and study this traffic were limited, GCHQ personnel manned a flat directly under Gordon Lonsdale's in Regent's Park in 1960 after he had been identified as a Directorate S illegal, if not the actual illegal *rezident*, in an effort to take advantage of his ground-wave transmissions, and MI5 collaborated in the development of **RAFTER**, an ingenious method of identifying illicit signals by amplifying unintended emissions from radio receivers thought to be in the possession of KGB operatives.

## COUNTER-GANGS

A counter-insurgency strategy originally adopted by the British in Palestine, counter-gangs were small self-contained paramilitary units which would engage the adversary with unorthodox tactics. In 1947 the targets were the Irgun and the Stern Gang, both Jewish terrorist groups which resorted to **abduction** and the bombing of civilians. The plan, pioneered by General Sir Bernard Fergusson, was to establish a plain-clothes capability to mount clandestine surveillance operations to identify suspects and then effect an arrest without the necessity of calling in uniformed colleagues. Accordingly the Palestine Police deployed two teams of ten men each, led by Alistair McGregor and Roy Farran, but the organisation was disbanded following the disappearance in May 1947 of a 16-year-old Irgun suspect, Alexander Rubowitz. Farran was charged with his murder and acquitted, leaving the crime unsolved.

Counter-gang tactics were refined further during the Mau Mau campaign in Kenya when hooded **defectors** identified fellow terrorists, and the policy of removing suspects to detention camps far from their villages served to reduce the power of the ringleaders who were tracked relentlessly in the bush by small, specially trained teams who achieved better success than the more conventional large-scale sweeps conducted by regular infantry.

The unorthodox tactics developed in Kenya and in the Malaya Emergency, where 'White Areas' were established entirely free of the influence of Chinese insurgents, also played a role in the defeat of the Indonesian guerrillas in Borneo. However, although the principles expounded by Brigadier Frank Kitson in *Low Intensity Operations* became recognised as an essential component in modern warfare, they were rejected by American strategists who invited Sir Robert Thompson to advise on pacification of the villages in Vietnam. Instead the CIA opted in 1967 to infiltrate, identify and neutralise the Vietcong infrastructure in rural villages. Sponsored by the CIA's Provincial Reconnaissance Units but managed by the Army of the Republic of Vietnam, teams of Vietcong defectors were granted amnesties in return for their assistance in penetrating Communist cells across South Vietnam. Their objective was to offer further amnesties and gain more defectors, especially from the elite Ban-an-ninh, and although an estimated 17,000 took advantage of the scheme, and another 28,000 were taken prisoner, approximately 20,587 refused to surrender and died in firefights until the operation was terminated in 1971. An unknown number of PHOENIX members and their families were abducted, tortured and murdered by the equally ruthless Ban-an-ninh.

Although often characterised by critics as an **assassination** program, achieving notoriety when William Colby was appointed director of Central Intelligence in 1973 after having supervised the operation, PHOENIX proved to be an exceptionally effective counter-insurgency measure. However, in a rural, Vietnamese environment there was inevitably an element of personal score-settling and unreliable denunciations motivated by other reasons, but intelligence suggested that PHOENIX was the most significant factor in undermining Vietcong morale, isolating its cadres from the village headmen, and requiring greater reliance on the more vulnerable regular troops of the North Vietnamese Army.

## COVCOM

A covert communications plan, abbreviated to COVCOM, is an agreed method of maintaining contact between **agent** and a CIA **case officer**. The precise nature of the plan will be closely held as disclosure of these **sources and methods** would alert an adversary on where to concentrate their counter-espionage resources. Broadly, the choices are *Treffs*, **dead drops**, one-way radio links, short-range transmissions, **secret writing**, or a combination thereof, the principle being not to burden an **asset** with incriminating equipment.

## COVER

The guise under which intelligence professionals operate is broadly divided into official and **non-official** cover. The former ranges from **diplomatic cover**, such as an attachment to an embassy, consulate, branch of the United Nations or trade delegation, which has the disadvantage of being closely associated with the represented country, and is thereby likely to attract hostile **penetration**. Professionals working under the latter, known in the Soviet system as **illegals**, have a long history of adopting commercial, academic and **journalistic** roles in support of their assignments overseas. This expedient had been a necessity because initially the Bolshevik regime failed to gain diplomatic recognition from the world's major powers, and therefore could not open and staff diplomatic premises overseas. Their Western counterparts are referred to as **NOCs**.

Between the two world wars the British Secret Intelligence Service, having relied upon military liaison posts during the First World War, placed their representatives overseas as Passport Control Officers. These were ostensibly employed by the Foreign Office, but were not considered part of the international diplomatic corps. In parallel SIS recruited sources among businessmen and journalists, but this practice was suspended after the arrest in March 1933 in Russia of a group of Metropolitan Vickers engineers who had regularly submitted reports to SIS. This incident attracted unwelcome attention to SIS which, thereafter, created a separate organisation known simply as 'Z' to insulate SIS from potential **blowback**. However, once hostilities began it was decided that all Z's **assets** would be absorbed into the PCO system, thereby eliminating the inherent security in compartmentalisation.

## COVER STORY

Known to Soviet era intelligence agencies as a **legend,** a cover story is a manufactured background to support an **alias** that has been adopted by an intelligence officer or **agent.** Unless it is very superficial, and intended only to be temporary, a cover story will be **back-stopped** and intended to withstand a certain amount of scrutiny although, being false, it will probably not hold up to much detailed research. A cover story may range from the standard assertion made by CIA operations officers, that they work for the State Department (where a telephone operator will support the tale, if contacted and challenged), to the more sophisticated commercial cover which may involve a **front company** or **proprietary.**

## COVERT ACTION

A uniquely American term, covert action is a description of clandestine operations conducted in support of an undeclared US government foreign policy goal. The spectrum ranges from propaganda campaigns, surreptitious participation in elections, to armed intervention, usually through the employment of contractors, mercenaries or other surrogates. Throughout its history the CIA has engaged in proxy conflicts, protected by **plausible deniability.**

## CRYPTO

All issues related to encrypted communications are referred to generically as crypto, an abbreviation for cryptographic. The term covers crypto equipment, being the sensitive communications devices employed to protect secret messages, and the personnel who are engaged in operating such equipment. Naturally, both are likely to attract the attention of hostile intelligence agencies seeking to gain illicit access to an adversary's systems.

## CULTIVATION

The process of assessing and nurturing a potential **agent,** known in CIA parlance as a **developmental,** is also referred to as cultivation. The target for **recruitment** will most likely be unaware that they have been selected by **a talent spotter** as a suitable candidate with access to the required information. The procedure takes many forms, but before investing time and resources in a particular quarry any agency will need to be satisfied that the person concerned is likely to prove amenable to a **pitch**.

## CUT-OUT

An intermediary designed to eliminate the risk of direct contact between two members of an espionage ring is known as a cut-out. In most circumstances that individual will have no knowledge of the persons who adopt this expedient to communicate in relative safety, and is therefore not in a position to compromise them. In the event that one of the parties has been compromised, the employment of a cut-out is intended to prevent the contamination from spreading.

> *Encounter* magazine was founded in 1953 by the poet Stephen Spender, who remained as literary editor until 1967, when it was revealed that the publication had been funded indirectly by the CIA which had sought to bolster intellectual support for the anti-Stalinist left in Europe. Among those who contributed to the journal were Hugh Trevor-Roper, Isaiah Berlin and A.J.P. Taylor. *Encounter* closed in 1991.

# D

## DAMAGE ASSESSMENT

Following a security breach, counterintelligence **analysts** will embark on a review of the impact sustained by an organisation, so that the appropriate counter-measures can be taken to mitigate the loss and avoid future repetition. Typically damage assessments, often referred to as post-mortems, remain classified for long periods because the survey itself will be likely to be immensely valuable to any adversary seeking to verify the quality of the information received or to identify how an **asset** was caught. Occasionally the damage assessment itself may become contentious, as happened when the US intelligence community's 1987 analysis of Jonathan J. Polland's betrayal of huge quantities of classified material from his post as a counter-terrorism analyst at the Naval Investigative Service was referred to by Secretary of Defense Caspar Weinberger giving evidence for the prosecution while the judge considered sentencing in February 1987. Weinberger specified harm to US foreign policy, the compromise of **sources and methods**, and an added risk to certain US personnel. The CIA's 165-page damage assessment was partially declassified in 2012 and listed 800 documents, many of them classified top secret or **codeword**, which Pollard had sold to his Israeli **handlers**. In addition there were an estimated 1,500 current intelligence summary messages which detailed US knowledge of the Palestine Liberation Organisation (PLO) headquarters in Tunisia; air defence systems in Tunisia and Libya; satellite imagery of Iraqi and Syrian chemical warfare production sites; Soviet arms shipments to Syria and other Arab states; naval forces, port facilities, and lines of communication of various Middle Eastern and North African countries; the MiG-29 fighter; and Pakistan's nuclear programme. There was also an assessment of Israeli military capabilities.

From a counterintelligence perspective, the information that the Israelis were not interested in was almost as significant as the reports they specifically requested in their **questionnaires** relating to Syria, such as details of a suspect research and development facility, an electronic intelligence system, **unmanned aerial vehicles**, a national command, control, and communications bunker in Damascus, the distribution of Soviet advisors, and issues relating to President Assad's health. Another high priority was a particular NSA manual covering Soviet radio traffic with Damascus.

Damage assessments may also function as a means of identifying systemic weaknesses which require attention to avoid repetition, although some of the details will be sanitised to protect sources and methods. Thus the damage assessment on the DIA analyst and Cuban **mole** Ana Montes omitted to describe exactly how she had been uncovered, and official accounts of the duplicity of Aldrich Ames or Robert Hanssen have not mentioned the role of any **defector**, or referred even indirectly to information received from Colonel Alexander Zaphorovsky.

## DAMAGE CONTROL

Once a **damage assessment** has been completed, and the impact of a particular **mole** has been quantified, an organisation that has suffered hostile **penetration** will take steps to withdraw **assets** likely to have been compromised, and reassign intelligence personnel deemed to be at risk. When, in January 1961, George Blake confessed to espionage, SIS undertook an immense exercise, code-named CRUET, to mark the personal files of everyone known to Blake, and therefore likely to have been compromised, with a traffic-light symbol of red and green colours to indicate the level of danger.

When, in 1975, Philip Agee published his exposé *Inside the Company: A CIA Diary*, hundreds of his former Latin America Division colleagues were identified by names, as well as many of their agents, causing huge disruption within the organisation.

At the end of October 1995 DCI John Deutsch told a closed session of Congress that Aldrich Ames had 'compromised more than one hundred US spies. Ten were executed. More fell under the control of the KGB.' In his testimony Deutsch admitted that policymakers, including Presidents Clinton and Bush, had not been informed of the tainted nature of the intelligence circulated until many months afterwards, and he revealed that the inspector general had named twelve CIA officers as having been responsible for several breakdowns in security and discipline, but as all but one were retirees, only one officer had received a reprimand.

## DANGLE

An apparently attractive intelligence target, ostensibly available for recruitment, may be nothing more than bait, but known as a dangle, deployed with the intention of drawing out an adversary in the hope that a **case officer** may be exposed in the act of making a **recruitment pitch** during what is termed an **operational game**.

## DEAD DROP

A hiding place in which a message, money, a **questionnaire** or other material may be deposited until its intended recipient can collect it is known as a dead drop and is an expedient to avoid a potentially dangerous personal meeting or *Treff* at which either party may be carrying something incriminating. Experienced **agents** will avoid frequent use of the same sites, and will rely on a system of innocuous signals to indicate a requirement to service a particular drop.

## DE-BADGE
The process of removing British military personnel from their regiment and then deploying them on clandestine operations is known as de-badging. During the West's support for the Mujahadeen in Afghanistan members of 22 SAS's **Increment** were de-badged to participate in **deniable** missions over the border from Pakistan. In October 1983 five Britons were apprehended, and one, carrying documents identifying him as 30-year-old Stuart Bodman, had been killed in July. His identification papers suggested Bodman was working under **journalistic cover**, posing as a correspondent for Gulf Features Services Ltd, a recently created British press agency not known ever to have filed a news report. However, in a clear case of **impersonation**, the real Bodman emerged in Kingston, west London, a fortnight later, a false passport application having been made in his name in November the previous year.

The others in the group were identified as Roderick Macginnis, Stephen Elwick, 'Tim, Chris and Phil', and according to newspaper reports in Britain, had been on a weapon-collecting mission for the Americans, with SIS's support. Ken Connor, one of the longest serving NCOs in the regiment, says that 'the SIS team began work in 1981, training the Mujahadeen mainly in the use of communications equipment, in safe-houses in Pakistan' and that 'by 1982 the team was carrying out the training in-country', but the project inside Afghanistan was abandoned when the team was ambushed and lost some of their documents.

## DECEPTION
The process of deliberately misleading an adversary is known as deception, and may have a long-term tactical objective, as defined by **strategic deception,** or a short-term goal, such as spreading **disinformation** to protect a valued **asset.**

Historically, Western intelligence agencies have fallen victim to some complicated Soviet-inspired deceptions, such as the Trust, an organisation that purported to consist of a widely based, influential group of anti-Bolsheviks scheming to overthrow the Communist regime. In reality the Trust was entirely manipulated and sponsored by the Cheka, with the intention of identifying and eliminating its opponents. In pursuit of its ruthless objectives, the Trust tempted numerous political activists, such as Boris Savinkov and Sidney Reilly, to venture into Russia and be accommodated at what were alleged to be **safe-houses**, but turned out to be anything but. Both men were arrested and are thought to have died in prison in 1925.

During the Second World War the NKVD mounted a major deception campaign on the Eastern Front through a network run by two Abwehr **agents,** code-named MAX and MORITZ who were in radio contact with the *Abstellen* in Sofia. Mystery surrounded the KLATT organisation until after the German surrender when analysts learned that MAX and MORITZ, actually Richard Kauder and Anton Turkul, had been **double agents** working for the NKVD, which supplied the Axis with authentic information, but led to many Red Army casualties, so as to enhance the channel's status. Initial study of the traffic by MI5 and the Radio Security Service had suggested that the information conveyed was so accurate, and so damaging for the Soviets, that it was inconceivable for anyone to contemplate that the breaches of security were intended.

Western agencies were duped by the Trust, and in the post-war era by Wolność i Niezawisłość (WIN) a similar supposed resistance network in Poland, partly financed by the CIA. These deception campaigns worked to some extent because the Soviets were willing to sustain considerable losses and make sacrifices, unimaginable to analysts in London and Washington, in support of the cause, an example of the perils of **mirror imaging**.

Deception was regarded in London as an essential component of all major military operations and, having been pioneered by Colonel Dudley Clarke in the Middle East, was practised with Operation MINCEMEAT in April 1943 to protect the Allied landings scheduled for Sicily, by floating a corpse ashore in Spain, laden with ostensibly secret documents; and then in Normandy the following year to divert Axis attention away from D-Day towards Pas-de-Calais. With the success of Operation FORTITUDE, a highly sophisticated and coordinated scheme, deception acquired a permanent place in the West's strategic planning.

## DECOY

The professional intelligence officer, or a **cooptee**, assigned the task of drawing away an adversary's surveillance resources from the scene of a genuine clandestine operation is a decoy.

## DEEP COVER

The term deep cover has different meanings in other intelligence agencies, but to the Secret Intelligence Service it is the posting under **diplomatic cover** of an officer who would be unlikely to be suspected of being an intelligence professional. This was often the case in Moscow where it was assumed that the SIS **station commander** would either be known already to the KGB, or would be discovered quite quickly through information from **locally employed staff,** who were all KGB surrogates, or through analysis of diplomats' work patterns. It was hoped that an officer under deep cover, often a woman, might escape the heavy surveillance and sometimes harassment experienced by the more obvious members of the station. In other SIS stations, where the convention was to declare the SIS station commander to the host community, there might also be an undeclared officer, deemed to be under deep cover.

## DEFECTOR

The individual who abandons their country to seek political asylum abroad is known by the not necessarily pejorative term as defector. The physical act of defection may be spontaneous or planned over a long period, and may be prompted by a variety of motives, noble and otherwise. Most major intelligence agencies have suffered defection, which is invariably followed by a **damage assessment** to mitigate the impact. The definition, from a counterintelligence perspective, is that an adversary switches sides and offers information, called a **meal-ticket,** in return for protection and **resettlement.**

## DEFENESTRATION

The involuntary ejection of an individual from a high window is referred to as defenestration. In March 1948 Jan Masaryk, the Czech foreign minister, was found dead in his ministry's courtyard in Prague. He was the last non-Communist member of a government which had seized power the previous month, and it was widely suspected that his death was not an accident. He was found wearing pyjamas, on the ground under the bathroom window of his apartment.

Another notorious case was that of President Anwar Sadat's son-in-law, Ashraf Marwan, who was suspected of having been an Israeli spy and of having warned his Mossad contact in 1973 about Egypt's plan to launch a surprise attack across the Suez Canal.

Allegedly Marwan had been in touch with Mossad since 1969 when he had approached an Israeli diplomat in London, offering to spy, and had delivered a warning in April 1973 that Egypt and Syria planned to start a war on 15 May. Consequently Israel had mobilised, an act that may have served to postpone the offensive. On 4 October he gave another warning and was debriefed two days later in London by Mossad's director, Zvi Zamir, on the very morning the conflict began. Marwan's dead body was found on the ground beneath the balcony of his fifth floor flat in Carlton House Terrace after midday on 27 June 2007.

## DENIED AREA

Environments in which conventional intelligence collection is hard, or downright impossible, such as Moscow, Havana, Beijing and Baghdad are termed denied areas by the CIA. During the Cold War the CIA was reluctant to establish a station at the US embassy in Moscow because of the pervasive security apparatus, ubiquitous surveillance and the degree of harassment experienced by the diplomatic community. Envoys and their families were required to live in designated compounds, access to which was controlled by the KGB, internal travel was restricted, and accommodation and local staff were provided by a monopoly state supplier.

## DEVELOPMENTALS

In CIA parlance a developmental is a prospective source currently under **cultivation** with the aim of **recruitment**.

## DIGRAPH

Within the CIA, cryptonyms for operations, locations, organisations, **agents** and individual sources were prefixed with two letters, known as a digraph, to indicate to the initiated the originating headquarters division or branch. To ensure continuing security, digraphs were changed on an irregular basis.

## DIPLOMATIC COVER

Most intelligence agencies have adopted the Soviet practice of placing some of their staff posted overseas under diplomatic, consular or other official **cover**. The advantage of this is that such individuals benefit from the protection offered by the 1961 Vienna Convention which grants immunity and other privileges to accredited diplomatic personnel.

During the First World War the Secret Intelligence Service negotiated permission from individual ambassadors to post staff to their countries under consular cover, but these arrangements were frowned upon by the Foreign Office so most SIS personnel working abroad did so under some military contrivance, such as the Permit Office or Military Transport Office, or on an attachment to an existing military liaison mission. In the interwar period, when SIS bureaux were equipped with radio transmitters and referred to as stations, agreement was reached with the Foreign Office that the Passport Control Officer (PCO) and his assistants could perform a dual role but would not receive formal recognition as consular staff, and would occupy separate accommodation. This was a semi-transparent cover and in most cases the PCO was declared to his hosts and fulfilled a liaison function, often cooperating on joint targets and exchanging information on common interests.

The Soviets meanwhile, in the absence of formal diplomatic recognition for the regime, and with great experience of clandestine operations overseas, embracing the spirit of *konspiratsia*, either ran illegal networks or by consent established trade missions which invariably concealed intelligence professionals.

## DIRECTED TRAVELLER

During the Cold War Western intelligence agencies conducted a series of operations known as the directed traveller programme which involved ordinary tourists, legitimate businessmen, academics and scientists who had been granted visas to visit the Soviet Union. Before departure suitable candidates were approached and asked for their cooperation. If willing, the **cooptee** would be invited to undertake a limited task during their stay, such as photographing a bridge or some other installation of interest to the military planners. Such volunteers were referred to as domestic contacts in the United States where the

CIA's National Resources Division maintained staff in many cities to complete a debriefing.

## DISCARD

The deliberate sacrifice of an **asset** in support of enhancing another source, individual or operation is known as a discard. The concept is controversial as it undermines the principle that **case officers** will always try to protect their **agents**. At the height of the Cold War, during the **monster plot** era, some Allied counterintelligence **analysts** came to believe that the Soviets had adopted a ruthlessly Machiavellian strategy of abandoning assets to protect more valuable sources, and in his memoir *Spycatcher* Peter Wright suggested that some very important and ostensibly successful cases, such as the recruitment of Oleg Penkovsky and Dmitri Polyakov, and the arrest of Gordon Lonsdale, were actually discards intended to shield a high-level hostile **penetration**.

Some counterintelligence analysts reinterpreted various apparent triumphs, such as the detection of John Vassall in 1962, as being discards. According to the revisionist theory, the KGB despatched Yuri Nosenko to the CIA as a **false defector** and enhanced his value by allowing him to disclose details that would identify Vassall, fully aware that Vassall had already been compromised by Anatoli Golitsyn in December 1961.

## DISCONNECTION

Often **case officers** may adopt an **alias** in dealing with an **agent**, and circumstances may require disconnection to prevent **blowback**. When MI5's Keith Wagstaffe **recruited** Stephen Ward in June 1961 he used the alias 'Mr Woods from the War Office' so Ward was unable to find him when he sought to acquire Wagstaffe's evidence for his defence after he had been charged with living off immoral earnings. Ward protested that 'Mr Woods' would be able to verify his claims about working for the Security Service, but Woods's telephone number had been disconnected. Unable to mount the defence he wished, Ward took his own life in August 1963.

## DISCUS
**A Short-Range Agent Communicator** (SRAC) developed by the CIA based on the original BUSTER device, DISCUS boasted a longer, line-of-sight range, an external battery charger and antenna, and the capability to encrypt and decrypt the text message automatically.

## DISINFORMATION
The English translation of the Russian word *dezinformatsia*, the term describes the technique of conveying false information to an adversary. Known generally as disinformation, this is regarded by the KGB as a separate discipline and a key component in a coordinated strategy to achieve specific political goals. Disinformation can range from the use of **active measures** or dirty tricks which may include the smearing of political opponents, the fabrication of documents and the manufacture of bogus news stories prepared for planting in the pages of sympathetic newspapers and periodicals by compliant journalists. Modern examples of disinformation include the circulation of fake photographs and other supposedly authentic material purporting to prove the CIA's involvement in the **assassination** of President John F. Kennedy, and the claim that HIV/AIDS had originated as an experiment with a dangerous virus conducted at Fort Detrick, Maryland.

Unlike propaganda, which is likely to be quickly recognised for what it really is, even if it has an impact in the short-term, disinformation is intended to be plausible and have a long-term effect.

## DOUBLE AGENT
When a spy consciously betrays his (or her) controller and collaborates with an adversary to deceive the original employer, that person has become a double agent. The concept was pioneered by the French Service des Renseignements before the Second World War, and was developed by MI5 in 1939 by the **recruitment** of Arthur Owens, an Abwehr agent living in London who was held in high regard by the Germans and equipped with a radio transmitter. Owens, code-named JOHNNY by the Hamburg Abstellen, was the first enemy spy of the conflict to be arrested, having been compromised by his correspondence to an accommodation address in Brussels. When detained, Owens offered to work as a double agent for MI5 to dupe his Abwehr controller and, code-named SNOW, participated in the **deception** until he

was judged untrustworthy and imprisoned in March 1941. By then he had been responsible for luring other spies to England, among them Goesta Caroli and Wulf Schmidt, who in 1940 also agreed to act as double agents. SNOW was also linked to G.W., CELERY, CHARLIE and BISCUIT, who were active members of his network.

The inherent danger in the management of any double agent is the possibility of a further betrayal, tipping off the original controller as to an **asset**'s role as a double agent. Cautious **case officers** equip their agents with a **security check** or a covert means of conveying an accurate report of their current status. In such circumstances the original case officer, having been tipped off to the **deception**, may seek to exploit the situation by running the source as a **triple agent**.

During the Second World War the Germans were adept at the skilful manipulation of captured enemy agents, and were also aware that Allied radio operators were dispatched on their missions with security checks to confirm their continuing liberty. Absence of the check was intended to indicate capture and transmission under duress.

The precise definition of the term double agent is important, and it is frequently misunderstood, or misapplied. For example, an agent who penetrates an intelligence agency, becoming a professional intelligence officer, and then passes information to an adversary, is simply a spy who happens to be an intelligence professional, but is emphatically not a double agent, although the spies Kim Philby, George Blake, Aldrich Ames and Robert Hanssen are sometimes mistakenly described as such. The distinction is significant because if any of these four was genuinely a double agent, the implication is that he deceived his Moscow controllers.

## DRAGONS

During the Cold War, as part of an operation code-named WRINGER, Western intelligence agencies supervised a chain of interview facilities in Germany, at Wiesbaden, Rhein-Main and Nuremberg, and in Austria, where returning scientists recently released from captivity in the Soviet Union were invited to provide information about the projects they had worked on, the location of research installations where they had been kept, and the names of others still engaged on Soviet programmes. The repatriated scientists were known generically as DRAGONS. Between 1947 and 1956 US Air Force interrogators based in Germany, and attached to the 7050th Air Intelligence Wing, interviewed some 300,000 former PoWs, in the course of which valuable intelligence was learned about, among many other sites, the ballistic rocket development laboratories at Khimkam north of Moscow, and at Perm and Samara.

## DRONE
*See* **Unmanned Aerial Vehicles.**

## DUBOK
The Russian word for 'little oak', a *dubok* in Soviet intelligence parlance is a hiding place or dead letterdrop where information can be exchanged without the risk of a personal encounter or *Treff* being held by a **case officer** with an **agent.**

## DUFF
The MI5 **code name** for **microdots** during the Second World War.

In 1941 MI5 experienced great embarrassment when it was revealed that a pacifist Quaker, Ben Greene, had been denounced as a Nazi sympathiser by an unscrupulous *agent provocateur*, Harald Kurtz, who had been paid for every person he denounced. The well-connected Greene took his case to the House of Lords and eventually won his release in January 1942.

# E

## EMERGENCY SIGNAL
During 'the Troubles' in Northern Ireland the British security authorities perceived a need for a method to transmit a clandestine signal in the event that a particular **agent** was in imminent danger of exposure or worse. The solution was a transmitter, disguised as a commonly sold domestic transistor radio, capable of sending a silent rescue request to the **asset's** **handlers.**

## ENGINEER

A particularly skilled bomb-maker will often be referred to by his adversaries as an engineer, a title that refers back to Northern Ireland where a former television repairman, Dessie Ellis, became highly experienced at constructing ingenious explosive devices which often included sophisticated anti-handling booby traps designed to kill anyone seeking to disarm them. He and another bomb-maker, Danny McNamee, wreaked havoc across England and Ireland in the 1980s.

Born and educated in Dublin, Dessie Ellis was regarded by the British authorities as an exceptionally talented opponent responsible for dozens of deaths. Arrested in July 1981 at his home in Finglas for possession of bomb-making equipment, he jumped bail and fled to Canada but was arrested in Buffalo, New York, in February 1982. He was extradited to Eire to be sentenced in April 1983 to ten years' imprisonment at Portlaoise. In November 1990, shortly before he was due to be released, he was extradited to London to face more charges, but after a year on remand in Brixton he was acquitted in November 1991 at the Old Bailey and deported.

Devices made by Ellis killed some fifty people in Northern Ireland and England, and they were characterised by their sophisticated electronics and detonation by remote-controlled, hand-held transmitters intended for use with toys.

The charges Ellis faced in 1991 related to the accidental discovery in October 1983 of an arms cache in the woods on the Harwick Estate around Whitchurch, near Pangbourne in Berkshire when 112 pounds of explosive, equipment ready to assemble radio-controlled bombs, command-wire-operated detonators, anti-disturbance devices, short-time-delay and long-time-delay devices were recovered, some of them bearing Ellis's fingerprints.

The materiel was found concealed in two buried plastic dustbins, and some of the fingerprints belonged to Gilbert ('Danny') McNamee, a PIRA bomb-maker from Crossmaglen, County Armagh. Forensic examination showed his fingerprints had also been on a bomb recovered in December 1983 in Phillimore Gardens, and another two arms caches, hidden in the Salcey Forest in Northamptonshire and the Annesley Forest in Nottinghamshire, found in January 1984. Those sites had been compromised by a pair of PIRA suspects who had been under surveillance when they had visited the caches accompanied by Natalino Vella. McNamee was sentenced to twenty-five years' imprisonment, escaped briefly from Whitemoor prison in September 1994 with Paul Magee, and eventually had his conviction quashed.

The Salcey location included two sub-machine guns, timing mechanisms and radio-control equipment, while at Annesley 113 pounds of commercial gelignite had been stored in two fermentation barrels. In January 1984 Vella, accompanied by his wife Claire, was watched by Special Branch detectives reacting to a tip from the Garda. The couple arrived at Heathrow from Dublin and met Kavanagh, together with two others, and then travel to Northampton railway station. They were driven to the caches in a Rover car which was eventually lost by its Special Branch surveillance during the journey back to London, but when it was found a plastic bag in the boot bore Kavanagh's fingerprint.

Under interrogation, Vella, a Dublin fish and chip merchant, acknowledged that he had been the PIRA quartermaster responsible for supplying weapons to the Active Service Unit which had carried out the London attacks. According to him, the actual bombers, Paul Kavanagh and Thomas Quigley, had exceeded their instructions and were to be withdrawn. Kavanagh, whose brother Albert had been shot by RUC officers during a bomb attack on a Belfast factory in March 1972, would be arrested in Belfast in March 1984. When questioned, Vella also conceded that he had visited the two arms caches to conduct an audit of the available weapons, completely unaware that he had been under observation.

Other fingerprints at the Pangbourne cache were linked to the PIRA bombers responsible for the atrocities at Hyde Park and Regent's Park in July 1982, and the bomb outside the Harrods department store in Knightsbridge. The cache was also found to be connected to a bomb placed under the car of the Royal Marines commandant, General Sir Stuart Pringle, in October 1981. Also recovered from Pangbourne were the keys to the car and laundry van used in the Ebury Bridge Road incident.

Fingerprints had also identified Ellis as the creator of several other bombs, including one that had been concealed in the laundry van which exploded in Ebury Bridge Road, near Chelsea Barracks, in October 1981, and on the bomb which detonated in an Oxford Street Wimpy Bar on 26 October 1981 as it was being disarmed by

Ken Howarth. Another of his bombs was defused in the Debenhams department store, and a fifth exploded outside the Wimbledon home of Attorney General Sir Michael Havers in November 1981.

Also compromised by the Pangbourne cache were Kavanagh and Quigley who were convicted in 1985 and sentenced to life imprisonment. The pair was accompanied by Gerard McDonnell, who had been Pat Magee's accomplice in plotting the Grand Hotel bombing in Brighton in October 1984, and was sentenced to life imprisonment in July 1986.

Another PIRA suspect implicated in the Hyde Park bombing was John Downey whose fingerprints were found on a car park ticket recovered from the scene. Downey had been convicted of PIRA membership in May 1974, and was thought to have been involved in the murder of two Ulster Defence Regiment soldiers, Alfred Johnston and James Eames, in a car bomb at Cherrymount, near Enniskillen in August 1972. Downey was arrested at Gatwick Airport in May 2013, while en route to Greece for a sailing holiday, but the prosecution case against him collapsed on a legal technicality.

The fifth member of the PIRA ASU was Belfast-born Evelyn Glenholmes. She was arrested in Dublin in 1986 but an attempt to extradite her to face charges in London failed. In 1991 she travelled to Havana where she spent five years representing PIRA, having been granted ambassadorial status. Her father, Richard Glenholmes, was also a PIRA activist, and he served ten years' imprisonment for having plotted to rescue the PIRA chief of staff, Brian Keenan, from Brixton prison in December 1979 using a hijacked helicopter. Keenan had been convicted in June 1980 of complicity in eight murders, and had been sentenced to eighteen years' imprisonment. The PIRA scheme to free him involved several well-known figures, among them Bobby Campbell, who was under surveillance and unwittingly led his Special Branch B Squad watchers to the top flat at 38 Holland Park where Bobby Storey and Glenholmes would be arrested. Also convicted at their trial on March 1981 were Margaret Parratt and Jacqueline O'Malley. Only Storey, the PIRA intelligence officer, was acquitted, but four months later he would be convicted of firearms offences in Ireland. Gerard Tuite, who was not present when the flat was raided, bur was anyway wanted on other charges, would be arrested in March 1982 at Drogheda and convicted in Dublin in July 1982 on terrorist offences committed in London four years earlier. He was sentenced to ten years' imprisonment.

The Special Branch surveillance operation had been initiated in October 1979 when the RUC reported that a telephone intercept had indicated that Campbell was about to visit relatives in Liverpool. The day after his arrival he was seen to travel to Euston and stay with his cousin, Margaret Parratt at her flat in New Southgate, in north London, and the following day went to meet Glenholmes. The PIRA team were then kept under constant observation for just over eight weeks, until the day before they had arranged to charter a helicopter from Battersea heliport, when the police intervened.

## ENGULF

This was a British **codeword** for a technical breakthrough in which sound recorded on devices planted inside the communications room of target embassies assisted cryptographers to read the traffic generated on cipher machines. This methodology proved effective against the Egyptian embassy in London during the Suez crisis in 1956 and was exploited in a refinement code-named STOCKADE which helped break French diplomatic codes.

## ESCAPE AND EVASION

During the Second World War selected aircrew and non-commissioned officers in units deployed to the front line, and therefore in danger of falling into enemy hands, underwent specialist training on an MI9 course held at a mansion, Caen Wood Towers, in Hampstead, north London. The estate, also known as Intelligence School 9 (IS9) and RAF Highgate, had previously been the home of a distinguished industrialist, Sir Robert Waley-Cohen.

The candidates were taught survival skills, equipped with concealed compasses, maps and hacksaws, and entrusted with a means of communication with the War Office after capture based on a code to be used in letters addressed to their families.

Once in the German PoW camp system, the trained personnel, who as NCOs were permitted to undertake work outside the camps unavailable to officers, were able to construct transmitters and maintain radio contact with MI9 in Britain, which was a branch of the Secret Intelligence Service.

The Kriegsmarine also introduced a secret method to maintain contact with PoWs in Allied hands through an ingenious but simple code that was entrusted only to officers and some senior NCOs. The system transposed certain letters of the alphabet into Morse, with A to I being a dot, and J to R a dash. The letters S to Z represented a space, and the objective was to write a message in Morse and then encrypt it using words with the appropriate first letters in ostensibly innocent correspondence that would pass the censor. As the two vital letters of the alphabet were I and R, the code was known as IRLAND, or Ireland, and it enabled captured personnel to send important information to the Kriegsmarine, which instructed the families of PoWs to submit any letters received from prison camps in America, Canada and Great Britain.

The Kriegsmarine, always anxious to hear details of particular engagements, or learn the circumstances of a U-boat loss or the capture of a surface vessel, also relied upon another, simpler code in which certain pre-agreed words, mentioned in a postscript offering greetings to a family member, indicated a cruiser or aircraft carrier.

Details of the Irland Code were quickly discovered by the admiralty's Naval Intelligence Division 1/PW personnel, who allowed the correspondence to continue in the hope of detecting some useful information. On one occasion in Canada in 1942 a letter revealed arrangements for the escape of Wolfgang Heyda, formerly the commander of U-434, from Camp 30 at Bowmanville on Lake Ontario. He was instructed to rendezvous near Pointe de Maisonette, New Brunswick, with U-536, but he was captured by Canadian Coastguards who had not been indoctrinated into a scheme to ambush the U-boat in the Gulf of St Lawrence, so the plan was abandoned.

Experience gained during the war was applied in the Cold War era, and MI9's activities were the subject of considerable secrecy, to the point that unauthorised disclosures about the same methods employed by US PoWs during the Vietnam War created great resentment.

## EXFILTRATION
The clandestine removal of an individual from hazardous territory is known as an exfiltration (the direct opposite of infiltration), and successful methods are rarely disclosed in the hope of repeating them.

In 1980 the CIA managed the escape of six Americans from Tehran by equipping them with Canadian passports and having them take on the roles of a location scouting party for a Hollywood movie production company. The Technical Services Division went to elaborate lengths to **backstop** the charade, as Tony Mendez later described in his account of the operation, *Master of Disguise* in 2000, which was followed by *Spy Dust* in 2003 and *Argo* in 2013.

In 1980 a senior KGB officer, Victor Sheymov, was exfiltrated from the Soviet Union in a CIA car, as he described in his 2013 autobiography, *Tiebreaker*, which included operational details that he had omitted from his first book, *Tower of Secrets*, published in 1993.

In 1985 Oleg Gordievsky was exfiltrated from Moscow by SIS in the back of a Ford Sierra by British embassy staff over the Vygo frontier crossing into Finland in an operation code-named PIMLICO.

Nikolai Khokhlov defected to the CIA from the NKVD in 1953 in Berlin and disclosed details of his mission to assassinate a Russian nationalist, one of the Kremlin's opponents in Germany. He would himself survive an attempt on his life when radioactive thallium was administered to him in Frankfurt. In 1958 he was resettled in San Bernardino in California, where he taught psychology at California State University, and he died of a heart attack in September 2007.

# F

## FABRICATOR

An individual who manufactures false information and conveys it to an intelligence professional is known as a fabricator, although in CIA parlance they can be 'smokers' to denote someone who blows smoke, not facts. Fabricators generally fall into two categories. Firstly, there is the intelligence officer who pretends to colleagues that successful recruitments have been made when in reality none exist. Such scams are usually financially motivated and involve payments to, and expenses supposedly incurred by, a fictitious source. Prior to the outbreak of the Second World War an experienced British intelligence officer, Sigismund Payne Best, based in The Hague, claimed that he had recruited a network of sources in Germany whose true identities were concealed by **code names** such as TABLETOP, CHAIRLEG and ARCHCHAIR. This expedient enabled Best to distinguish between his authentic agents and his invented sources. More recently, another SIS officer in Paris reported that he had acquired a source inside a French Communist trade union. He was exposed, and dismissed by SIS, when he was required to hand his source over to another **case officer.** When challenged he admitted that he had constructed most of his **asset's** reporting from open sources.

The second category includes agents who deceive their employers by peddling false material. Into this group falls Juan Pujol, the Spaniard code-named ALARIC who persuaded his Abwehr controller in Madrid that he had reached England when in fact he had travelled no further than Lisbon. Pujol's talent for invention would later be exploited by MI5 when it was recognised that he could be run very successfully as a **double agent,** and thus was enrolled as GARBO.

The pitfalls of reliance on a fabricator were demonstrated when the Bundesnachrichtendienst began to supply the US Defense Intelligence Agency with information about Iraq's chemical weapons which had been provided by a refugee, Rafid Ahmed Alwan, then living in Munich. Code-named CURVEBALL, Alwan had left Iraq in 1999 and would be responsible for some 200 reports relating to weapons of mass destruction being prepared by Saddam Hussein's regime in the months before the coalition's invasion in 2003. In reality, Alwan had used the internet to manufacture his accounts of mobile laboratories and accidents involving biological weapons.

## FALSE DEFECTOR

In 1963 the CIA Counterintelligence Staff became enamoured of the concept of the false defector, believing that the KGB planned to despatch staff officers to the west, posing as authentic **defectors,** thereby establishing a channel for **disinformation**. The proposition would split the Allied counterintelligence community and leave the KGB **defector** Yuri Nosenko incarcerated, on the authority of the

US attorney general, in a specially constructed cell block at Camp Peary between September 1965 and October 1967. The same motive resulted in another **defector**, the KGB **illegal** Yuri Loginov, being sent back to the Soviet Union in July 1969 as part of a **swap**.

During the **molehunt** era the cases of numerous defectors were re-examined to spot KGB **deception**, and there was always some suspicion about the *bona fides* of five who were subject to a lengthy investigation. Oleg Tumanov, for example, ostensibly a seaman who swam to the Libyan shore from the destroyer *Spravedlivy* in November 1966, was recruited as an editor for *Radio Liberty*'s Russian broadcasts in Munich, but disappeared suddenly in February 1986, following the defection of Viktor Gundarev in Athens. According to his autobiography, *Tumanov: Confessions of a KGB Agent*, which was published in 1993 he, like the rest of his family, had been a KGB professional and his unscheduled return to Moscow had brought his **penetration** mission to a close. However, according to Oleg Kalugin, Tumanov was a genuine defector who was traced to Munich by the KGB and pressured into cooperating.

**Analysts** also expressed doubt about Yuri Krotkov, a well-known Soviet writer and filmmaker who defected while on a visit to London in September 1963. Although he was not a KGB officer, Krotkov revealed that he had occasionally acted as a KGB **cooptee,** and recalled that he had participated in a **honeytrap** to compromise the French ambassador in Moscow, Maurice Dejean. He also revealed that John Watkins, formerly the Canadian ambassador in Moscow, was a homosexual who had also fallen victim to entrapment.

After his defection Krotkov continued to write and in 1967 published *The Angry Exile*, a critique of post-war social conditions in Moscow. Two years later he gave evidence to the Senate Committee on Judiciary under the name 'George Karlin' and in 1979 published *Red Monarch*, a semi-satirical biography of Josef Stalin. Krotkov was **resettled** in the United States, but he was never fully accepted as an authentic defector, and he eventually died in Spain in 1982.

It has been argued that the whole concept of the false defector is flawed because no intelligence agency would risk placing a staff officer, and their acquired knowledge, at the disposal of an adversary.

## FALSE FLAG

The **case officer** making a **pitch** to a **recruitment** candidate who misrepresents the country or agency seeking to gain that person's cooperation by **deception** is said to be operating under a false flag.

When the British embassy employee Harry Houghton was recruited by the KGB in Warsaw in January 1952 he was given the impression that he was being **handled** by the Polish UB. After he returned to London in February 1953 the charade continued until August 1957 when Mieczyslaw Reluga defected from the Polish embassy in London. Worried that Houghton would fear for his safety at the apparent breach of security, his KGB contact Aleksandr V. Baranov admitted that he was not a Polish officer. In fact the KGB's anxiety proved unnecessary as Houghton then revealed that he had always suspected he was being run by Russians, and not Poles. As a **cover** for his later contacts with the **illegal** *rezident* in London, Konon Molody, Houghton claimed after his arrest in January 1961 that he had been a victim of a false-flag recruitment as he had been led to believe that Molody was a US naval intelligence officer named Commander Alec Johnson.

In 1982 an American purporting to be a CIA officer approached a woman working at the US embassy in East Berlin and asked for her assistance in a sensitive investigation into one of her colleagues suspected of being a **mole**. She was requested to supply details about the embassy staff and copies of documents, which she did until she became increasingly uncomfortable in her role and confided her concerns to another diplomat who exposed the charade. The man impersonating the CIA officer was identified as Robert G. Thompson, a former member of the US Air Force Office of Special Investigations who had been imprisoned in May 1965 but released in a spy **swap** in April 1978.

In 1989 Philip Agee, a **renegade** CIA officer who had left the Agency in 1968 and then defected to the Cuban DGI, made a very similar attempt by convincing a junior member of the local station in a Latin American capital that her confidential assistance was required in a drug investigation. Agee posed as a member of the inspector general's staff and produced a personal letter from the director of Central Intelligence, William Webster, requiring her to participate in enquiries relating to the misuse of Agency pouches to smuggle narcotics.

Eventually the young officer had doubts about the authenticity of the director's letter, and when she disclosed the details of what had happened Agee's role was revealed. Additionally, the FBI discovered that the address in New York she had been given to communicate with was linked to a DGI officer.

Other false flag operations include Mossad's creation in 1955 of a supposed Bundesnachrichtendienst office in Germany to interview scientists working on ballistic missile development in Egypt. Zeev Avni, who had been born in Berlin, posed as a BND officer to persuade the rocket experts, many of them former Nazis, to disclose details of their work and identify their colleagues. In the mistaken belief that they were being interviewed by an authentic German intelligence officer, all agreed to cooperate.

## FAMILY JEWELS

On 2 February 1973 James Schlesinger replaced Dick Helms as director of Central Intelligence, and he quickly made himself unpopular with the CIA's Directorate of Operations by requiring the immediate retirement of a large number of career officers. He also commissioned a review of the CIA's domestic activities in anticipation of being called to give evidence before the House Armed Services Committee, and was alarmed to learn that the DO had given support to an ex-officer, E. Howard Hunt, who had been employed in the Nixon White House as a security adviser, and had been indicted on charges of breaking into the office of the Los Angeles psychiatrist who had treated Daniel Ellsberg, the **analyst** who had leaked the Pentagon Papers. The DCI ordered his deputy director for Operations, Bill Colby, to review any other questionable or illegal activities, and in May 1973 directed all 'senior operating officials of this Agency to report to me immediately on any activities now going on, or that have gone on in the past, which may be construed to be outside the legislative charter of this Agency'.

Schlesinger then added a further instruction, that anyone linked to Hunt and the Watergate burglars should identify themselves to the management. The task of compiling what would become known as 'the Family Jewels' was given to Colby and the CIA's inspector general, William V. Broe. However, later in 1973, after only a few months in the post, Schlesinger was appointed Defense secretary, leaving Colby to take on the role of DCI. Colby briefed the chairman of the House Armed Services Committee on the existence of the list, but did nothing more. However, in December 1974 he was questioned about the document by the *New York Times* journalist Seymour Hersh, and acknowledged its existence, although not the content, which amounted to 693 typed pages of a loose-leaf folder, covering nineteen topics; it would not be declassified until June 2007:

1. Imprisonment of the Soviet defector Yuri Nosenko at Camp Peary that 'might be regarded as a violation of the kidnapping laws.'
2. Wiretapping, codenamed MOCKINGBIRD, of two journalists, Robert Allen and Paul Scott, in 1963.
3. Surveillance, codenamed CELOTEX II of Jack Anderson of the *Washington Post*, and his associates Brit Hume, Leslie Whitten and Joseph Spear.
4. Surveillance, codenamed CELOTEX I, of the *Washington Post* reporter Michael Getler.
5. Break-in at a photographic studio in 1971 of a former CIA employee who was under surveillance and living with a Cuban espionage suspect.
6. A break-in, codenamed REDFACE I, at Anatoli Golitsyn's office in Silver Spring, Maryland.
8. Mail opening at Kennedy Airport, codenamed SR/POINTER, from 1953 to 1973 of letters addressed to and from the Soviet Union.
9. Interception of mail from San Francisco, codenamed WESTPOINTER, addressed to China between 1969 and 1972
10. Monitoring in 1972 of the World Assembly for the Peace and Independence of Indo-China meeting in Paris which called for disruption of the US Republican national convention in San Diego. One delegate, Rennie Davis, the founder of the Anti-War Union, had been sponsored by ex-Beatle John Lennon.
11. Drug tests conducted on military volunteers at Edgewood Psychiatric Hospital on Long Island, New York.

12. Links to the assassins of Rafael Trujillo.
13. A plot to assassinate Patrice Lumumba, who was later murdered by the Belgians.
14. Surveillance of a Miss King while on two visits to the United States, and on her friends in Detroit in 1971 after she had reported a plot to kidnap Vice President Spiro Agnew.
15. Surveillance, code-named BUTANE, of Victor Marchetti in 1972.
16. Retention of '9,900-plus' redundant files on the foreign contacts of the anti-war movement, of whom one third were Americans.
17. Polygraph experiments on job applicants to the sheriff of San Mateo County, California.
18. Testing of direction-finding signals equipment in 1971 in Miami Beach designed to detect illicit transmissions made by illegals.
19. Provision between 1969 and 1971 to the Washington D.C. police of specialist monitoring equipment during anti-Vietnam war demonstrations.
20. Operation MERRIMAC, the penetration of an anti-CIA group by a woman between 1967 and 1971 who was later handled by the FBI.
21. Operation TWO-FOLD, the training in 1971 of an anti-corruption unit in the Bureau of Narcotics and Dangerous Drugs.
22. Employment of Mafia mobster Johnny Roselli, in a failed plot to assassinate Fidel Castro.

## THE FARM

Within the CIA the training area at Camp Peary, near Williamsburg in Virginia, is known as 'the Farm'. Amounting to 9,000 heavily wooded acres in York County, supposedly under the authority of the Department of Defense, the site is surrounded by a chain-link fence and was acquired by the US Navy as a training facility in 1942. It was then employed as a PoW camp to accommodate Kriegsmarine crews required, on security grounds, to be kept in isolation from the general PoW population. The Farm now includes a 5,000-foot runway and housing for National Clandestine Service candidates. In 1961 the CIA also acquired a peninsula at Harvey Point, near Hertford in North Carolina, for much the same purposes.

The property also included a purpose-built prison block where KGB defector Yuri Nosenko was incarcerated between September 1965 and October 1967 on the authority of the attorney general.

## FELLOW TRAVELLER

An individual who is ideologically sympathetic to the Communist movement but does not openly espouse the cause, but may act as an **agent of influence**, is often referred to as a fellow traveller. Such a person may occupy a position that would preclude holding such views, and make it impossible for them even to acquire membership of an underground Party branch.

## FERRET FLIGHT

Aircraft on missions to penetrate potentially hostile airspace do so to test the local ground defence systems. Such intruder flights may be intended to provoke the local radar stations to activate their equipment, thus allowing monitors to assess their range and frequency, or to scramble interceptors. The resulting information allows a potential adversary to identify the strengths and weakness of the radar coverage in particular areas and to develop counter-measures.

One of the first ferret missions was flown in May 1943 against a Japanese radar site on Kiska Island in the Aleutians. Between May and September 1943, the 16th Reconnaissance Squadron flew 184 missions in the Mediterranean and identified 450 enemy radar stations.

By their very nature these flights are inherently dangerous. Ferret flights into Soviet airspace between 1945 and 2000 resulted in the loss of twelve aircraft and the death of sixty-nine aircrew. A further eighty-one Americans died in incidents involving Korean and Chinese air defences over the same period, and in 1992 the National Security Agency confirmed that sixty-four cryptographers had died on air reconnaissance missions during the Cold War.

## FIELD NAME

During the Second World War Special Operations Executive **agents** were assigned a field name which identified them in messages to headquarters and to fellow members of their **circuit**. The system was intrinsically insecure and breached the general principle that individual **assets** should not know their own **code names**.

## FINISHED INTELLIGENCE
Within the United States intelligence community intelligence assessments derived from classified sources and ready for distribution by CIA Directorate of Intelligence **analysts** to authorised consumers, such as policymakers and other agencies, are known as finished intelligence. Very often the precise nature of the source of the content will have been sanitised to avoid a leak.

## FIREMAN
Within the Secret Intelligence Service those personnel based at headquarters who are immediately available for short-term assignments overseas are known as firemen. They will undertake missions which, for whatever reason, cannot be completed safely by officers staffing the local station. Most likely there may be a **recruitment** or similar challenge, such as the collection of material concealed in a cache by a **defector,** that could be compromised if it involved officers vulnerable to hostile surveillance or already known to the host country's security apparatus. In CIA parlance, the equivalent term is a visiting case officer (VCO).

In his memoirs, *The Big Breach*, Richard Tomlinson recalled how he had flown to Moscow under **journalistic cover** to recover papers that had been hidden by a defector before his departure, aware that they were too dangerous for him to smuggle out of the country. Tomlinson's task had been to shake off any surveillance, find the cache and deliver the contents to the embassy so it could be sent to London in the diplomatic pouch, free of inspection.

In a similar mission in November 1992, following the defection of the KGB archivist Vasili Mitrokhin from Latvia, SIS sent an officer to Moscow to recover a milk churn buried under his *dacha*, which he claimed contained his notes of documents he had copied from Directorate S's records. The officer completed his mission successfully and Mitrokhin's vast collection, smuggled out of the KGB's headquarters over twelve years, provided SIS with an unprecedented insight into the KGB's past operations.

# FIVE EYES

The Five Eyes are the signals intelligence agencies of the United States, Great Britain, Canada, Australia and New Zealand. The cooperation in the collection, analysis and distribution of signals intelligence (SIGINT) between these five English-speaking countries became known by the term, but dates back to the seven-page Britain–United States signals intelligence treaty made in Washington, DC in March 1946 and officially known as the Britain–United States Communication Intelligence Agreement (BRUSA). The document built on the foundation of an earlier pact made in June 1943 between Sir Edward Travis, then deputy director (Signals) of the Government Code and Cipher School (GC&CS, later GCHQ), and the US Army's deputy chief of Staff, General George Strong, which had standardised SIGINT procedures, allocated interception responsibilities, applied analytical resources and regulated distribution. This arrangement was then reinforced by a second signed in October 1944 relating to SIGINT operations in the Pacific. Negotiated by OP-20-G for the US Navy and Alan Hillgarth and Travis for GC&CS, the agreement linked American cryptographers on Adak and Guam to the British network based at Colombo and Melbourne.

The BRUSA parties were the US Army–Navy Communication Intelligence Board, the US Army–Navy Communication Intelligence Coordination Committee and the London Signal Intelligence Board, represented by Edward Travis, Eric Jones and Harry Hinsley from GCHQ. The final document was signed in Washington, DC on LSIB's behalf by the Special UK Liaison Officer, Patrick Marr-Johnson.

In March 1953 BRUSA was replaced by the UK–USA agreement which added Australia, Canada and New Zealand to a partnership covering the interception and exchange of external communications. The terms of the treaty provided the foundation for the pooling of collection facilities among the participants, and the sharing of the product. It also noted the transfer of the National Security Agency's interception facility in Hong Kong to Okinawa. The text of the original document was not declassified until June 2010.

Since 1953 the term Five Eyes has been taken within the international intelligence community as a shorthand for wider security and intelligence cooperation by the five participants beyond signals intelligence, and while it is true that there is significant liaison in those fields, and that SIGINT collaboration has been extended to include Norway, Denmark and Germany, the degree of cooperation within the Five Eyes is unmatched elsewhere.

## THE FORT
The SIS training facility at Fort Monckton, on the coast near Gosport in Hampshire is often simply referred to as 'the Fort'. It provides a secure environment for briefings, small-scale exercises, and the grounds, adjoining a golf course, are equipped so visitors attending the clandestine infiltration course can practise scaling chain-link fences.

## FREDS
A derogatory term used by the British Intelligence community in Northern Ireland during the 1970s for Provisional IRA turncoats who acted as **agents** and would identify other republican volunteers, either from photographs taken covertly from unemployment benefit offices where the paramilitaries collected their welfare payments, or in person, concealed in surveillance vehicles. Freds and police inform-ants were referred to by PIRA as **touts**.

## FREIKAUF
The German term for the ransom paid by the Federal Republic for the release of prisoners by East Germany, *Freikauf* was also used to refer to the **swaps** made during the Cold War to exchange those arrested on espionage charges. Altogether some 34,000 individuals, catego-rised as political prisoners, were among the 215,000 whose freedom was bought for an estimated $2.4 billion in hard currency.

## FRIENDS
The British Secret Intelligence Service is widely known as 'the friends', and is referred to as such by regular members of the Foreign Service who are reluctant to mention 'Six' or 'SIS' a reticence that dates back to the post-war era, before the passage of the Intelligence Services Act 1994, a period when the organisation was unacknowledged.

## FRONT COMPANY

A **commercial cover** used by an intelligence agency to provide plausible employment for an officer or agent is known as a front company or, to the CIA, as a **proprietary**.

Prime Minister Anthony Eden's order to SIS to assassinate President Nasser so outraged Anthony Nutting, Selwyn Lloyd's Minister of State at the Foreign Office, that he not only resigned his ministerial appointment, but also his seat in the House of Commons. Out of loyalty to Eden, Nutting maintained a discreet silence over the precise reason for his permanent departure from politics.

## G

## Gs

Also known as 'the Super Gs', the FBI's Special Surveillance Group is the American equivalent of the **Watcher Service,** being an organisation of specialists trained to keep suspects under discreet surveillance, undetected.

## GANGPLANK PITCH

The tactic of making a covert offer to a suspected intelligence officer as they leave their host country is known as a gangplank pitch. The term originates in the practice, widely deployed during the Cold War, when a fellow professional might be discreetly slipped a note disclosing the instructions that should be followed if they wished to take up an offer of recruitment. Usually the **pitch** would give an address in a neutral country to which an innocent postcard could be mailed in order to signal acceptance of the terms, or **meal-ticket**, which would also be itemised.

The technique had three objectives: firstly, to confirm to the target that their true occupation has been compromised, or their **cover** blown. Secondly, to offer an opportunity for the target to respond to an authentic offer which the recipient could be sure had been conveyed by someone, such as a uniformed customs or immigration officer, who could not possibly be an *agent provocateur*. Thirdly the gangplank pitch, as a counterintelligence instrument, had the benefit of disrupting an adversary's operations by presenting the target with a dilemma about how to declare, as was required by duty, the offer to colleagues who might suspect that the offer was an indication sophisticated **operational game**.

## GAVRILOV CHANNEL
Established by the CIA's Burton Gerber, then chief of the Soviet Division, and his Counterintelligence Staff counterpart David Blee, the Gavrilov Channel was a backchannel line of communication with the KGB's Leonid Shebarshin who headed the First Chief Directorate, and Anatoli Kireyev, head of the First Chief Directorate's counterintelligence branch.

Named after a nineteenth-century Russian poet, the link was used to assure Moscow that the American journalist Nicholas Daniloff was not an Agency **asset**, and to seek assistance when the Beirut station chief, Bill Buckley, was abducted in the Lebanon.

## GOLD SOVEREIGNS
Before and during the Second World War SIS gained a reputation for making payments to agents in the form of gold sovereigns, a currency that instilled instant trust, but as it became known in the Balkans that SIS personnel often wore money belts, it exposed them to additional risk. At least one SIS officer, David Russell, is believed to have been killed in such a robbery in Romania in June 1943.

## GRAYMAIL
The defence tactic of deterring a prosecution from presenting evidence in open court for fear of compromising national security is known as graymail. The option for the authorities is either to limit the criminal charges to those alleged offences which can be safely supported by less damaging evidence, or to submit to defence demands for disclosure of classified material that would harm the interests of the state.

Graymail is a common strategy in litigation involving intelligence personnel because of the nature of their duties, and the authorities have responded to the challenge by seeking the courts' permission to exclude the public from the hearings, adduce testimony from witnesses hidden behind screens, or to impose restrictions on reporting of the evidence. In Great Britain courts have often sat *in camera*, and until 1996 ministers were able to issue Public Interest Immunity Certificates (PIIC) which had the effect of suppressing certain evidence, most commonly details concerning the names and addresses of witnesses when there was a genuine fear for their safety.

The Common Law status of the PIIC was challenged in 1992 following an application made during the prosecution of an SIS **agent,** Paul Henderson, in respect of his claim to have acted at SIS's direction. The judge ruled in favour of the defendant and rejected the terms of the PIIC, so the trial collapsed, and the government agreed that thereafter all PIICs would be considered as applications to the court, and not orders that could be appealed to a higher court.

In May 1961, at the end of a brief trial held *in camera* at which he pleaded guilty to five charges under the Official Secrets Act, George Blake was stunned to be sentenced to a total of forty-two years' imprisonment. He had calculated that the maximum sentence for his admitted breach of Section 1 of the Official Secrets Act was a term of fourteen years, but the judge, Lord Chief Justice Parker, ordered three of the convictions to be served consecutively, not concurrently.

In the United States the 1980 Classified Information Procedures Act gave the power to trial judges to hear secret evidence in private, so as to avoid harmful public disclosure. Nevertheless, defendants retained the right to obtain the judge's approval to present potentially damaging national security information to the jury. The Act also provides a protocol for lawyers to make applications to the trial judge *in camera*, but it does not serve to protect the information if it is relevant to the proceedings. For instance, charges against the NSA **analyst** Ronald Pelton were reduced in 1986 when he was prosecuted for espionage so as to avoid further public disclosure of classified operations. He was convicted of selling information to the KGB between 1980 and 1983 for $35,000. He was sentenced to three concurrent life sentences, but was released in November 2015.

In Britain the prosecution of Katharine Gun, a GCHQ linguist who leaked internal communications to the *Observer,* was dropped in February 2004 when it appeared likely that the defence would seek an order for the disclosure of the attorney general's advice to the Cabinet regarding the legality of the invasion and occupation of Iraq in 2003. Although the defence asserted that the decision not to proceed amounted to proof that the government would not risk the attorney's advice being made public, the Crown Prosecution Service insisted that the reason for withdrawal was counsel's advice that in the adverse political climate of the time there was not the required likelihood of a conviction, and a real chance of the jury returning a perverse verdict.

The SIS assassin sent to Nicosia to shoot the EOKA terrorist leader Colonel George Grivas was a former wartime SAS officer, Stephen Hastings. At the last moment, when a political settlement over the future of Cyprus appeared imminent, the sanction was rescinded and Hastings was withdrawn. He was later elected to the House of Commons.

# H

## HANDLER

An alternative term for case officer, a **handler** is the intelligence professional who recruits and manages human sources.

## HOME OFFICE WARRANT (HOW)

A warrant to intercept the mail and telephone conversations of a suspect is often a central part of any counter-espionage investigation and in Britain, prior to the 1986 Interception of Communications Act, such authorisation was given by the Secretary of State for Home Affairs, or in an emergency the permanent under-secretary (PUS) at the Home Office. In 1938 the private secretary in the office of the PUS, Sir Alexander Maxwell, responsible for handling requests for

HOWs was Jenifer Hart, a woman later suspected of being a Soviet spy recruited when she was an Oxford undergraduate.

Similarly, Judith Coplon, a Department of Justice employee, was the person entrusted with handling FBI applications for surveillance warrants, and she would later be convicted of espionage for the NKVD.

## HOMING DEVICE

An electronic beacon which transmits a continuous signal so its location may be monitored is technology that has been exploited in the counterintelligence environment. For example, the movement of target vehicles may be kept under observation from a safe distance, thereby reducing the danger of compromise.

Modern applications rely on satellite triangulation, and can be traced back to the portrayal in the movie *Goldfinger* in 1964 of James Bond's Aston-Martin fitted with a rolling map displaying his quarry's Rolls-Royce as it was driven across France to Switzerland. Reportedly President Lyndon Johnson was so impressed by the apparatus that he asked the FBI director J. Edgar Hoover whether the Bureau possessed such equipment. Hoover allegedly replied with the lie 'We're working on it.'

## HONEYTRAP

An operation designed to compromise a target by using blackmail is known as a honeytrap. The technique was favoured by Oleg B. Gribanov of the KGB's Second Chief Directorate which was credited with using CIA officer Edward Ellis Smith's relationship with his maid Valya in 1956 as leverage to obtain his cooperation. A homosexual, John Vassall, was imprisoned in London in 1962 after he had been entrapped in June 1955 while serving at the British embassy in Moscow, and the Canadian ambassador, John Watkins, was caught in similar circumstances. In the same year the French air attaché, Colonel Louis Guibaud, shot himself after he had been photographed in a compromising situation. Similarly the French ambassador, Maurice Dejean, was removed from his post after an affair with a **swallow,** the ballerina Larisa Kronberg-Sobolevskaya; and the British ambassador, Sir Geoffrey Harrison, was recalled in 1968 when he admitted his seduction by his chambermaid, Galya Ivanova.

The CIA has eschewed such tactics, on the practical grounds that an individual persuaded to collaborate under pressure will seize the first opportunity to turn the tables on the oppressor and, according to Burton Gerber, a former Moscow station chief, the ethical grounds that such behaviour is immoral and reprehensible.

The British have been more expedient, exercising discreet leverage from an indiscretion, such as MI5's accidental discovery of the illicit trysts held by the KGB's Oleg Lyalin with his secretary, Irina Templyakova, in London prior to his defection in August 1972. MI5's caution was influenced by the 1961 debacle in which the Soviet assistant naval attaché, Eugene Ivanov, had been identified as a womaniser and likely candidate for defection.

## HONOURABLE CORRESPONDENT

French citizens, often businessmen, journalists and doctors, who work part-time for the DGSE are known as honourable correspondents. They cooperate willingly with the organisation, and in French culture such an approach is considered a privilege, although the financial inducements are limited. The appointment of Pierre Marion, formerly the chairman of Air France, to head the DGSE in June 1981 was widely perceived as an acknowledgment that *la piscine* had made a significant commitment to industrial espionage.

## HOUSE

The process of identifying a property connected to a suspect is known as 'housing' and will probably be the result of physical surveillance. The importance of housing is that even when a target is unidentified, the best method of obtaining that individual's true name is to find their accommodation. Confirmation of a house or apartment will open up numerous potential leads, including associated tax, utilities, electoral lists, insurance data, vehicle registrations and driving licence, and other relatively open-source information.

In 1952, when a suspected member of the KGB *rezidentura* in London, Pavel Kuznetsov was the subject of informal, unscheduled surveillance by a member of MI5's **Watcher Service**, he was spotted holding a meeting on a park bench in Wandsworth with an unidentified young man. When the meeting was over, the MI5 watcher followed the unknown youth to his home, and thus was able soon afterwards to name him as William Marshall, a member of the Diplomatic Wireless Service. Subsequently surveillance was extended to both men and they were caught red-handed at a park *Treff* in April 1952. Marshall was convicted of espionage and sentenced to five years' imprisonment.

> The tactics adopted by modern guerrillas dates back to the Peninsular War when Spanish irregulars harassed French forces throughout their country. In consequence, the French Grande Armée suffered a series of setbacks, including the ambush known as the battle of Arlabán in May 1811. The guerrilla activities greatly assisted the British and Portuguese regular forces led by the Duke of Wellington.

# I

## ILLEGAL

Agents operating outside the protection of diplomatic immunity are generally known as illegals, although the term is usually employed in connection with Directorate S of the KGB's First Chief Directorate. Specialists in this discipline, referred to as 'Line N', either adopt the role of an illegal for overseas assignments, some of which last many years, or act as illegal support officers, attached to the local **legal** *rezidentura* providing money, documents and other assistance to their undercover colleagues, with whom they will communicate through the expedient of **dead drops**.

During the Cold War this elite organisation inherited the tradition established before the Second World War when the NKVD's foreign networks, in the absence of formal diplomatic representation in many target countries, were largely directed and controlled by a group of cosmopolitan professionals, often respectfully called the old **Chekists**.

In the United States the NKVD's first illegal *rezidentura* was accommodated in New York by Amtorg, the Soviet trading company and commercial **cover,** and from 1934 was headed by the illegal *rezident,* Gaik B. Ovakimian, who had arrived in 1932 under chemical engineer cover, and succeeded Valentin Markin when the latter was killed in a bar brawl two years later. Ovakimian would be arrested in May 1941 after the FBI had extracted an incriminating statement from one of his sources, Dr Maurice Cooke, acknowledging that he had been recruited to steal industrial secrets. Ovakimian was deported to Moscow in return for three American women held in Soviet gaols. Ovakimian was replaced by his deputy, Jacob Golos, **alias** Jacob Baisin, who ran a travel agency, World Tourists Inc., in Manhattan, who then died of a heart attack in November 1943.

As well as the Soviets, the greatest investor in illegals is thought to have been the Cuban DGI which, according to documents copied by the KGB **defector** Vasili Mitrokhin, deployed 650 illegals to South American destinations staged through Prague over a period of four years. All were equipped with authentic passports from various Latin American countries, but with **alias** identities.

## IMPERSONATION

One method of acquiring **alias** identification, usually for the use of an **illegal,** is for an intelligence professional to adopt the identity of an authentic individual in circumstances in which the sponsoring agency is confident that there is little or no risk of exposure. This procedure has gone awry on at least two occasions when the unwitting donor has turned out to be alive.

In April 1988 a man posing as Erwin van Haarlem was arrested in London and exposed by DNA testing not to be of the Dutch parentage he claimed, but actually an StB officer, Vaclav Jelinek, who began his mission to London in 1975. He worked as a Hilton hotel manager, but in 1977 was reunited by the Red Cross with his mother, Joanna van Haarlem, who had been searching for her son for years, having given him up for adoption during the war. Surprised by this development, Jelinek perpetuated the **deception,** but was betrayed by an StB **defector** in 1988, and in 1989 was sentenced to ten years' imprisonment. Upon his return to Prague in 1994 he successfully sued the new Czech government for compensation and published an account of his experiences as an illegal. Meanwhile, Joanna van Haarlem traced her real son, a factory manager in the Czech Republic.

In March 1985, in a not dissimilar case, a Polish UB officer, Jerzy Kaczmarek, was arrested in Bremen while living as Janusz Arnoldt, an alias he had adopted in 1977. The real Arnoldt had been placed in an orphanage in 1947 but Kaczmarek employed the Red Cross to trace his birth mother Hildegard, then living in West Germany, and turned up, claiming to be her long-lost son. The shock of the reunion killed her, but the rest of her family welcomed Janusz and he found a job in Bremen as a civil servant dealing with immigration issues, and joined the Social Democrats. The impersonation was exposed in 1985 when the real Janusz Arnoldt materialised and denounced his substitute, but three days later he too suffered a fatal heart attack.

A search of Kaczmarek's home revealed espionage paraphernalia including a short-wave radio, a photographic laboratory, a brief-case with false compartments and a nutcracker **concealment device** in which his ciphers were hidden. He was detained for ten months before being included in a **spy swap** in Berlin in February 1986 and **resettled** in Poznan.

The FBI's knowledge of Soviet tradecraft in relation to illegals dates back to July 1963 when a raid on the Washington apartment of Alexandre Sokolov, **alias** Robert Baltch, and his wife Lise-Lotte Sokolov, alias Joy Ann Garber, revealed, in a wealth of other incriminating espionage paraphernalia, a pair of forged US passports in the names of James O. Jackson and Bertha R. Jackson. The passports were entirely false, although when checked some of the details proved authentic. The genuine James Jackson, an athletics coach living in Texas, had been issued with a passport bearing the same number on the same date, and he had used it to travel across eastern Europe in May 1961. Bertha's passport had been issued to a Harry Lee Jackson, an advertising executive from Maryland who had visited Europe in July 1961, and apparently had inadvertently provided the GRU with an opportunity to copy the contents.

The real Robert K. Baltch turned out to be a Catholic priest from Dormont, Pennsylvania, whose parents had been immigrants from Lithuania. They had returned home in 1933, having acquired US citizenship, and had taken their son and daughter with them. After the war, in March 1947, the entire family had travelled back to America where Robert had been ordained, and had even applied for a renewal of his US passport. At the time the imposter was obtaining a marriage licence in lower Manhattan, the real Robert Baltch was serving his congregation in Amsterdam, an industrial town in upstate New York. As for Joy Ann Garber, she also existed, as a married woman in Norwalk, Connecticut. Doubtless the GRU had obtained details of Robert Baltch's passport details, probably in Moscow soon after his father had applied for passports for his family at the US embassy in Moscow back in 1940. The use of Joy Garber's identity was rather more unusual. In the various official papers she had signed since her arrival in the US, the illegal masquerading as Joy Ann Garber had correctly given her birth details as 16 May 1930, at Springfield, Massachusetts. Curiously, when the FBI checked the original record it was discovered that Joy Ann's parents had been Ossip and Sonia Garber, her father being the photographer who had been convicted with eight others in a fraudulent passport racket in New York in 1939. He had been released from prison in 1940, and had died in 1951.

In October 1964 espionage charges were dropped against Sokolov and his wife. They were deported to Prague, and he died in Moscow in 1973.

## IMPULSE
The KGB term for a clandestine signals intelligence collection facility usually located in the *rezidentura* of an overseas embassy. The GRU equivalent was known as ZENIT.

## INCREMENT
The small group of 22 Special Air Service Regiment's sabre squadron personnel who have undergone 'incremental training' to work with the Secret Intelligence Service are known as the Increment. They are considered qualified to act as bodyguards and undertake other roles in support of SIS missions, such as the operation in April 2011 to open a backchannel and negotiate with Libya's breakaway National Transitional Council. The SIS officer was accompanied by seven protection staff from the Increment, but they were surrounded and detained by a group of anti-Ghadaffi rebels. The SIS team, which had just landed from a pair of Chinook helicopters, was finally released after the intervention of the British ambassador, and returned to Malta aboard HMS *Cumberland*.

## INDUCTION ANTENNA

During the First World War technicians on the Western Front routinely attempted to intercept the enemy's landline communications by tracing the relevant target cables and splicing the wires so as to gain unauthorised access to the traffic. This technique was hazardous and time-consuming, and risked compromise because of the interference with the integrity of the cable, but it was later discovered that laying another cable alongside the target had the effect of an induction antenna and successfully picked up the signal with only a small loss of strength. Thereafter the use of this technique became widespread.

The principle of the induction antennae was later applied to other targets, and was particularly successful when the National Security Agency tapped Soviet underwater cables near the naval bases at Murmansk and Petropavlovsk, and the Libyan landline in the Gulf of Sirte which connected Benghazi to Tripoli. Those operations, betrayed by NSA **analyst** Ronald Pelton in 1982, resulted in the recovery by the Soviets of an ingenious pod which had been placed over the cable, and later put on display at the Red Army Museum in Moscow.

## IN OBSCURA

The moment when an intelligence professional is positively free of hostile surveillance is known as *in obscura*, regarded as an opportunity to change appearance or undertake some other **operational act** that, if observed, might serve to compromise the individual or operation.

## INTRUSIVE SURVEILLANCE

Some surveillance techniques are considered especially sensitive because of their intrusive nature, and among them is a procedure, known as a remote administration tool (RAT) developed by the Federal Bureau of Investigation at its Operational Technology Division laboratory in Quantico. This consisted of a computer program that, when downloaded onto a target computer, activated the webcam without switching on the indicator light. No statistics have been published regarding the grant of warrants to exploit invasive methods, but the issue became public in February 2014 during an FBI investigation into a fraud in Houston, Texas.

The secret strategy behind the campaign conducted against the Turks by T.E. Lawrence ('Lawrence of Arabia') was to cut the Ottoman landline communications, usually by destroying the telegraph poles that ran alongside the railways, thus forcing the enemy to rely on wireless transmissions. This traffic was then intercepted by a British signals intelligence organisation using antennae sited on top of the Pyramids.

# J

## JARK

The **homing devices** inserted into paramilitary weapons in Northern Ireland, so the security authorities could track their movement, were known as jarks. The task of finding, **tagging** and then monitoring the contents of hidden caches of weapons and explosives became a significant preoccupation during 'the Troubles'. Jarks proved an efficient method of remotely identifying the precise location of a particular weapon, often enabling a car carrying terrorists to be interdicted before it could be fired.

## JIB

The Jack-in-the-Box, abbreviated to JIB, was a device which enabled a pop-up dummy to replace a passenger in a vehicle when a **rolling car meet** was in progress. Designed for use in **denied territory** the JIB was developed in 1980 by the CIA's Office of Technical Services from an inflatable doll purchased to deceive hostile surveillance. Packed into a briefcase, the mechanical figure, with an authentic-looking head but a folding wooden torso, would spring into action when required, and disappear equally quickly. The JIB was intended to demonstrate that a passenger seat was occupied, either to conceal the absence of the real passenger who might have slipped out temporarily to fulfil some **operational act**, such as servicing a **dead drop** or holding a *Treff*, or occupy the seat until an agent jumped into it. In May 1982 the JIB was employed successfully to facilitate a meeting with Adolf Tolkachev.

In September 1985 Edward Lee Howard's wife Mary, who had undergone a CIA training course before a planned deployment to Moscow, used just such a device to assist her husband's escape while supposedly under intense FBI surveillance. Once Howard had jumped from the vehicle he was replaced by a home-made mannequin, leaving the FBI surveillance team with the impression that both had driven back to their home in Santa Fe after a dinner at a local restaurant. The ruse worked and Howard's absence was not noticed until after he had caught a flight out of the country. At the time of his escape, Howard was under investigation as a suspected **mole,** having been dismissed from the Agency two years earlier for misconduct exposed during a routine **polygraph** examination. Having admitted to petty theft and drug use, Howard had been fired, and then had approached the Soviets in Vienna, although his identification would be part of Vitali Yurchenko's **meal-ticket** when he **defected** in August 1985.

## JOURNALISTIC COVER

As the role of a journalist is so close to that of an intelligence officer, recruiting confidential sources and drafting reports in a specific format, many journalists maintain contact with the intelligence community, and intelligence professionals occasionally recruit journalists as agents or adopt journalistic covers themselves. Certainly the New China News Agency, the TASS news agency, and Novosti have all provided slots for, respectively, the PRC's Ministry of State Security, the KGB and GRU.

In 1916 SIS set the precedent by the purchase of the Reuters news agency, through an intermediary, Roderick Jones, buoyed with a secret British government guarantee of financial support. He liaised with Raymond Henniker-Heaton, formerly the editor of *You*, 'the magazine of practical psychology', who was appointed to run SIS's Section X, the organisation's press liaison department.

Jones would be appointed a director of Cable and Wireless and then director of Propaganda when the Ministry of Information was created. Numerous overseas offices were opened for the sole purpose of gathering intelligence, and both during and after the Second World War several Reuters correspondents pursued a parallel clandestine career. Peter Brown, formerly the *Morning Post*'s correspondent in Belgrade, joined Reuters before he was recruited by David Footman into SIS's political section as an expert on left-wing movements in Europe. Leslie Smith, who spent much time in pre-war China, joined SIS's Southeast Asia staff; Brian Connell, latterly ITV's chief commentator on foreign affairs, went into Naval Intelligence, while Courtenay Young became an MI5 **molehunter**. Frederick Vanden Heuvel, a colourful SIS officer, masqueraded as the assistant press attaché at the Berne embassy throughout the war, and his SIS colleague Wilfred Hindle, who masterminded many of SIS's anti-Soviet operations, wrote *Portrait of a Newspaper and Foreign Correspondent* while based at SIS's station in pre-war Budapest.

The famous Australian Far East hand, Richard Hughes, became a legend on the fringes of the espionage world, and scooped the world in February 1956 by his exclusive interview in Moscow with Guy Burgess and Donald Maclean. Hitherto, there had been no news of 'the missing diplomats' and it was Hughes who broke the story that the pair had defected to the Soviet Union. Together with his SIS contact, Michael Wrigley, Hughes was immortalised first by Ian Fleming in *You Only Live Twice*, as Dikko Henderson, and then by John le Carré, in *The Honourable Schoolboy*, thereby placing a semi-official imprimatur on the close relationship between intelligence professionals and writers, of the kind established in Vienna immediately after the war when Graham Greene relied on Bill Hutton for authentic local colour while researching the background to *The Third Man*. Hutton, a North Country newspaperman before the war, had won his Military Cross at Anzio and fought behind the Afrika Korps lines with the Long Range Desert Group. Fluent in Russian, he had been a key figure in the quadripartite occupation, although his official post was supposedly limited to press liaison.

In the post-war era SIS developed very close links with Mercury, the news agency set up by Ian Fleming, who despatched Ian Colvin to Berlin, Donald McCormick to Tangier, Antony Terry to Vienna and Cedric Salter to Barcelona. All had enjoyed considerable wartime intelligence experience, ranging from SIS, through Naval Intelligence, to SOE. In fact it was SOE which acquired most of SIS's journalistic activities, principally the Britanova news agency, which in 1940 came under the amorphous umbrella of the Ministry of Economic Warfare. Britanova was a hugely successful, ostensibly independent organisation that was eventually to grow into a post-war SIS front, the Arab

News Agency (ANA), with branches in Amman, Baghdad, Beirut, New York, Paris and Jerusalem, distributing material in English and Arabic to almost every Arab newspaper, and even to All-India Radio.

Once ANA was well established, two others followed, Near and Far East News (NAFEN) and NAFEN Asia, both with the same directors in control: Alan Hare, then a serving SIS officer, and Adelaide Maturin, a secretary in the wartime SOE who later switched to SIS. While ANA covered the Middle East, NAFEN opened offices across Africa and in both India and Pakistan. However, SIS was forced to abandon ANA as a **cover** for its Middle East operations in August 1956 when Jim Swinburn, the agency's manager in Cairo, was arrested and convicted of espionage. His entire network of more than thirty sources was rounded up, and a huge quantity of incriminating documents was found at his flat, so the ANA was absorbed into Reuters. At that time the senior ANA staffer, based in Cyprus, was Tom Little, a Fleet Street veteran who had worked with *The Times* and the *Economist*, and the fact that both Little and the ANA were SIS **assets** was so well known that, according to Colonel Abd-el-Qader Hatem, who was a senior member of Nasser's Organisation of Free Officers, Little was fed 'with misleading information which they knew would go the British secret service'. Eventually ANA and NAFEN, operating from offices neighbouring Reuters headquarters in Fleet Street, lost their separate identities and British propaganda was channelled through conduits controlled by the Foreign Office's Information Research Department (IRD), which itself was staffed by a high proportion of SIS personnel.

Anthony Cavendish joined United Press after his premature departure from SIS's Vienna station in 1955, and experienced many hair-raising adventures because his SIS connections had become well known to his KGB adversaries. When *The Sunday Times*' Insight team turned its attention on Kim Philby, for a series of articles that were eventually published in October 1967, long before the public had any inkling of the scale of his treachery, or even that he had disappeared to Moscow, details of the research undertaken by Philip Knightley, David Leitch and Bruce Page were leaked to SIS by the paper's editor-in-chief, Denis Hamilton. Later a director of Reuters, Hamilton had joined *The Times* in 1946. He consulted the current SIS Chief, Sir Dick White, and Sir Denis Greenhill, then Chairman of the Joint Intelligence Committee, who held several meetings with

*The Sunday Times* editor, Harry Evans, to persuade him to abort the project. Greenhill failed, but did get Hamilton's consent to an arrangement which gave SIS advance notice of every disclosure the Insight reporters intended to make.

The Insight journalists were largely hostile to the intelligence establishment and were determined to pursue what they perceived to be an astonishing Whitehall cover-up of the damage Philby had inflicted. In the end SIS begged Evans at least to protect the identity of Philby's oldest friend, I.I. 'Tim' Milne, who was still operational at the time of publication, being the SIS **station commander** in Tokyo. Both Tim and his younger brother Tony, then working at headquarters, having returned from the SIS station in Montevideo, had dedicated their lives to SIS, and had been cruelly betrayed by Philby, and their public exposure could ruin whatever prospects remained for them, as well as putting Tim's life at risk. Evans accepted SIS's argument, and Milne's name was kept from the public until he retired from SIS the following year.

In a reversal of European practice, the CIA is prohibited by Congress from employing journalists, the American press corps being highly sensitive to the charge that its members report to the US government after Senator Frank Church's committee revealed in 1976 that fifty US newsmen had been on the CIA's payroll. Anxious to disassociate the Fourth Estate from the administration, the media demanded and obtained from Congress a special status intended to protect it from external pressure, reinforcing a commitment made by George Bush when he was DCI: 'The CIA will not enter into any paid or contracted relationship with any full-time or part-time news correspondent accredited by any United States news service, newspaper, periodical, radio or television network or station.' Although not enshrined in federal law, like the statute which prevents the CIA from recruiting from the Peace Corps (or any former member within five years of departure), the rule is enforced with, as the former DCI, Admiral Stansfield Turner testified, only very rare exceptions. An identical rule applies to members of religious orders and US AID, but to no other group, although he did recall a single instance when, during the 1979 Iranian embassy hostage crisis, the CIA contemplated recruiting an American correspondent believed to have access to the Tehran compound. However, in the event, the scheme was abandoned.

The CIA's rule, of course, only applies to Americans, leaving foreign reporters open to the Agency's blandishments. The veteran Middle East photographer Claude Salhani, who is of Egyptian origin but brought up in the Lebanon, acknowledges that much of what he did while covering the civil war in Beirut made him very attractive to numerous intelligence agencies.

On one occasion in 1975 he was invited to spend three days in a training camp run by the Popular Front for the Liberation of Palestine General Command, a faction headed by Ahmed Jibril and his subordinate, the notorious Abu Abbas. The camp, the size of a small village, hewn out of the side of a mountain, had provided facilities to almost every terrorist organisation on the globe, teaching tactics and weapon handling to revolutionaries from Latin America, the Basque country, Corsica, Northern Ireland and Germany. 'Intelligence services such as Israel's powerful Mossad, Britain's MI5 and France's SDECE would have paid dearly to learn more about this "University of International Terrorism". It was a rare opportunity for me to be allowed to enter such a place,' recalled Salhani, who was to rub shoulders with Baader-Meinhoff gunmen, Red Army Faction plane hijackers and Provisional IRA bombers. Some years later, in March 1981, he was covering for UPI the seizure of a Boeing 720 which had landed in Damascus when he accidentally discovered a way of eavesdropping on the cockpit conversations during the two weeks of tense negotiations conducted by the Syrian authorities by using his car's FM radio:

> This led the resident CIA station chief in Damascus to approach us, wanting to know how UPI had obtained all this information only moments after the exchanges took place between Brigadier-General Kholi and the hijackers ... Cables had been frantically flying back and forth between the CIA's headquarters in Langley, Virginia, and the Syrian capital as the Americans desperately tried to discover more on the fate of the Americans held hostage aboard the plane.

Salhani never let on to his source, but eventually both the CIA and the Syrians realised how the news was leaking.

When Turner was first appointed DCI, by President Jimmy Carter in March 1977, he dined with his British counterpart,

Sir Maurice Oldfield, who appalled his guest by suggesting that the media represented a useful and highly economic source of information. Describing SIS as 'stymied by not being able to keep pace with the technical revolution ... and by spiralling costs', he recalled that Oldfield had suggested that plenty of good foreign intelligence was available domestically, without the hazard of sending agents into hostile territory, through the use of journalists, academics and businessmen:

> International journalists keep in touch with key thinkers and politicians in countries where they've served.
>
> Although contacts of these kinds aren't likely to have access to the inner secrets of the local Politburo or Cabinet, they will have an excellent feel for the state of the economy, the degree of societal unrest, or the prospects for incipient political movements. I began to ponder the advantages and disadvantages of collecting information from our own citizens, though I was amused at the old spymaster's primary lesson was not how to recruit a secret agent or to effect some other esoteric technique of espionage, but how to make use of resources openly available, at no risk to anyone.

Turner professed himself shocked by, yet attracted to, Oldfield's observations, but soon discovered that the conventional relationship that had existed between the CIA and the media had been all but destroyed. In the good old days a foreign correspondent found it useful to exchange ideas with someone who had access to different sources of information, and there was always the hope the station chief would let slip a good lead. The station chief often found that the newsman had a circle of acquaintances, which the station chief hoped to tap indirectly. Since both parties were basically trying to learn as much about the country where they were posted, they had much in common. Almost all the relationships between the CIA and journalists were informal. Most were no more than informed conversations on subjects of mutual interest, a comparing of notes. Some few developed to the point where the newsman agreed to seek specific information needed by the CIA. In even fewer cases the CIA paid the reporter to work actively for it.

In contrast the British Army in Northern Ireland was found to be issuing bogus press credentials to its undercover personnel. An undertaking was sought (and received) that the **deception** would cease, for fear of compromising authentic journalists, the cause having been taken up by the National Union of Journalists, which expressed outrage that its members could have been placed in jeopardy unnecessarily.

The danger for journalists with intelligence connections have been illustrated by CBS's George Polk who was shot in Salonika in May 1949, supposedly a victim of Greek Communist rebels. ABC's Bill Stewart died on television in 1980, at the hands of the Nicaraguan militia, and David Blundy, then working for the *Sunday Correspondent*, was shot in November 1989 while covering the civil war in El Salvador.

The death of David Holden, chief correspondent of *The Sunday Times*, who was widely thought to be linked to SIS, was found dead with a single bullet wound to the back of the head in a Cairo suburb in December 1977, is proof enough that the occupation is full of potential risk. He had flown in from Amman a few days earlier, and the classic execution style of his murder inevitably led to speculation that he had been the target not of a random robbery, but a deliberate liquidation.

In March 1990 *Observer* journalist Farzad Bazoft, who had been arrested on espionage charges in Baghdad, was hanged. Bazoft had been detained after visiting the Al-Qaqaa State Establishment at Iskandariya, half an hour south of the capital, where he had attempted to take soil samples, apparently in an effort to find out what had caused a massive explosion at the site on 17 August, when several hundred people were rumoured to have been killed. Saddam Hussein ignored pleas for clemency and Bazoft, who was of Iranian origin but travelling on temporary British travel documents, was executed, after which the Mukhabarat released an extract from his personal address book containing the London telephone number of Yaacov Nimrodi, a legendary Israeli intelligence officer who had spent much of his career running the Mossad station in Tehran. The controversy increased when the Home secretary disclosed that Bazoft had maintained contact with the Metropolitan Police Special Branch, reporting on Iranian refugees and political activists, and had concealed from the *Observer*'s editor, Donald Trelford, his criminal conviction for armed robbery, a sentence which he had served at the very time he had pretended to have been taking a course in journalism at Birmingham University. According to Simon Henderson of the *Financial Times*, who wrote *Instant Empire*, Bazoft was working for SIS and on the day of his arrest at Baghdad airport had successfully handed the Al-Qaqaa soil sample to 'Michael', his **handler** at the British embassy, who had promptly despatched it to London for analysis.

The task of covertly monitoring the movement of suspect vehicles through the deployment of clandestine cameras was pioneered in Northern Ireland. A computer system, codenamed GLUTTON, accumulated details of car index numbers and then made the data available to mobile army patrols conducting vehicle check-points during the counter-terrorism operations in the 1970s.

# K

## KEYHOLE
A **codeword** security classification originally introduced to protect reconnaissance satellite imagery from a specific series of orbiting 'birds', KEYHOLE acquired a generic value covering the whole spectrum of intelligence collection from space.

Established initially in 1956, the CORONA programme was intended to replace the U-2 reconnaissance aircraft with a photographic satellite system. After a dozen launch failures, the first successful flight occurred in February 1960, described as a weather satellite. The very first batch of pictures included sixty-four Soviet airfields and twenty-six surface-to-air missile (SAM) sites that had hitherto been undetected.

By the time the programme ended in May 1972, ninety-five satellites had been launched, and twenty-six missions failed, in a total of 146 attempts, at a cost of $820 million. In twelve years 800,000 images had been captured of 600 million square miles of the earth's surface, of which 1.65 million were inside the Soviet Union. Classified as TALENT-KEYHOLE, the imagery had been processed by 1,500 technicians at the National Photographic Interpretation Center. Although the CORONA series provided vastly more imagery than the U-2, the satellites were hard to manoeuvre, operated in a polar orbit only and could not provide stereo pictures.

The CORONA satellites mapped much of the Eastern Bloc, the People's Republic of China and the Middle East, and the declassified imagery has now been released to the INMOS facility at Brookings, in South Dakota. Launched in December 1976, the KH-11, the first space-based platform to use digital technology and transmit near-real-time images, provided eye-in-the-sky images from Moscow whenever it was in position and clouds did not obscure the target.

## KNOCK-IN

In the parlance of CIA **polygraph** examiners, an incriminating admission made by a test subject, usually of illicit drug use, is known as a knock-in.

## KONSPIRATSIA

In the Soviet era clandestine operations were conducted under the principles of *konspiratsia* as established by the original **Chekists**, the Bolsheviks who saw themselves as the sword and the shield of the revolution. *Konspiratsia* encompasses everything associated with a covert life and includes living under alias, using fake travel documents and exercising vigilance for hostile surveillance. Within the KGB there was no greater professional compliment that to be described as an 'old Chekist', a recognition that an officer had adopted the spirit, behaviour, self-sacrifice and ideological commitment of the early revolutionaries.

In January 1980 the CIA created Studio Six, a fake Hollywood movie production company, to infiltrate a rescue team into Tehran to escort six American diplomats to Switzerland. Led by Tony Mendez of the Office of Technical Support, the group pretended to be members of a film crew scouting in Iran for locations for *Argo*, a science fiction project. They were issued with Canadian passports.

# I

## LEGALS

Intelligence personnel benefiting from the diplomatic immunity offered by the Vienna Convention are often known as 'legals', to distinguish them from their counterparts who operate under **non-official cover.**

## LEGEND

The false background for an individual assigned a mission as an **illegal** abroad, by the KGB's Directorate S, was known in Soviet circles as a legend. The phrase was adopted by Western intelligence agencies to indicate a fabricated personal and family history, usually involving **tomb-stoning** or **impersonation.** During the Cold War Western counterintelligence **analysts** noted that Line N personnel had some common characteristics, such as the journey taken to their operational destination, which invariably meant transiting through a third country, such as Finland and Argentina. They also detected a pattern in the construction of legends or fake biographies which depended on passports confiscated during the Spanish Civil War, or birth certificates issues in municipalities in Canada and Soviet-occupied Karelia, where there were no longer any records that could be verified independently.

In the case of Kaarlo Tuomi, a GRU illegal found by the FBI in New Jersey, he had been born to a Michigan farming community in November 1916 but had been taken by his parents to Russia in 1933 and settled in Kirov. After military service in the infantry Tuomi had been recruited by the GRU and trained as an illegal by Dmitri Polyakov. After several training missions to Europe he returned to the United States, via Paris, Brussels and Montreal, in December 1958 on a GRU assignment and travelling as Toivo Robert Mustonen. He crossed the Canadian border to Chicago by train and then resumed his true identity, of Rudolph K. Tuomi to begin the procedure required for applying for his own authentic passport. However, FBI Special Agents Jack O'Toole and Joe Diffley intervened and, over ten days in a hunting cabin, persuaded him to become a **double agent.** Tuomi initially pretended to cooperate but three months later tipped off his GRU controller, so becoming a **triple agent,** and eventually admitted this to the FBI in September 1962. He was compromised in July 1963 by the arrest of two other GRU illegals, Alexandre V. Sokolov, **alias** Robert Baltch, and his wife, 'Joy Ann Garbler'. Accordingly Tuomi, who anyway had been recalled to Moscow, ostensibly for a vacation, was **resettled** in Minnesota, published his memoirs *Lost Spy* in Finnish in 1984, and died in Palm Beach in 1995.

## LETTERBOX
As a method of indirect communication between an agent and case officer, the letterbox avoids the necessity of a personal meeting at which both parties could be placed in jeopardy. Letterboxes are either dead letterdrops, better known as **dead drops**, or **live letterboxes**, which are generally individuals who act as **cut-outs** whose sole function is to relay correspondence.

## LINE-CROSSER
Low-level **defectors**, often opportunistic military personnel, are known disparagingly as line-crossers. They are generally of low intelligence value as they can probably only disclose information of a local, tactical value. During the 1950s there was a steady stream of line-crossers from the Soviet zones in Austria and Germany, and rumours abounded that some had been unceremoniously returned as common deserters to the gentle mercies of the Red Army. However, at a meeting of the British Joint Intelligence Committee in June 1947 the director of Naval Intelligence, Admiral Edward Parry:

> raised the question of Russian defectors in the British zones in Germany and Austria. He said that he could get very little help from the Americans who were passing all the bodies on to the British after a short interrogation. The numbers were increasing and he was anxious to find some way of disposing of the bodies. He could not send them back, firstly because this would discourage others, and secondly because after interrogation they would have valuable information to impart to the Russians. The Secretary then handed round a note on the Ministry of Labour scheme for bringing DPs into this country. It was suggested that possibly Russian defectors disguised as Czechs or Balts could be included.

## LIQUIDATION

In MI5 parlance the liquidation of a case means that it is to be terminated as no longer of any operational interest. The relevant file would be consigned to Registry for permanent storage and the **case officer** reassigned.

## LIVE LETTERBOX

An individual who receives and redirects mail on behalf of an espionage organisation, either consciously or unconsciously, playing the role of a *post restante*, is known as a live letterbox, and their purpose is to act as an intermediary or **cut-out** so as to conceal a potentially incriminating link between two co-conspirators. In FBI parlance, a live letterbox is known as a **mail drop**.

Prior to the First World War the British Security Service MI5 identified Karl Gustav Ernst, a north London barber with a shop in the Caledonian Road, as a live letterbox and from November 1911 routinely monitored his mail until the outbreak of hostilities, when he was arrested. Ernst had come under suspicion when the former German naval attaché in Washington, DC, Captain Hubert von Rebeur-Paschwitz, had been seen to visit him late at night after he had attended the funeral of King Edward VII in May 1910 as a member of the Kaiser's entourage.

Study of Ernst's correspondence revealed that he and another hairdresser, Wilhelm Croner, were at the centre of an espionage network which answered to the Kaiser's spymaster, Gustave Steinhauer, and had been in existence since 1910. All the members of the organisation were watched, and a spy in the Royal Navy, George Parrott, was arrested in July 1912 although the fact that he had been compromised by the **mail cover** on Ernst was concealed at his trial. Then, in January 1913, Croner committed suicide, leaving Ernst to deal with his widow, Marie Kronauer, who would be detained in June 1914.

The intercepted correspondence showed that Ernst was paid £1 10s a week, but had been greatly concerned by the arrests of other German agents. It also proved that he had recommended others for recruitment, among them Richard Berger **alias** Roger Symmonds; W.E. Andrews, an employee of the Woolwich Arsenal; and one Edward Evans.

A British subject born in Shoreditch in December 1871, Ernst was taken into custody at Brixton and on 13 November 1914 was sentenced at the Old Bailey to seven years' imprisonment by Mr Justice Coleridge, which he served at Portland Prison.

Shortly before the outbreak of the Second World War there was a very similar episode when an Abwehr live letterbox, Mrs Jessie Jordan, came under surveillance in Dundee. A Glasgow-born hairdresser, Jordan had met a German waiter in Perth and had spent the First World War in Germany until he died of pneumonia, which had prompted her return to Scotland. Her large volume of foreign mail had attracted the attention of her local postman and in January 1938 her correspondence with Box 629 Hamburg revealed her clandestine role, receiving letters from the United States and redirecting them to addresses on the Continent.

The Hamburg address had been compromised by an MI5 **double agent**, Christopher Draper, a former RAF pilot who had been in contact with the Abwehr since 1933. Draper had been recruited by Dr Hans Thost, the London correspondent of the Nazi newspaper *Völkischer Beobachter*, who had been expelled in November 1935.

Interception of Mrs Jordan's letters led MI5's Guy Liddell to travel to the Washington, DC in January 1937 to alert J. Edgar Hoover to her correspondent in New York who signed himself 'Kron' (Crown). The FBI's Leon Turrou quickly identified Kron as Gunther Rumrich, a US Army deserter, and he was arrested in February 1937, charged with his participation in a plot to acquire American passport blanks, and imprisoned for two years. The interrogation of Rumrich produced another further lead, contaminating his brother Gustave, a student at Prague University, who was also a spy and was arrested by the Czech authorities. He was found to have been in contact with another Abwehr live letterbox in Dublin, run by Mrs Gertrud Brandy, and scrutiny of her mail showed her to be in touch with a French merchant navy officer, Ensign Jean Aubert, who was arrested at the end of 1938 and shot at Toulon on 6 March 1939.

The FBI also arrested Erich Glaser, who had served in the US Army in Panama with Rumrich, and Rumrich's courier, Johanna Hoffmann, employed as a hairdresser aboard the SS *Europa*. Another spy implicated was Otto Herman Voss, then working for the Sikorsky Airplane Company in Farmingdale, and he in turn identified Willy Lonkowsky and Carl Eitel, both Abwehr agents who had already returned to Germany. A further fourteen others were indicted, and when the ringleader, Dr Ignatz Griebl, who was named by Hoffmann, was questioned by Turrou, he admitted that he had been involved with the Abwehr since January 1937 when he and his mistress, Kay Moog, had travelled to Germany aboard the *Europa* and been recruited by members of the crew. They had suggested that Moog move to Washington, DC, and make herself useful by entertaining administration officials. After he completely incriminated himself, Greibl agreed to work as a double agent and entrap Karl Herman, whom he described as the Gestapo's chief in New York. A search of Herman's home revealed a mass of evidence and he quickly revealed the extent of his network and claimed to have been working under duress.

Turrou's investigation identified eighteen conspirators, and the fourteen of those still at liberty were subpoenaed to attend a grand jury in May 1938, but none turned up. Like Greibl, who returned to Germany on the SS *Bremen*, they had fled the country.

Apparently unaware that Box 629 was thoroughly compromised, the Abwehr continued to use the channel and it would be used to communicate with another MI5 double agent, Arthur Owens, code-named SNOW.

Alain Mafart, a DGSE officer involved in Operation SATANIQUE was identified as a suspect in the New Zealand police investigation of the sabotage of the Greenpeace ship *Rainbow Warrior* in Auckland in July 1985 when he was caught altering a receipt to inflate his expenses. Allan Galbraith, the Scottish detective who led the enquiry, demanded to know why, if Mafart was really a Swiss honeymooner who was not travelling on business, as he insisted, he had altered a bill issued by the Dorne Valley Tearooms from $8.50 to $58.50. Caught in the lie, Mafart confessed, implicating his alleged wife, Dominique Prieur, while the remainder of his team, led by Louis-Pierre Dillais, escaped on the French nuclear submarine *Rubis*. Mafart omitted that detail from his 1999 memoirs, *Carnets Secrets d'un nageur de combat* (*The Secret Diaries of a Combat Diver*).

# M

## MAIL COVER

The term used by the Federal Bureau of Investigation for the execution of a mail intercept warrant on an individual or a specific address. While it is universally recognised that spies generally do not exchange incriminating information by post, precisely because of the fear of interception, a study of a target's mail greatly assists investigators to gain an understanding of contacts, lifestyle, habits and interests, all of which can prove immensely beneficial.

On 17 March 1950, in the aftermath of the Klaus Fuchs case, MI5's Guy Liddell explained the importance of letter interception to his sceptical director general, he had recorded that Sir Percy Sillitoe:

> had criticised the fact that only a letter-check had been put on in 1947 and this in spite of the fact that we knew that in general practice, spies did not communicate their secrets through the post. He said that the purpose of the letter-check was to get some idea of the man's general background and the names of the people with whom he was communicating and the kind of circles in which he moved. This was often a valuable pointer to further enquiries in other directions and possibly to an approach to someone with whom he was found to be innocently in quite intimate touch.

## MAIL DROP

Known also as a **live letterbox**, but known to the FBI as a mail drop, this is an individual who allows their home to be used as an accommodation address for espionage, in an effort to circumvent likely interception of mail at the addresses more closely associated with the true correspondents.

In 1941 Customs inspectors on the Texas border accidentally stumbled over evidence that the NKVD communicated with agents in Mexico from the *rezidentura* at the Soviet consulate general in New York through an elaborate system of **cut-outs**, among them Rose Biegel who lived in Prospect Park, Brooklyn. She was married to Luis Arenal, and his sister Angelica was married to David Siqueiros, the prominent Mexican artist and Communist who had been imprisoned for leading an armed attack on Trotsky's home in 1940.

The communications revealed by the US Bureau of Censorship in November 1941, and investigated over the next two years, consisted of twenty-four encrypted messages, concealed in **secret writing**, which served to incriminate an entire network of espionage suspects, among them Lydia Altschuler (of New York), Mrs Pauline C. Baskind (New York), Mrs Frances Silverman (Yonkers), Fanny McPeek (Brooklyn), Barnett Sheppard (Great Neck, Long Island), Mrs Ethel Vogel (New York) and Helen Levi Simon Travis (Armada, Michigan). All had links to the Communist Party of the United States of America and family connections to other spy-rings. Indeed, Mrs Travis had been employed by the *Daily Worker* under the name Maxine Levi. At the heart of the organisation was Anna Vogt Colloms (Croton-on-Hudson), a courier and CPUSA member who was found on 12 August 1943 to be carrying enciphered correspondence over the border from Mexico to the United States. Her role was mentioned as courier 'A' in a fragmented VENONA text from the Mexico City *rezidentura* dated 14 March 1944:

[49 groups unrecoverable] by which letters were received from ARTUR and HARRY [Jacob Epstein] and also about surveillance of NONA [Ruth Wilson] and the courier 'A' who came to the COUNTRYSIDE [Mexico] for liaison with HARRY but achieved nothing.

The messages, written on apparently blank sheets of paper in a box of stationery which was confiscated temporarily, were copied and eventually decrypted to reveal a well-advanced NKVD plot to free Trotsky's murderer, Ramón Mercader, from his prison. Heading the plot was Epstein, a CPUSA member, formerly of 958 Madison Avenue, who had fought in the Spanish Civil War with the Abraham Lincoln Division of the International Brigade. His wife had also served in Spain, as a nurse.

A veteran CPUSA member, Colloms was employed as a teacher at the Washington Irving High School in lower Manhattan and acted as an intermediary with Jacob Epstein and his wife Ruth Wilson, American emigres in Mexico City who were coordinating

the NKVD's scheme for Mercader's escape. The decrypted letters identified Louis S. Bloch, a movie operator, born in Lithuania
and formerly employed by the Soviets, as a contact for the other
couriers, and he had already been identified by the FBI as a link
to Mikhail A. Shalyapin, a member of the NKVD *rezidentura* at
the Soviet consulate-general in New York, who appeared in the
VENONA traffic code-named STOCK. His wife, Zoya Semenovna
Myakotina, was officially listed as a typist at the consulate-general,
but surveillance suggested she was also a **cooptee**, performing intelligence duties too.

The box of stationery had been given back to Mrs Colloms on her
return journey from Mexico City three weeks later, but the paper had
been replaced. When she reached New York she gave the box to Ethel
Vogel, who then passed it on to Ruth Wilson.

When the NKVD learned that Colloms might have been compromised, a new route for the correspondence was established, via an
address in Santiago, Chile, belonging to an individual identified only
as ALEX. However, Moscow suggested that the code to be employed
should come from the 1942 Pocket Book edition of W.F. Kernan's
*Defense Will Not Win the War*, a copy of which was promptly
acquired by the FBI to facilitate access to further messages. Some
indicated that the NKVD planned to establish a clandestine transmitter in Buenos Aires to open direct communications with Moscow.

The FBI's enquires in Mexico City, known as the ALTO case, were
headed by the **Legat**, Birch D. O'Neal, and concentrated on texts
from Anne Sayer, an **alias** adopted by the German émigré writer Anna
Seghers, at 338 Insurgentes, the home she shared with her husband,
Professor Laslo Radvanyi. During the following years cryptanalysts
successfully read much of the correspondence and gained an insight
into how Pavel Klarin, formerly the NKVD *rezident* in New York,
was able to distance the Soviet embassy from his ring of **illegals**.
Nevertheless, his reliance on ideologically sound volunteers meant
most of his contacts were known Communists.

When Elizabeth Bentley defected in November 1945 she told the
FBI how she had been instructed by her lover, Jacob Golos, who had
been the NKVD's illegal *rezident* in New York, to visit Brooklyn to
collect mail addressed to Rose Arenal from Mexico. Code-named
GREGORY by the FBI, she was questioned almost continuously for

three weeks by Special Agents Thomas G. Spencer and Joseph M. Kelly and identified several dozen of Golos's contacts.

## MAIN ADVERSARY

During and after the Cold War the Soviet intelligence agencies invariably referred to the United States as 'the main adversary'.

## MASINT

The acronym for measurement and signature intelligence, MASINT is the technical intelligence collection discipline of monitoring indicators to establish a pattern so **analysts** can study the data over the long term and spot potentially significant, tell-tale changes. The term covers a wide spectrum of **remote sensors,** such as those resembling javelins which were dropped over the Ho Chi Minh trail during the Vietnam War to collect seismic evidence of troop movements; devices concealed as tree stumps to count aircraft rotations at strategic airfields located far from cities and protected by dense cloud cover; and air-sniffers designed to sample the atmosphere in the Himalayas to detect Chinese nuclear tests.

## MATRIX THEORY

Intelligence **analysts** often illustrate their craft by describing a jigsaw puzzle consisting of individual pieces drawn from various sources (open sources, diplomatic reporting, defence attaché reporting; PoW interrogation; measurement and signature intelligence (**MASINT**); overhead reconnaissance; signals intelligence and human intelligence).

## MEAL-TICKET

The price paid by a **defector** for **resettlement** is known as a meal-ticket and will likely comprise valuable information, perhaps including the identity of individual spies, or sufficient detail about their activities to compromise them.

## METKA

Also known as 'spy-dust', this powdery substance, composed of nitrophenyl-pentadien and luminol, was employed by the KGB in support of Seventh Chief Directorate surveillance operations. The chemical was sprayed surreptitiously onto a target's clothing and would be invisible to the naked eye but reflected brightly when illuminated under ultra-violet rays. Samples were detected in 1976 and in 1985 the KGB **defector** Vitaly Yurchenko confirmed that the method was used against targets in locations where the necessary equipment had been installed at **choke-points**. The CIA, having been advised that the compound was potentially carcinogenic, arranged for the State Department to deliver a formal demarche on the subject, but the Soviets continued to use METKA as a highly effective method of **tagging** suspects, sometimes applying a substance known as NEPUNE-80 to a target's shoes by impregnating a door mat.

Detailed information about the KGB's surveillance techniques employed in Moscow were first disclosed in 1964 by the defector Yuri Nosenko who described a clear liquid applied to the roof of a target vehicle which identified it to watchers placed on tall buildings equipped with the detection apparatus, thus allowing it to be tracked across the city.

## MICE

The mnemonic for Money, Ideology, Coercion and Ego, MICE is intended to convey the four principal motivations for traitors who betray classified information. Much research has been undertaken to identify the character flaws that make an individual liable to pass secrets to an adversary, and the CIA completed a lengthy study, code-named SLAMMER, to find the common denominators in examples of breaches of security when the culprit was available for interview, often in prison.

Money is quite obvious, and there is overwhelming evidence that individuals with financial problems, often a consequence of a difficult divorce, are very vulnerable and some may resort to the sale of classified documents in desperation. A common denominator is that the vendor will approach a diplomatic mission with a proposal, thus enabling the counterintelligence authorities to monitor landline calls and interdict the **pitch**. During the Cold War ideology was a significant factor, and certainly some of the adherents to Communism did not receive significant remuneration. Furthermore, the pool of Communist Party members in target countries gave the Soviet services an advantage in identifying potential recruits, and avoiding hostile **penetration** by having the local apparatus undertake background checks to confirm the political credentials of any candidate.

Political conviction, of course, may be nothing more than a convenient or more acceptable explanation for treason than simple avarice, although in many cases ideology does not present an obstacle to self-advancement. This is especially true of scientists, technicians and members of the business community who have been recruited by the Chinese Ministry of State Security and been allowed to enrich themselves in the process.

In November 2009 Kendall Myers, who had spent the seven years before his retirement from the State Department in 2007 as an **analyst** in the Bureau of Intelligence and Research, was arrested, along with his wife Gwendolyn Steingraber Myers. Both had spied for Cuba over a long period, almost thirty years, but apparently had not received much in terms of financial compensation.

Coercion, or compromise, implies a degree of pressure or blackmail, and it is not unusual for an espionage suspect to attempt to adopt the role of a victim. However, leverage exercised by a manipulative case officer, even if that person has pretended to be the victim's protector from some other ill-intentioned individual, may engender resentment, and in such circumstances the target may seize the opportunity to turn the tables on a perceived tormentor. Accordingly, coercion is not always a guarantee of a source's reliability. In the case of John Vassall, he claimed after his arrest in September 1962 that the KGB contact who had blackmailed him when he was caught in a homosexual **honeytrap** in Moscow, had in fact tried to shield him from a more senior officer, allegedly the person really responsible for his predicament. He seemed unable, or unwilling, to recognise that it was indeed his immediate contact who was masterminding his situation. When confronted with the chance to confess, Vassall proved cooperative, made a full statement and pleaded guilty at his trial.

Egotism, or sometimes resentment at having been passed over for promotion, is not uncommon as many agents have manifested narcissistic tendencies, believing themselves to be cleverer than their contemporaries, This intellectual arrogance, the conviction they could not be caught, is a common trait and may also contribute to a desire to confess after arrest, to prove the scale of what they perceive as having been their success.

## MICRODOT

One method of surreptitious communication is the reduction of a photograph down to a size that can only be read by a microscope or similar specialist equipment. Concealment of such a tiny item is relatively easy – it can be placed, for example, under a postage stamp. Detection of microdots is correspondingly difficult, although during the Cold War MI5 developed a process involving neutron activation.

Microphotography was developed by the Germans before the Second World War and was disclosed to MI5 in 1940 by a **double agent**, a photographer code-named RAINBOW. The technique became widespread in 1941, having been entrusted to another **double agent**, code-named TRICYCLE, and was referred to by MI5 as **DUFF**.

American knowledge of microdot technology dates back to the examples surrendered to the FBI in February 1941 by William Sebold, a naturalised loyal American who, after a visit to his family in Germany, had reluctantly agreed to contact four other Abwehr agents for whom he carrying a microdot **questionnaire** and was to provide a shortwave radio link to speed their communications with Hamburg. The microdot technique patented in 1938 by Zeiss, purported to solve the problem of carrying potentially incriminating documents and messages. Photographing the item, and then reducing it in size by a ratio of 200:1 to a dot that could only be read with a microscope, required specialist knowledge, training and equipment, but was a major breakthrough in concealed writing which, hitherto, had depended on secret inks which could be detected under appropriate lighting conditions, or by chemical treatment. The FBI hired an optical expert, James E. Dunlop, from the medical laboratory at Johns Hopkins Hospital to study photo-reduction methodology. His study proved invaluable when the German espionage networks in South America came to rely on the technique after their clandestine radio links were tracked by US direction-finding and their stations closed down.

In the absence of a transmitter, the Abwehr chief in Mexico, Georg Nicolaus, code-named MAX, became dependent on microdots concealed in the ordinary mail, but most of his postal drops in Europe were known to the British Security Coordination (BSC) censors in Bermuda who conducted the most detailed physical examination of all the transatlantic mail. All sea and airmail to and from the western hemisphere was channelled through Bermuda and Trinidad where BSC had established large Imperial Censorship facilities. Nicolaus's traffic became known as the MAX case, and the title of the summary reports were 'The Mexican Microdot Case'. The BSC censors in Bermuda examining eastbound Mexican mail had been alerted to watch for microdots early in December 1941, and a month later the first example was detected, followed quickly by a further twenty, all to or from Mexico and linked to MAX. His alternative mail route was to a PO box address in Chile, run by Isabel Pederit de Reiner, who had the contents radioed over the PYL-REW link, which of course was also the subject of American Radio Intelligence Division monitoring until it was closed down in November 1942.

Utterly compromised and increasingly isolated, Nicolaus was withdrawn from Mexico in May 1942, aboard the *Drottingholm*, together with other internees scheduled for repatriation, but when they arrived in New York to embark on the voyage home they were searched by the FBI. Nicolaus was found to have six microdots concealed in his shoe, so he was separated from the other detainees and kept at the Greenbrier resort at White Sulphur Springs, West Virginia, a camp prepared for German diplomats, until the end of hostilities, when he finally supplied the FBI with a lengthy statement about his wartime activities, having previously steadfastly refused to answer any questions about his activities in Mexico. Naturally the FBI had wanted to prosecute Nicolaus for possession of the microdots, which contained US war production information and details of a new crew escape system fitted to American submarines, but the State Department insisted that such a move would violate the terms of the safe-conduct agreement negotiated with the Mexicans, and even refused to allow him to undergo a hostile interrogation.

As a means of covert communication the microdot survived into the Cold War, and a variation of the technique was employed to conceal a tiny message, micro-engraved by laser, in an advertisement on an inside page of the European edition of the February 1983 edition of *National Geographic*, which was passed in 1983 by a CIA **case officer** in Moscow to an **agent**, Colonel Vladimir Mikhailovich Vasilyev, code-named GTACCORD. The text was virtually unreadable without the aid of a 30x magnifier.

## MIDRASHA

Mossad's training academy is located north of Tel Aviv on the Haifa Road, directly opposite the Country Club resort on Highway 5 at Herzliya, and identified only as the prime minister's summer residence.

## MIRROR IMAGING

Inaccurate intelligence assessments made by **analysts** who fall into the trap of judging an adversary's behaviour by their own standards of logic, are said to be the result of mirror imaging. The problem often lies at the heart of misjudgements made on vital strategic issues, such as the assumption in 1962 that Nikita Khrushchev would not risk worldwide condemnation by deploying nuclear missiles to Cuba; the belief in 1982 that General Leopoldo Galtieri would not attempt an amphibious assault on the Falkland Islands in the autumn; and the assessment in 1990 that Saddam Hussein would not invade and occupy another Arab country. In each of these examples, analysts were proved wrong, and reviews of the relevant intelligence estimates suggested that the leaders under scrutiny, Khrushchev, Galtieri and Saddam, were driven by entirely different factors than those considered a priority by external commentators and academic experts. Khrushchev was convinced that the delivery of ballistic weapons to the Caribbean would strengthen his hand when negotiating the removal of NATO-controlled Thor IRBMs from RAF airfields in eastern England, thirty Jupiters at Gioia del Colle in Italy, and sixteen Jupiters deployed at US Air Force sites near Izmir in Turkey. On these points the Kremlin's strategy succeeded, in part because CIA analysts did not understand the true nature of the Soviet gamble.

The failure in relation to the Argentine invasion and occupation of the Falklands was all the greater because there was a distinct escalation in the political rhetoric in Buenos Aires, accurately monitored and reported by the local British embassy, but Whitehall was taken completely by surprise.

When Saddam Hussein was interrogated by the FBI's George L. Piro in January 2004 he readily acknowledged that his preoccupation had been a fear of Iran and a determination to demonstrate Iraq's strength, to the point of perpetuating the myth that his country had developed covert stocks of weapons of mass destruction so as to deter Tehran's perceived aggression.

## MOLE

In 1626 Sir Francis Bacon mentioned a mole as a spy in his *Historie of the Reign of King Henry*, and although the reference is slightly ambiguous, it is widely thought to be the origin of the term which came into more common usage with the publication by John le Carré of *Tinker, Tailor, Soldier, Spy* in 1974. The accepted definition of a mole is a spy who is already committed to a particular ideology and makes a deliberate effort to penetrate a host country's intelligence structure with the intention of gaining promotion and inflicting maximum damage.

## MOLEHUNTER

Counterintelligence officers in pursuit of hostile **penetration** are often referred to as molehunters, and their roles can be categorised as the search for a spy where there is firm evidence of the existence of a leak, and the investigation of a specific suspect who has been identified as a probable candidate.

Evidence of penetration, sufficient to initiate a molehunt, is likely to consist of information from a **defector** who can confirm that a specific item has been compromised, but does not know the culprit. Thus in 1961 the KGB officer Anatoli Golitsyn demonstrated that he had seen very particular NATO documents, thereby prompting investigations in France and Britain that led to the arrests of George Paques and John Vassall respectively.

## MONSTER PLOT

Critics of the CIA's Counterintelligence Staff, and its long-serving chief James Angleton in particular, refer what is described as his interpretation of the KGB's strategy during the 1960s as the 'monster plot', a Machiavellian view of wholesale **deception** perpetrated by the Kremlin to mislead the west about the true nature of Soviet policy. Allegedly the viewpoint, often denigrated as a conspiracy theory, was originally espoused by the KGB **defector** Anatoli Golitsyn, who asserted that some later defectors, including Yuri Nosenko, were **false defectors**, and that the CIA and MI5 had suffered high-level hostile **penetration**. The **molehunts** conducted during this period shortened several careers, and led to the suspicion that at least one potential defector, Yuri Loginov, was a **plant**. The chief protagonists in the debate were Pete Bagley, Bill Hood and Ray Rocca, whose positions against Nosenko were opposed by John Hart and Cleve Cram.

## MOSCOW RULES

The conditions under which clandestine operations are conducted in hostile territory were known as Moscow Rules during the Cold War because of the ubiquitous nature of the local security apparatus supervised by the KGB's Seventh Chief Directorate. The environment was so unfavourable that for many years the British Secret Intelligence Service did not run a station in the embassy, and advised the Americans to adopt the same policy, asserting that Soviet surveillance was so aggressive as to amount to active harassment, making even the most routine duties hard to accomplish. When the Central Intelligence Agency did deploy officers to Moscow they quickly succumbed to KGB provocations, and Edward Ellis Smith was forced to withdraw in 1956 after he had been compromised in a **honeytrap** by his attractive maid Valya.

CIA personnel posted to the Moscow station underwent a training course, known as 'the Pipeline' in which counter-surveillance techniques were taught. Candidates were instructed in the art of spotting Soviet mobile surveillance, usually conducted from Volgas and the smaller Zhigulas, which were distinctive because they were generally cleaner than other vehicles on the road and, most unusually in the Soviet capital, displayed that most coveted of equipment, windscreen wipers.

Members of the CIA station in Moscow, when on an operational assignment, were equipped with a concealed SRR-100 radio receiver and scanner, worn under their clothes which monitored frequencies used by KGB street surveillance teams, allowing the appropriate counter-measures to be taken. The device, held in place by a Velcro harness under the armpit, was tuned to the channels reserved for the Seventh Chief Directorate on 103.25 MHz. Intercepted signals were then relayed via an **induction antenna** looped around the neck to a tiny, custom-made earpiece. Eavesdropping on the KGB transmissions had shown that the teams communicated with a number code which was either spoken, or presented as clicks, and that 'twenty-one' ('*dvahd-tsaht awdeen*') meant 'target in sight'.

When, in July 1977, Martha Peterson, the CIA case officer assigned to handle Aleksandr Ogorodnik was detained in the act of laying a **dead drop** on the Krasnokaluzhsky Bridge, her earpiece went undetected even after the KGB had found and removed the scanner attached to her bra. The remainder of her equipment is on show at the SVR's private museum above the officers' club behind the Lubyanka building.

Unlike their Western counterparts, Seventh Chief Directorate surveillance teams were not averse to resorting to overt harassment tactics, such as the bumper-lock, in which the tailing vehicle would follow its target so closely that they occasionally connected.

## MOUSETRAP
The conversion of a supposed **safe-house** into a site occupied by an adversary intending to attract suspects to the property and then detain them is known as a mousetrap, a term coined by the French resistance during the Second World War when the German counter-intelligence agencies demonstrated considerable skill in penetrating, manipulating and ultimately controlling a large number of *reseaux* ostensibly directed from London.

The Arab News Agency in Cairo was SIS's journalistic cover in Egypt, managed by James C. Swinburn. Having been arrested in August 1956, he was tried in May 1957 for espionage and sentenced to five years' hard labour at the notorious Barage prison. The Agency's most famous correspondent, Tom Little, later worked for the *Economist* and *The Times*, even though he had been thoroughly compromised by the Egyptian Mukhabarat. In his defence Swinburn's principal agent, Sayed Amin Mahmoud, claimed that his ten sub-agents were entirely notional, and simply a means to fabricate his expenses. The court disbelieved him and he was sentenced to death.

# N

## NARRATIVE

Non-committal and deliberately ambiguous in terms of accuracy, a narrative is often given as the description of an account, true or false, of a particular event by the intelligence community.

## NATURAL COVER

Intelligence personnel and their agents who do not operate under **alias** and use their genuine profession as a **cover** for their clandestine activities are said to be working under 'natural cover'. In 1945 the Secret Intelligence Service drafted a report on future requirements for infiltrating agents into the Soviet Union:

> We should thus use trade and finance as our primary channel. HMG will play a greater role in the trade and finances of the USSR than could have been anticipated several years ago. We thus have at our disposal two distinct and totally satisfactory covers:
>
> a) official cover – government finance and economic missions, commercial attachés and junior commercial representatives in consulates.
>
> b) natural cover – businessmen, industrialists, specialists, engineers, chemists, etc., or trained intelligence personnel accompanying them on their visits to the USSR.

The first American intelligence agency to deploy personnel overseas undercover was the FBI's Special Intelligence Service which in 1942 posted 300 special agents under **commercial cover** to South America. One of the first, Kenneth Crosby, was a qualified stockbroker based at a Merrill Lynch office in Buenos Aires. But other legitimate firms were approached to provide cover. Among these were General Motors, Republic Steel, Guaranty Trust, Sterling Products, Republic National Bank of New York, the Grace National Bank, the meatpackers Swift & Company, and the Texas Oil Company.

The CIA's Clandestine Service was assigned the task of recruiting and managing personnel operating under **non-official cover** through the Office of External Development, an organisation shrouded in additional layers of secrecy. The only limits on the recruitment field are clerics, American journalists and current members of the Peace Corps.

## NON-OFFICIAL COVER (NOC)

Intelligence personnel who work in hostile environments without the protection of the diplomatic privilege afforded by the Vienna Convention are NOCs, and are vulnerable to arrest and worse. In the Russian experience NOCs are known as **illegals**, to distinguish them from **legals** employed under diplomatic or consular **cover**.

Probably the best-known NOC of recent times is Valerie Plame, the co-author in 2007 of *Fair Game*, who joined the CIA in 1985 and was posted to the Athens station four years later. Thereafter she appeared to drop out of the Agency and in October 1993 attended a year's course at the London School of Economics, but in reality she had become a NOC and ostensibly worked for a **front company**, Brewster Jennings & Associates, which operated as a business consultancy in Brussels. In 1997 she transferred to the CIA's Non-Proliferation Center as an **analyst** assigned to the Iraq Task Force, and the following year married Joe Wilson, an American diplomat. She resigned from the CIA in January 2006.

## NOTIONAL AGENT

A non-existent source, created to fulfil a specific purpose, is termed a notional agent. During the Second World War MI5's celebrated **double agent** GARBO ran a network of twenty-four sub-agents, none of whom existed outside his imagination, although the reporting from each was carefully recorded and filed so as to prevent any tell-tale internal contradictions that might have compromised the **deception**.

Even before GARBO arrived in Britain he was fabricating reports for his Abwehr controller in Madrid. He had invented a source in Liverpool, supposedly a Swiss named William Gerbers, who had submitted regular reports from a vantage point overlooking the Mersey. As this spy was likely to be far too dangerous during the hard-to-miss preparations for the imminent invasion of North Africa, his demise was arranged, and the appropriate death notice was placed in the *Liverpool Daily Post* on 19 November 1942.

Suitably impressed, the Germans sent his widow their condolences, and the offer of a pension.

The prelude for GARBO was CHEESE, supposedly a radio operator in Cairo recruited by Renato Levi in 1941 to run his organisation in his absence. His subordinate was identified as a Syrian of Russian extraction named Paul Nicosoff ('pull knickers off') by Levi's impish case officer, the peacetime playwright and theatrical producer Evan Simpson. The Abwehr never doubted Nicosoff, but their desire actually to meet his principal source, code-named BGM (for 'Blonde Gun Moll') resulted in Simpson having to indoctrinate a Cretan member of the local Security Intelligence Middle East (SIME) staff to impersonate her.

## NUMBERS STATION

A method of one-way voice communication, broadcasts on short wave radio of an expressionless voice reading out ostensibly random numbers come from what are termed numbers stations. The intended recipient is an agent who tunes in to the channel at the appointed time and decrypts a particular sequence, probably with the aid of a **one-time pad**.

SIS's technical adviser, Major Frank Quinn, laced a box of Kropje chocolates, a popular Egyptian sweet, with a lethal toxin as part of a plan to assassinate President Nasser, but the project was abandoned in favour of a better scheme involving poison gas. That too proved impracticable.

O

## ONE-TIME PAD (OTP)

Most sensitive intelligence communications are encrypted either by sophisticated machine-generated ciphers or by the employment of manual one-time pads. The standard OTP consists of a list of five-figure groups which can be used as additives for a text which has been transformed into numbers by simple transposition. The advantage of the OTP is the lack of repetition, as the pad will only be used once. Only pairs of OTPs are manufactured, and each page will only be used once and then destroyed, thus eliminating the vulnerability of other cipher systems. The OTP's disadvantage is the time-consuming nature of the encryption and decryption procedure.

OTPs are generally regarded as the most secure encipherment ever devised, but during the Second World War cryptanalysts at Bletchley Park concentrating on the German Foreign Ministry OTPs and led by John Tiltman discovered that their supposedly random five-figure groups had been generated by a machine made by Lorenz.

## OPERATIONAL ACT

Any act of a professional nature by an intelligence officer is known as an operational act, and is an indicator of their true role. Suspects under surveillance may compromise their mission by manifesting behaviour that identifies their true calling.

## OPERATIONAL GAME

When in a counterintelligence context one or other side initiates contact with an adversary for a specific purpose, perhaps to entrap a known **case officer**, dangle a **double agent** or mount some **provocation**, the action is described as an operational game or, in Russian, *operativinaya igri*. The intended outcome is some advantage, which may be nothing more than a distraction to preoccupy an opponent, or a disruption to prevent them from taking a particular course. During the Cold War such activities were commonplace in Moscow where the KGB sought to identify members of the CIA station and prevent them from conducting their job, which was in part to attract potential sources for **recruitment** and manage existing **agents**. In reality, because of the scale of hostile surveillance and harassment, Agency personnel found the environment exceptionally challenging and very few assets were successfully handled in the city, thus limiting prolonged contact to safer locations overseas.

## ORCHESTRA

Shortly before the outbreak of the Second World War the Soviets established three espionage networks, known as the Red Orchestra, based in Belgium but with branches in France, Great Britain and Germany; the Black Orchestra, operating in Italy and the Vatican, and a Yellow Orchestra in the Far East.

The existence of the Red Orchestra was discovered in 1941 by a German counterintelligence investigation initiated in Belgium and code-named ROTE KAPELLE (Red Chapel). By then the two principal **illegals** who had created the organisation, Leopold Trepper and Viktor Guryevitch, had left the country, but in December a **safe-house** in the Etterbeck district of Brussels was pinpointed by German radio direction-finding equipment and raided. A GRU officer, Lieutenant Anton Danilov, who previously had been posted to Paris as an assistant military attaché in 1938, and had also worked in that capacity in Vichy, was arrested. Soon afterwards another Soviet illegal, Mikhail Makarov, was taken into custody when he called at the house. Both men resisted their interrogators, but eight months later, in July 1942, the Abwehr radio direction-finders closed in on the attic of a house in Laeken where they found a German Communist, Johann Wenzel, who had been trained as a radio operator in Moscow. Initially Wenzel refused to cooperate, but his past traffic, copies of which were recovered from his home, revealed a hitherto undiscovered branch of the Rote Kapelle based at the very heart of the Reich. After eight weeks of torture in Berlin, Wenzel was returned to Brussels and installed with a guard and his radio equipment in an apartment in the rue Aurore, where he cooperated fully. Meanwhile, a study of his previous messages compromised a German Foreign ministry employee, Ilse Stoebe, who was arrested by the Gestapo in Hamburg. Before she was executed on 22 December 1942 Ilse implicated the three most important members of the German Rote Kapelle: Harro Schulze-Boysen of the Air Ministry; Arvid von Harnack, a university lecturer who ran a widespread organisation with sources in both the Abwehr and Kriegsmarine; and Rudolf von Scheliha, a diplomat in the information section of the German Foreign Ministry. Once Ilse Stoebe had named Schulze-Boysen and Harnack, their entire network, amounting to eighty sub-agents, was rounded up and either hanged or beheaded without delay.

The subsequent RHSA investigation concluded that Harnack and Schulze-Boysen, both Communist activists for many years, had only been recruited by the GRU quite recently, in 1941. They had been given a radio transmitter by Alexander Erdberg, of the Soviet Trade Delegation in Berlin before its withdrawal in June 1941, but they never achieved direct contact with Moscow, as intended. In August 1941 Viktor Guryevitch had given them another set, but again they failed to establish direct contact and instead had relied upon couriers to pass messages to the Soviet embassy in Stockholm and to Wenzel in Brussels. This was the fatal flaw in an otherwise well-organised network.

Certainly the quality of the material reaching Moscow from Berlin was unprecedented, for among the members of the ring were Herbert Gollnow, an Abwehr liaison officer at Hitler's headquarters responsible for supervising clandestine air operations on the Eastern Front; Leutnant Wolfgang Havemann of naval intelligence; and Horst Heilmann, an Abwehr cryptographer who was having an affair with Schulze-Boysen's wife, Libertas. All were interrogated and then hanged at Ploetzensee prison. Scheliha, a more experienced Soviet agent, suffered the same fate. He had been recruited while serving at the German embassy in Warsaw in 1934 and had been paid for his information through a Swiss bank. As well as being compromised by Ilse Stoebe, he was incriminated by Heinrich Koenen, a German Communist who parachuted into Osterode in East Prussia in October 1942 with instructions to contact Ilse. By the time he landed she was already in the hands of the Gestapo, and when he was arrested on 22 October he was found to be carrying a receipt confirming a transfer of $7,500 to Scheliha's bank account.

The Black Orchestra was headed by a Ukrainian nationalist, General Anton Turkul, who, though espousing anti-Bolshevik views, was actually a Soviet agent and was supported by another Soviet spy, Ilya Longe. Turkul remained in Rome until 1943 when he was persuaded to flee the advancing Allies and move to the Abwehr's protection in Sofia. Both Longe and Turkul were interrogated by MI5 after the war, and it was concluded that both men had actively worked for Moscow.

The Yellow Orchestra was headed by Mamamoto Enomoto, a Japanese journalist from Osaka working for the *Mainishi Shimbun*, who had been posted to Budapest in 1938 at his request after he had witnessed atrocities in Nanking which had gone unreported. Disillusioned, he had then made a visit to Moscow where he had been recruited by the NKVD after having declared that he was on a mission for Domei Tsushinsha, a Tokyo news agency with strong links to Japanese military intelligence. In Budapest Mamamoto acquired a young girlfriend, Drago, and was cultivated by Richard Kauder, a Soviet agent who would soon agree to work for the Abwehr office in Vienna.

Mamamoto operated across the Balkans and was closely associated with Riochu Omeida, the Japanese press attaché in Sofia, and Colonel Otto Hatz, the Hungarian military attaché in Budapest. He was also going through the motions of reporting for his Japanese Domei Tsushimsha network which, he claimed, was headed by Colonel Onodera Makoto, the military attaché at the Japanese embassy in Stockholm. Thus both Mamamoto and Riochu, while pretending to be active on behalf of the Japanese and the Abwehr, actually remained loyal to the NKVD. To assist his frequent travel in and out of Hungary Mamamoto recruited the chief of the Bulgarian police, Colonel Kotsarov, and Peter Matejeff, head of the Bulgarian intelligence service. In March 1943 Mamamoto was appointed interpreter to a delegation to Berlin headed by General Okamoto Kiotomi, the Japanese director of Military Intelligence, who was accompanied by Colonel Kotani of the Armoured Corps, Captain Onoda of the Imperial Navy, and a senior Foreign Ministry official, Yosano. The tour took a month and its report, intended as a candid assessment of Germany's military strength, was completed in July 1943 and highlighted recruitment problems, fuel shortages and a dangerous reliance on synthetic lubricants. It also detailed the areas under partisan control.

Mamamoto was arrested by the Americans in Vienna in February 1946 but transferred to Naples from where he and Drago, now his wife and pregnant, were to be shipped to Japan. While on the voyage the Mamamotos disembarked in Ceylon where their child was born. They later reached Osaka, but Mamamoto's role as a Soviet spy would remain unknown until October 1979 when a KGB officer, Major Stanislas Levchenko, defected to the CIA and revealed that Mamamoto, by then long since dead, had been a major Soviet source code-named GREY.

## ORDER OF BATTLE

The basis of any counterintelligence operation will be an understanding of the individuals and roles of an adversary, which in a Cold War context required surveillance to identity the structure and membership of an opposing organisation. In a counter-terrorism environment the objective is not dissimilar, the necessity being to name, **house** and monitor a suspect.

The term comes from the fundamental military intelligence requirement to know the strength and capability of a potential enemy, to assess whatever information can be gleaned so as to develop a wiring diagram illustrating an opponent's command and control architecture.

During the Cold War it was widely believed that one effective method of compiling the membership of the local CIA station was to identify the ownership of vehicles left in the car park after 4.30 p.m., when most of the regular US State Department diplomats would go home, leaving behind their CIA colleagues who, because of the nature of their double duties under **diplomatic cover,** invariably worked later. Inevitably a professional intelligence officer would exhibit a characteristic **pattern of life,** such as use of payphones and visits to restaurants, and a home life that suggested a sensitivity to the threat of eavesdropping not shared by regular diplomats.

## OWN GOAL

When a terrorist is killed by the premature detonation of their own device, usually as a consequence of inexperience or a mistake in the construction of the timer or detonator, this is known as an own goal, a term borrowed from football.

On the advice of MI5, which feared the Provisional Irish Republican Army might drive a car bomb onto the Channel Tunnel's shuttle service, the designers opted not to adopt the conventional arrangement of separating drivers from their vehicles during the journey. At that time suicide bombers were unknown and MI5 had not anticipated that Islamic extremists would engage in so-called martyrdom actions.

# P

## PAPERMILL

The source of forged documents and spurious propaganda material is often referred to disparagingly as a papermill. During the interwar period one particularly adept White Russian, Vladimir Grigorievich Orlov, formerly General Wrangel's intelligence chief, made a reputation for himself by establishing a facility in Berlin that churned out a huge quantity of plausible, but bogus, correspondence, directives and pamphlets supposedly generated by the Comintern in Moscow. He also produced his own self-serving intelligence bulletins. The consequences of his counterfeiting activities would be profound, and include his suspected involvement in the notorious Zinoviev Letter.

Orlov had been sent to western Europe in the spring of 1920 to set up an intelligence network, at a time when the White Guards had lost the Civil War and their last troops were being pushed into the Crimea. Orlov's task was set out by Major General Nikolsky, who was then stationed in Sevastopol. Dated 19 May 1920, and addressed to the military attaché in Italy, Nikolsky advised that he had sent Orlov to organise a secret anti-Soviet agent network which would communicate with the General Staff. Orlov had taken the entire White Guards intelligence headquarters staff with him and between 1920 and 1923 was based in Strenski Karlowtzy, near Belgrade, where operations were directed by generals Kusonsky, Shatilov, Miller and

Stanislavsky, with Orlov running the agents until the organisation moved to Paris in 1924. According to a post-war Soviet assessment:

> The anti-Bolshevik activities inside Russia were directed by General Kutepov (mutinies and uprisings). Prince Sergei Nikolayevich Trubetskoi was in charge of information and intelligence. Cossack affairs were looked after by General Krasnov. All three were subordinate to the Grand Duke Nikolai Nikolayevich.

An NKVD investigation conducted in 1945, after the Paris *rezidentura* had acquired Orlov's archive in Belgium, concluded that his branch in Berlin had been subordinate to General Kutyepov and Prince Trubetskoi. It also identified some of Orlovs's agents, among them Mechislav Kuntsevich, allegedly a member of the staff of the 'secret service of the Foreign Office', who received 2,000 francs a month; Lieutenant Sonakhovsky,'an employee of the British Police department', who received 1,000 francs a month; and Nina Sokhatskaya, described as 'head of the London network', who took office expenses and a monthly salary of 2,000 francs.

The Soviets had received contemporaneous reports of Orlov's plots from an informant, Nikolai Kroshko, code-named A/3, who successfully penetrated the forger's immediate circle:

> The most interesting thing is what Orlov is doing at the moment. Together with Nelidov he is preparing forged documents for sale to British intelligence. At present are for sale: French intelligence codes, a manual of naval signals, blueprints of factories etc. All this is printed at the Schwale printing works in the Trirsche Strasse. Big money is involved. Through Nelidov the design of a Soviet AA gun is being offered for sale (in fact this is the design of a French gun).

Although born into a poor family, Kroshko had been educated at a gymnasium and in 1918 had escaped from the Germans to join General Anton Denikin's army. Later he turned up in Poland, where he worked with Boris Savinkov, but by 1920 he had become disillusioned and was recruited to spy on the Whites for Moscow. He proved to be a versatile, well-connected source, with contacts among the Nazis and the Stahlhelm auxiliary police. One of his greatest coups was the overnight removal of two suitcases full of documents from the Denikin-Wrangel military mission in Berlin so they could be photographed by the *rezidentura*. However, he only received Orlov's approval after he had made two secret visits to Moscow, in 1925 and 1927. Thereafter he was indoctrinated into the OGPU's forgery techniques and made impressions of Orlov's keys to his apartment and laboratory. When Orlov departed for Mecklenburg, Kroshko removed the proof of his forgeries, among them the two notorious documents which purported to implicate Moscow in a plot to bribe US Senators Blore and Norris to gain diplomatic recognition for the Soviets. These forgeries were later handed to the US government and resulted in Orlov's prosecution in Berlin in February 1929. This forced Kroshko to flee, and he was subsequently given a post at OGPU headquarters.

Orlov sold forgeries to the British, and A-3 also reported to Moscow that, 'the Estonians are selling to the Germans and the British, through Orlov (paying him 10 per cent commission), material on Soviet armaments and fortifications (Krasnaya Gorka and Kronstadt), obtained by Estonian Intelligence'.

In 1930 a 'former Russian naval lieutenant' named Kerr, who had 'worked with the English', turned up in Berlin and was identified by the OGPU as Arkady Petrovich Kerr, born in Odessa, who had served with the British mission to Archangel under General Miller. Kerr had been evacuated to Britain and then travelled on special assignments to Reval and Riga. When he arrived in Berlin to 'study the work of emigrant organisations against the Bolsheviks', an official in Moscow noted on the margin of a report submitted by the Berlin *rezidentura* that, 'This is comrade Viktor.' Kerr's real mission was to penetrate the Brotherhood of Russian Truth, a White Guards organisation which provoked this response when its objectives were published:

The Brotherhood of Russian Truth disseminates anti-communist propaganda, creates trouble whenever possible for the Soviet Administration, organises acts of terror against commissars and unrepentant communists, organises and unites all men ready to fight in secret fighting units, provokes mutiny in the ranks of the Red Army and its final object is a general armed rising.

One of the Brotherhood's leaders in Berlin was Aleksandr N. Kolberg, a former tsarist public prosecutor who had long worked in Orlov's organisation under the **alias** Lomonosov, and specialised in the forgery of Soviet and Comintern signatures. Kolberg was recruited by Kerr for the British, never realising that he had already been signed up by the OGPU. Some of the material supplied by Orlov and his friends was of quite high quality and, according to A-3, Orlov possessed the signatures of Bustrem, Trilisser, Yevdokimov, Ausem, Rakovsky, Proskurov and Smirnov. 'The forgeries look very real,' wrote A-3. 'The signatures are extremely well imitated by Kolberg and their authenticity was enhanced by the fact that Orlov, an experienced specialist, managed to convey the very essence of the style of Soviet correspondence.' Orlov was also responsible for the forged documents which resulted in a celebrated libel action brought by the car manufacturer Henry Ford against Herman Bernstein, a journalist who published a series of articles in the American press accusing Ford of 'ideological anti-semitism and direct participation in anti-semitic pogrom organisations', citing his links with anti-semitic White emigrant groups, complete with documents purporting to link Ford to a group of Russian anarchists in Constantinople.

Ford 'is collecting material against Bernstein in every country' reported A-3, 'and it is on this that Orlov bases his schemes. He has already been in touch with the representatives of Ford and Boris Brasol (who acted for the supporters of the Grand Duke Cyril in America) and has promised to supply "genuine material", compromising Bernstein.'

Coincidentally another forger, Druzhelovsky, came to Orlov's assistance in May 1925 while under interrogation at the Berlin Polizeipraesidium where, in an effort to exonerate himself, he incriminated several others, including Bernstein, whom he accused of working for the OGPU. 'This accusation served as the basis for Orlov's work,' wrote A-3. 'The aim of the forgeries was dual: first, to compromise Bernstein by showing that he was a Soviet agent, and second, by depicting the Soviet government as a "Jewish gang".' The forgery scheme described by A-3 was based on events which allegedly had taken place in 1922, and linked Bernstein to the Cheka through an intelligence network in Constantinople headed by Colonels Baliyev and Akatsatov, who routinely kept an eye on the monarchists. Bernstein's role had been to plant **deception** material in the press, but the Constantinople *rezidentura* broke contact with him because of his excessive demands for money. Meanwhile, Orlov created an entire correspondence between the Cheka and the Constantinople *rezidentura*, matched with a series of fabricated instructions from Moscow on the struggle against anti-semitism 'employing the most drastic means', together with a number of orders 'on the protection of Jews' and relations with the Jewish sections of the Communist parties. 'This second lot of forgeries', A/3 reported, 'is very subtly and skilfully constructed and forms the basis for the Protocols of Zion, but executed with great care and ingenuity.'

Orlov's trump card was the genuine register of the Kharkov Cheka for 1922, supplied to him by a former Cheka official named Sumarokov, code-named JASHIN, who later became one of Orlov's assistants. When Orlov wanted to substantiate newly created correspondence, he simply inserted an additional page between the real ones. 'A lot of money was spent on this work', wrote A-3, 'and technically it was of the highest quality. Russian paper was used and the stamps and register pages with headed columns were fabricated on the basis of photocopies of the originals. All the stamps were those in use in 1922.'

Orlov intended to sell all the forgeries, together with the registers, to Henry Ford and A-3 reported that Orlov, 'in a communicative mood ... boasted that in the past year he had earned 12,000 Deutschmarks'. However, Orlov was not always so plausible, and in May 1929 Moscow learned that:

> Curie (from the Deuxieme Bureau of the French General Staff), in a conversation with a prominent member of the White emigrant movement, recalled the unsuccessful collaboration of the French with Orlov, who simply deceived them by fabricating false information on the USSR.

Despite the OGPU's **penetration** of Orlov's network, it did not receive advance warning of his involvement in the notorious Zinoviev letter, and the first report on the subject, from the Berlin *rezidentura*, was received on 11 November 1924, and distributed to Vyacheslav Menzhinsky, Genrikh Yagoda, Artur Artusov and Nahum Eitingon, and claimed that:

According to certain information, which requires checking, the Zinoviev letter was allegedly fabricated in Riga by Lieutenant Pokrovsky (who worked with Biskupsky, connected to Guchkov), who has in his possession Comintern stationery and made it up from extracts of Zinoviev's speeches with something extra added, and as this was a circular, not a letter, it bore no signature. Pokrovsky, who is in contact with the British coun-terintelligence service, told them that he had information that an important letter would be sent that day by post from Riga to an agreed address belonging to the British Communist Party, which was allegedly given to him. He then posted the letter which was duly intercepted by the British. Its further fate is known.

This was followed by a second report, dated 20 November 1924 and addressed to Mikhail Trilisser, the Chief of the OGPU's Foreign Department. Again the culprit was named as Ivan D. Pokrovsky:

Attached please find a copy of a report from one of our sources on the 'Zinoviev letter' of 12 November 1924. According to information received by us, Zinoviev's letter to London was written in Riga by the White Guards intelligence organisa-tion. The author of the letter is Pokrovsky. The letter was sent, through Polish intermediaries, from Riga to London by post and addressed to a well-known English communist, MacManus. The British police who keep tabs on the latter's correspond-ence, photographed the letter and handed it over to the British Foreign Office as genuine.

On 18 Mau 1925 the Berlin *rezidentura* had reported that:

On 10 May, Orlov received a semi-encoded letter from Pokrovsky, who informs him that he had thought up 'a new kind of dirty trick to play on the Bolsheviks' by forging something and he asks Orlov if the ordered stationery and stamps are ready.

Orlov expresses surprise about the stamps as he is not sure which exactly are needed.

The OGPU's information about Ivan Pokrovsky's participation, received in November 1924, came from two independent sources and was later confirmed by Aleksander F. Gumansky, another of the White emigres in Berlin, who alleged that Pokrovsky headed an organisation in 1924 which forged large quantities of Soviet documents that were then distributed to Orlov in Berlin, to Shevich in Paris, and to other buyers. The forgeries, based on genuine Communist Party decrees, but with extra names added, were so good that an Englishman had been sent to Riga specifically to work with the organisation.

General Korneyev was a Russian officer of English origin who had been granted British citizenship during the First World War, and in the autumn of 1924 had requested material that could be used against the British Labour Party in the forthcoming General Election. Pokrovsky responded by sending Korneyev samples, among them the Zinoviev letter. This formed the basis of a scheme in which a copy of the letter was sent by registered post to the Soviet embassy in London. At the same time, the Metropolitan Police had been tipped off so the letter was intercepted, photographed and replaced with a blank sheet of paper which was delivered to the Soviet embassy with two policemen watching who acted as witnesses. The postman obtained a signature to confirm receipt, and when Zinoviev's letter was published in the British press, the Foreign Office requested the Soviet embassy to inform it of the contents of a letter delivered to it against the official's signature. The embassy's only answer was that the envelope had contained nothing more than a blank sheet of paper.

Some years later Gumansky fell into Soviet hands and underwent a lengthy interrogation before his execution. When the issue of the Zinoviev latter was raised he insisted that:

It was fabricated in Riga by a certain Pokrovsky, a really talented person, who worked for the British since 1920. British Intelligence in Riga did not establish contact with other British stations in connection with this assignment. I got to know Pokrovsky in 1925 when he was in Berlin on his way to Hamburg from where he was leaving for Brazil. I was invited to meet him by Orlov and in the presence of Orlov himself, the husband of his sister (whose name I have forgotten) and, if I remember rightly, Kolberg. He told us the following: 'My chief, Captain Black, suggested that I should compose a letter addressed to the British communists. I drafted it but not on proper paper and without a signature, not knowing how it would be used. This was before the general elections. Immediately after the elections Black told me that if I left Europe he would make me a downpayment of £500 and arrange for a monthly pension of £15 to be paid to me over a period of two years. He advised me to go to Brazil. I agreed to this proposal as I had long wanted to leave Europe. The British vice-consul in Riga offered to buy my archives for £500. I sold all the old rubbish and am now on my way. He told Orlov the next day that Black was also leaving for Brazil.

In another part of his testimony Gumansky returned again to the Zinoviev letter:

The Uruguayan documents were fabricated by Pokrovsky, the author of the Zinoviev letter, and Aleksander Zelinsky. Pokrovsky got £500 for the Zinoviev letter and a recommenda-tion in Buenos Aires, with the help of which he got a job with the Argentinian political police. In 1933 Pokrovsky moved to Montevideo where, with the support of the British Intelligence Service, he again was employed by the local political police as an expert on communist affairs.

## PARALLEL DIPLOMACY
The British Secret Intelligence Service euphemism for exercising covert influence over foreign political leaders is parallel diplomacy. This is unlike the more familiar backchannel method. It can occur when SIS opens a deniable line of communication with a terrorist organisation, as happened when Frank Steele established a discreet link with the Provisional IRA in October 1971, and Alastair Crooke was posted to Gaza in 2003 to open negotiations with Hamas. Similarly, SIS has been credited in using its leverage over Archbishop Makarios during the Cyprus independence talks in London in 1959,

and on Kenneth Kaunda prior to the Lancaster House talks to resolve Rhodesia's future in 1979.

The advantages of parallel diplomacy are that the discussions can be conducted in private, without the media pressure to announce results that arises in the case of its shuttle equivalent, as so often practised by professional envoys, and that the participants can be confident that their candour will not result in leaks. The contact may also exploit the personal relationships that probably have developed over a period of many years.

The example was followed in 2001 by the public appointment of the CIA director George Tenet to broker a peace agreement in the Middle East.

## PAROLE

The prearranged recognition words exchanged to identify two previously unknown individuals meeting for the first time, usually an agent and **case officer**, is termed a parole, or sometimes a protocol. The phrases chosen are innocuous, so no harm is done if addressed to the wrong person.

When the cipher clerk Igor Gouzenko **defected** in Ottawa in September 1945 he removed more than a hundred documents from the GRU *referentura*, including a file containing instructions for the British physicist Alan Nunn May, code-named ALEK, to meet his Soviet contact upon his return to London. Dr May was directed to rendezvous with his Soviet contact in Great Russell Street, opposite the British Museum. May was to walk from the Tottenham Court Road, reaching Museum Street at exactly 8 p.m. with a copy of *The Times* under his left arm. He would be met by a man holding *Picture Post* in his left hand who would ask 'What is the best way to the Strand?', to which ALEK would reply 'Well, come along, I am going that way.' The directions concluded: 'In the beginning of the conversation ALEK says "Best regards from MIKEL".'

In the event the plan was aborted, most probably by the Soviets after a tip from Kim Philby, although the area was placed under surveillance by MI5 which set up a **static observation post** in a nearby pub, employed vehicles to drive up and down Great Russell Street, and briefed the legendary MI5 agent Klop Ustinov to act the role of a Russian spy in case May showed up on his own.

After the RAF signals intelligence intercept operator Douglas Britten was recruited by the KGB in 1962 he was issued with a map to illustrate his rendezvous near Pinner tube station, and was given the parole, 'Could you tell me the way to the local library?' to which Britten was to reply, 'Unfortunately not. I don't live here.'

## PASSEUR

During both the First and Second World Wars the men and women who regularly crossed international frontiers as couriers, either carrying contraband or acting as guides for evaders, were known as *passeurs*. This dangerous occupation has its origins on the Dutch border in 1915 when agents crossed into neutral territory to smuggle messages from Belgian **train-watchers** to SIS's headquarters staff.

In the Second World War there were *passeurs* who regularly crossed the demarcation line between Nazi-occupied France and Vichy, and others who escorted escapees across the Pyrenees into neutral Spain. Most notably, one young *passeur*, Alexandre de Marenches, would become chief of SDECE in 1970.

## PATTERN OF LIFE

During any intelligence investigation, and especially those conducted in a counter-terrorism role, the first priority is to establish a suspect's pattern of life. The route taken will depend on the information already available, and whether it relates to a named individual, an address, a vehicle or a telephone number.

In the case of a name, a check will be made on the agency's own indices, and the Criminal Records Bureau, to ascertain the identity. Further, an enquiry will be made with the tax authorities to establish any current or past employer; with the appropriate issuing authorities to obtain details of any passport application, driving licence, television licence, insurance cover, entry on the electoral roll, bank account, credit card and credit reference status. The local police collator may also have a record of the individual or their address.

Alternatively, a check will be made with the Land Registry, the local council tax authority, the insurance fraud bureau, and details of any driving licence held at that address, or telephone landline registered there. The property's water, electricity and gas use will reveal consumption and indicate the number of occupants, as will the electoral roll.

If a vehicle is identified, the ownership records and insurance details can be checked to determine the name and address of the registered keeper, and if the index number has been flagged by the police on behalf of Special Branch or is known to be associated with drugs or crime.

If a mobile phone or landline is known, the metadata, being the date, time and duration of calls over the past two years, plus details of all movements with an accuracy of a few hundred metres, including unbilled calls, can be recovered. The service provider will also disclose payment details, linking the phone to an address, bank or credit card.

This information creates a pattern of life, long before physical surveillance is activated, or any warrant is required to authorise electronic or **intrusive surveillance**. Anomalies in the pattern of life, such as use of a hard-to-trace prepaid mobile phone, possession of more than one mobile phone, contamination by contact with other flagged suspects, dubious behaviour, such as the occasional removal of the mobile phone battery (a measure often taken by criminals to conceal their movements temporarily), will attract attention and may form the basis of a decision to widen and deepen enquiries.

Once a target has been **housed**, arrangements can be made to establish a **static observation post** in the vicinity, which will involve tracing anyone in the street or neighbourhood with a current or past security **clearance**.

In a counter-terrorism context, establishing a suspect's pattern of life assists in prioritising limited surveillance resources, and identifying **radicalisation**.

## PENETRATION

Hostile penetration of an intelligence agency is both the ultimate goal of a counterintelligence adversary, and the greatest danger for any organisation. Penetration can be accomplished either by inserting an agent into the target organisation, or undertaking the successful recruitment of an established officer.

The long-term development of a **mole** who is directed to join a target organisation is a rare event, perhaps best illustrated by the notorious Cambridge Five, of whom four, Kim Philby, Guy Burgess, Anthony Blunt and John Cairncross, had been recruited as Soviet

**assets** before they were encouraged to seek employment in branches of the British intelligence apparatus. By the end of the Second World War Philby, Burgess and Cairncross had joined the Secret Intelligence Service, while Blunt had served in MI5 from 1940 until 1945. Philby would remain an SIS officer until his dismissal in December 1951, and continued in contact with his SIS friends until his defection in January 1963. Blunt too would stay in occasional touch with the KGB until his acceptance of an immunity from prosecution in April 1964. None of the Cambridge Five was ever arrested or convicted of any crime related to espionage.

Enhanced background screening, which might have identified suspicious political affiliations of the kind enjoyed by the Cambridge Five, was introduced in 1949, but the vetting procedures were designed to exclude applicants for security clearances who have character flaws and vulnerabilities, rather than to identify spies. Thus, most detected spies on both sides of the Atlantic have been granted clearances, and virtually all the world's intelligence services have suffered severe, high-level penetration, including Great Britain's SIS (Kim Philby, John Cairncross and George Blake), MI5 (Anthony Blunt) and GCHQ (Douglas Britten and Geoffrey Prime); Canada's RCMP Security Service (Gilles Brunet and James Morrison); France's SDECE (Jacques Foccart); Israel's Mossad (Zeev Avni); Sweden's SÄPO (Stig Bergling); Federal Germany's BND (Heinz Felfe, Hans Clemens, Gabrielle Gast and Gydrun Hofer) and BfV (Hans Joachim Tiedge and Klaus Kuron); and Estonia's KaPo (Uno Puusepp).

As arguably the world's principal target for penetration, the myriad United States intelligence agencies have endured numerous cases, including the FBI (Robert Hanssen, Richard Miller and James Earl Pitts); CIA (Aldrich Ames, Jim Nicholson, Karl Koecher, Sharon Scranage and Larry Wu-Tai Chin); DIA (Ana Montes); NIS (Jonathan Pollard); IRB (Kenneth Myers); NSA (David Boone, Jack Dunlap, Robert Lipka and Ronald Pelton).

As well as intelligence agencies, foreign ministries are also attractive targets for penetration, and those of Great Britain (Donald Maclean, Guy Burgess and Edward Scott); Federal Germany (Helge Berger, Alfred Frenzel, Dr Hagen Blau, Leonore Heinz); Norway (Arne Treholt and Gunvor Haavik); Japan (Shoji Hiroshi, Takamore

Shigeru and Higurashi Nobumori); and France (Boris Lvovich) were the focus of sustained attention by the Soviets during the Cold War.

Although hostile penetration can prove a catastrophe for any organisation, most intelligence agencies accept the risk as an occupational hazard and recognise that a service is bound to become a target for an aggressive adversary. Thus many counterintelligence branches will adopt the pragmatic attitude of acknowledging the likelihood and, having eliminated one case, simply proceed to pursue the next, confident of its existence.

James Angleton's conviction that the KGB had penetrated the CIA ensured that his Counterintelligence Staff was permanently in pursuit of moles, and although he and his subordinates received considerable opprobrium for having adopted this posture, the policy of continuous vigilance, in the belief that current penetration was under way, was effective in the protection of the Agency's secrets.

Suspected but unproven penetration creates an exceptionally difficult environment in which to recruit sources and maintain liaison relationships. SIS was widely untrusted until 1985 when it was able to demonstrate that having run Oleg Gordievsky inside the KGB for eleven years was indicative of its integrity. Other agencies have experienced serious but undeclared penetration. The French SDECE had at least two cases, and the DST came to suspect its own director, Marcel Chalet. MI5 continues to deny it was penetrated, although acknowledges that there was sufficient evidence to launch a **molehunt** which investigated its director general, Roger Hollis, and his deputy, Graham Mitchell.

Near certainty from external sources that an organisation has been penetrated, in the absence of internal evidence, is equally debilitating. GCHQ spent many years seeking a Soviet mole code-named BARON, and the DST pursued a spy with the KGB cryptonym GARMASH. Without a satisfactory conclusion, such molehunts can severely undermine morale. Equally, in an inconclusive case, when a spy has been detected, but it has proved impossible to gain the evidence to bring a criminal prosecution, as happened to the Australian Security Intelligence Organisation, and the FBI with UNSUB DICK, the results are damaging.

# PIANIST

In the vocabulary of wartime Soviet intelligence personnel, a radio operator was known as a pianist.

# PINCH

The theft of cryptographic material for the purpose of acquiring a crib to assist a cryptanalytical attack on a target cipher is known as a pinch. During the Second World War the British undertook several missions to pinch the Kriegsmarine's Home Waters Enigma key known as *Heimisch*, later HYDRA, and broken briefly by the Allies in June 1941, following the capture of cryptographic material from the *München*. More documents, relevant to the DOLPHIN key, seized on 11 May 1940 from a patrol boat, *Schiff-26*, enabled six days of DOLPHIN traffic to be read retrospectively for the previous month, from 22 to 27 April. In March 1941, a force of British commandos and Norwegian volunteers, code-named Operation CLAYMORE, attacked the German-occupied Lofoten Islands, and a party from HMS *Somali* boarded an armed trawler, the *Krebs*, and recovered a box of Enigma rotors and the key list for February. Consequently, DOLPHIN traffic for April succumbed, and then the messages from 1 to 8 August were read retrospectively. This was followed by breaking the daily keys for 18 and 19 September, and thereafter DOLPHIN was read with a delay of no more than 36 hours until the end of hostilities with the exception of a three-week period from 1 March 1943, when new bigram tables were introduced and required reconstruction by the cryptographers.

Pinches involving a burglary were discouraged because, if the enemy realised confidential cipher material had been compromised, the necessary counter-measures would be instated, thereby nullifying any potential advantage. Indeed, a plan by Office of Strategic Services personnel to burgle the Japanese naval attaché's office in Lisbon was cancelled at the last moment because, unknown to the officers concerned, the cipher had been solved already.

During the Cold War the CIA's Staff D, headed by Carleton A. Swift and then Bill Donnelly, was responsible for break-ins at diplomatic premises across the world in an effort to assist the National Security Agency. Staff D was considered so secret that it was kept separate from the Directorate of Operations, and gained an impressive reputation for success without ever causing the Agency embarrassment. Staff D would later be replaced by the Special Collection Service, a joint NSA/CIA unit with its own discreet headquarters in Beltsville, Maryland, although its existence was compromised by the FBI's Robert Hanssen, who supplied his Soviet and then Russian **handlers** with details of the organisation's size, budget, performance and targets. In 2013 details of the SCS were made public by documents disclosed by Edward Snowden.

## PISCINE

The headquarters of the Direction Générale de la Sécurité Extérieure (DGSE) on the Boulevard Mortier in Paris is known as *la piscine* because of its proximity to the municipal public swimming pool nearby. The organisation, largely staffed by military personnel, is directly answerable to the Elysée Palace and therefore has a very high degree of political support, acting as an instrument of political power. This became evident when the **blowback** from the *Rainbow Warrior* affair in New Zealand was adroitly shelved by President François Mitterand's administration and never became a scandal on the scale of Watergate, principally because the entire DGSE operation had been authorised by the president personally. The insertion of the word *piscine* in any conversation is intended to convey the authority at least of the current DGSE chief. The Gallic difference in cultural attitudes to intelligence collection is most obvious among the **honourable correspondents**, who regard a request for assistance from the DGSE as a privilege and duty, irrespective of an occupation, such as journalist or doctor, that in other countries would make the request be considered offensive or unwise.

The DGSE, often called 'the deck' by Allied services, because of its previous incarnation as the Service de Documentation Extérieure et de Contre-Espionnage (SDECE) has acquired a reputation for engaging in industrial espionage, not least because of the appointment of the former Air France director, Pierre Marion, as SDECE's chief in June 1981.

SDECE played a role in the 'dirty war' against Algerian nationalists and the Organisation Armée Secrete (OAS) which campaigned to retain French control over the colony. The conflict was marked by SDECE's controversial employment *les barbouzes* ('the bearded ones') who identified, abducted and assassinated opponents of Paris's official policy.

## PITCH

The moment a prospective agent is invited by a recruiter to engage in espionage is known as the pitch and, depending upon the circumstances, may place the **case officer** in jeopardy by revealing himself (or herself) as a professional intelligence officer. Such an encounter in hostile territory may involve considerable risk because of the possibility that the target might react badly, reject the offer and perhaps report the incident to the local security apparatus. Other varieties include the **gang-plank pitch** and the **cold pitch**. Some CIA personnel, borrowing a phrase from the real estate business, call the recruiter 'the closer'.

The pitch will be the culmination of a period of research and **cultivation** after the target has been identified by a **talent spotter** as a potential candidate for recruitment, and the objective of a carefully choreographed introduction known as the **bump**.

The pitch may be made by a **legal**, being an intelligence professional operating under diplomatic cover, or an **illegal** who may have put themselves in danger by engaging in an act of espionage without the benefit of diplomatic immunity.

## PLANT

The deliberate establishment of a false source of information for use by an adversary is known as a plant. During the CIA's **molehunt** into the 1985 breaches of security which culminated in the arrest of Aldrich Ames, the KGB made several attempts to misdirect the investigation by offering false leads, one of which was a plant who, in January 1986, alleged through an anonymous source in Germany (who later turned out to be a KGB-controlled **double agent**) that the security of the CIA's communications had been compromised by the successful **penetration** of its principal radio facility at Warrenton, Virginia. The information, hand-delivered by letter to a CIA officer in Bonn, contained some genuine information about Gennady Varenik (an **asset** in the KGB's Bonn *rezidentura* code-named GT/FITNESS) and correctly named his CIA case officer as Chuck Leven. The anonymous source was treated with caution, but large sums of money were delivered to a designated **dead drop** in East Germany.

An inevitably lengthy investigation finally concluded that no such breach had occurred, and that the entire tale, delivered in six letters, had been a skilfully constructed ploy. Although, according to 'Mr X', Varenik had been caught two months earlier, in November 1985, when his father had accidently discovered some compromising espionage paraphernalia, the CIA thought that this was not the real explanation, especially as Varenik had been detained in East Berlin.

Similarly, another KGB source, Aleksandr Zhomov (GT/PROLOGUE), sold his CIA **handlers** over a period of three years dozens of supposedly authentic internal Second Chief Directorate documents which seemed to disclose how the KGB's ubiquitous surveillance on US embassy staff had been responsible for identifying the CIA agents lost in 1985. Once again, Zhomov, who had approached Jack Downing, then chief of the Moscow station while on a train to Leningrad in June 1988, was finally exposed as an elaborate hoax, presumably intended to divert the CIA from the existence of a well-placed mole within the Soviet/Eastern European Division.

## PLAUSIBLE DENIABILITY

The capacity for a political leader to be misleading about previous advance knowledge of, or authorisation for, a high-risk operation is known as plausible deniability. In such circumstances it is, of course, essential for the individual's reputation that no contradictory evidence should emerge.

On 2 May 1960 President Dwight Eisenhower was assured by DCI Allen Dulles that the **cover story** for a U-2 aircraft's intrusion into Soviet airspace, that a NASA weather research flight from Turkey had flown off-course because of an innocent navigational error, would not be challenged because the aircraft must have broken up at very high altitude, and there was no chance that the pilot, who had also been equipped with a suicide needle laced with curare, could have survived.

Once the US Air Force had issued the **cover story**, and speculated that the pilot might have become unconscious and strayed into Soviet airspace while the aircraft was under the control of the automatic pilot, the Kremlin revealed on 6 May that F. Gary Powers was very much alive, in custody, and declaring himself to be a CIA employee who had flown from Peshawar in Pakistan. Dulles promptly offered his resignation to Eisenhower, who refused to accept it.

## PLAYBACK

The manipulation of an adversary's means of communication, such as a radio transmitter captured during the Second World War, is known as playback. The German combined counterintelligence agencies proved to be exceptionally adept at engaging in this type of **deception**, with catastrophic results for the resistance organisations sponsored by Special Operations Executive in France and the Netherlands. In Holland the Abwehr and Sicherheitsdienst began with one prisoner and his transmitter, and exploited the playback or *Funkspiel* until some fourteen **circuits** had been established.

## PLEA BARGAIN

Expediency, and the need for the compilation of a comprehensive **damage assessment** may require the prosecuting authorities to reduce the gravity of criminal charges, or make a recommendation to the sentencing judge, during the trial of a defendant accused of espionage. The celebrated Washington attorney Plato Cacheris successfully negotiated life imprisonment instead of the death penalty for his clients Aldrich Ames and Robert Hanssen in return for their cooperation in creating a detailed analysis of the scale of their betrayals. Similarly, the DIA **analyst** Ana Montes incriminated a DGI **access agent** and former State Department employee, Marta Rita Velazquez, for a reduced sentence of twenty-five years' imprisonment. However, Velazquez resigned from her post in 2002 and fled to Sweden before she could be arrested.

## POCKET LITTER

Casual items, such as keys, photos, wallets and ticket-stubs which are intended to convey a false impression, or offer support to an **alias**, are often referred to as pocket litter. A classic example is the case of 'Major William Martin', an entirely bogus British officer whose body was placed in the sea off the Spanish coast near Huelva in April 1943 as part of an ingenious MI5 **deception** operation code-named MINCEMEAT. The cadaver was actually that of a homeless Welsh alcoholic, Glyndwr Michael, but the plan called for him to be dressed as a British courier entrusted with sensitive documents.

Confident that the body would be searched by the Spanish authorities MI5 officers went to elaborate lengths to fabricate Major Martin's personality and private life by preparing the appropriate pocket litter, which revealed the existence of a fiancée, an overdraft with Lloyds Bank, a St Christopher medallion to indicate that he was a Roman Catholic, a receipt for the purchase of an extravagant engagement ring from a Bond Street jeweller, and the ticket stub of a London bus. The objective was to create a plausible life for a non-existent person, and the ruse succeeded. When the body was found in the sea by fishermen the Spanish alerted the Abwehr and provided access to the briefcase chained to Martin's wrist. Although Abwehr **analysts** expressed some doubts about the authenticity of the documents in the case, the identity of Major Martin was not challenged, and he was buried in a local cemetery under that name, an episode that later inspired Duff Cooper's novel *Operation Heartbreak*, and the officially sponsored non-fiction account in *The Man Who Never Was*.

## POLYGRAPH

The US intelligence community sets considerable store by the polygraph examination, a device which records physical reactions to questions posed by the operator, and many security **clearances** are dependent upon passing a test.

Often called a lie-detector, and sometimes called being 'on the box' or being 'fluttered', the polygraph combines a monitor of respiration, blood pressure, pulse and sweat (measured by the galvanic conductivity of skin) and was used regularly from 1948 by the US Counterintelligence Corps. In 1965 a CIC operator, Sergeant Glen Rohrer, defected to Czechoslovakia and took a machine with him, which subsequently was subjected to close scrutiny by Soviet Bloc intelligence officers. When Aldrich Ames sought the KGB's advice about beating the machine in April 1991, he was told to get a good night's sleep as there was no reliable antidote. On the event the examiner was concerned about his possible deception regarding a question about unauthorised contact with foreign nationals, and he was recalled for a second session by the Employee Branch of the CIA's Polygraph Division, on the recommendation of John F. Sullivan.

Ames passed this second exam and Sullivan later recalled 'I saw no anomalies in the charts, nor did anyone else who looked at them, and the test was deemed no deception indicated.'

Ames had undergone a test in May 1986, eleven months after he had made the 'big dump' of classified material, which he had handed to his KGB contact, Viktor Cherkashin on 13 June 1985. On that occasion the test had been administered by a woman who had previously known Ames and Rosario, then his mistress, who would become wife, at the Mexico City station in 1982. When the examiner had been posted temporarily to Mexico, Rosario had taken her shopping, an encounter that she had reminded Ames of. Ames was arrested in February 1994 and made a **plea bargain** to avoid a death sentence. Both of his 1991 polygraph examiners, who had not been informed that he was under investigation by **molehunters** and considered a suspect for the 1985 losses, left the CIA.

In October 1995 Harold ('Jim') Nicholson failed the first of three polygraphs, and was arrested at Dulles Airport in November 1996. None of his three examiners was informed that he was already the subject of a molehunt and in his confession Nicholson admitted to having spied for the KGB since June 1994 when he had been the station chief in Kuala Lumpur. He also said that the Soviets had tried to train him to beat the polygraph. Although the failed polygraphs were credited with his exposure, he had in fact been identified as a spy by GT/AVENGER, a CIA **asset** who also provided vital evidence against Ames and Bob Hanssen.

Operators, trained first at Fort Holabird, Maryland, and later at Fort Huachuca, Arizona, were instructed that some applicants with a guilty conscience seeking a clearance might opt to avoid the test and work in an unclassified environment, thus proving the device's deterrent effect.

The first CIA polygraph test was administered in August 1948 to Robert B. Bannerman, the deputy director of Support. Thereafter 123 examinations were conducted until January 1949, and all applicants were tested, with just 8 per cent declined a job, of which 92 per cent had failed the polygraph. Between 1952 and 1979 the CIA Office of Security often disapproved applications for security clearances, but never on the basis of a bad test result, but only because of admissions made as a consequence of an examination indicating deception.

FBI polygraphs conducted by Ken Schull on Brian Kelley, a senior CIA counterintelligence officer suspected from 1997 of being a Soviet **mole** code-named KARAT, indicated he had been entirely truthful and cooperative, yet the examiner later disclosed that he had come under pressure from headquarters to change his verdict. Kelley was cleared when incontrovertible evidence incriminating Hanssen was supplied to the FBI by Colonel Alexander Zaporozshky, a former senior KGB officer who came out of Russia in November 2000 and was quietly **resettled** in Virginia.

The only spy known to have been caught as a direct result of deception identified by a polygraph was a CIA officer, Sharon Scranage, who came under suspicion while stationed in Accra, Ghana, in 1985.

At the end of the Cold War the CIA concluded that a large number of East German and Cuban DGI assets were really **double agents**. Most had passed their polygraphs, thus leaving the impression that perhaps some professionals really had found a technique of beating the machine.

The perception that polygraphs did not really work influenced British attitudes, and after a trial with the devices the British Intelligence community rejected proposals for their introduction as an aid to completing background screenings for security **clearances**. According to Brian Stewart, formerly the SIS **station commander** in Hong Kong, his chief, Maurice Oldfield, once boasted to him that he had beaten the polygraph when had had taken a test.

## POST-USEFULNESS SYNDROME

A **defector** who has undergone **resettlement,** or an **asset** who no longer has any operational value may succumb to post-usefulness syndrome, which may be interpreted as a manifestation of underlying narcissism or attention-seeking. The syndrome is associated with claims that the individual has further, hitherto undisclosed information, or is in a position to re-establish their lost status.

## PROPRIETARY

In the CIA's parlance a **front company** which exists solely for the purpose of giving false employment to its personnel is known as a proprietary. They range from business consultancies and aircraft charter companies to import–export firms, organisations that will not attract unwelcome attention in the environment in which they operate. Wholly owned CIA companies are also known as 'Delawares', referring to the state of their original incorporation.

Not all the staff working for a proprietary may be aware of its covert ownership, usually concealed through a complicated web of deliberately obscure trusts, foundations, management consultancies and proxies. In the case of Air America, a charter aircraft company active in Southeast Asia in the 1960s, it grew to be one of the largest airlines in the world, employing 6,000 pilots, ground staff, and administrators, and flew numerous routes in addition to the work undertaken on behalf of the CIA.

Other identified proprietaries in the same field are Southern Air Transport, Intermountain, Continental Air Services, and Civil Air Transport. The CIA's aircraft-servicing branch in the Pacific, Air Asia, based in Taiwan, employed some 2,000 staff prior to its sale in 1975.

Proprietaries are usually deniable, arm's-length operations, and when John T. Downey and Richard G. Fecteau were shot down on an illegal flight over China in November 1952, they spent many years in prison, being released in March 1973 and December 1971, respectively. Similarly, in May 1958, Allen Pope was captured by the Indonesians while on a clandestine flight to resupply rebels in Sumatra and imprisoned for four years. In 1986, two Southern Air Transport crewmembers, William Cooper and Wallace Sawyer, were killed, and their cargo kicker, Eugene Hassenfus, was captured when their C-123 was shot down over Nicaragua during an airdrop to the Contras.

Who was Stuart Bodman, supposedly a British journalist killed by Soviet troops near Bagrami in Afghanistan in July 1983? His alleged employer, Gulf Features Services Ltd, turned out to be phoney, and both his passport and international driver's licence had been issued to an impersonator, the real Stuart Bodman never having travelled abroad. The Afghan government later claimed that Bodman was one of five men in civilian clothes, carrying video cameras and satellite communications equipment, who had been intercepted after they had crossed the border from Taramengal.

## Q

## QUESTIONNAIRE

The shopping list supplied to an agent by a **case officer** to direct the **asset** towards information required is usually in the form of a questionnaire and reflects the needs of the agency's clientele. Such a document is, of course, itself quite sensitive as it may disclose the strengths and relative weaknesses in that service's existing knowledge, and therefore have a considerable counterintelligence value.

Before and during the First World War the German Admiralstab issued its agents in England with lists of priority targets for collection, thereby indicating which topics the organisation knew least about. Prior to the outbreak of hostilities, captured questionnaires tended to concentrate on the collection of naval data, as illustrated by the lists supplied to Walter Rimann, Adolph Schroeder (**alias** Frederick Gould), and Armgaard Graves in 1912; Fred Manasse in 1913; and Peter Gregory, Lina Heine, and Albert Rodriguez in 1914.

In his correspondence with Schroeder, the German spymaster Gustav Steinhauer posed as 'C.F. Schmidt' and on 30 October 1912 offered him £200 for the 1909 *Gunnery and Torpedo Manual*, with addenda, and £200 for the 1912 *Annual Report of the Torpedo School*. A few days later, on 5 November, he asked whether the ships of the Second and Third Fleets, the crews of which were usually kept in barracks, had been manned, and further whether the Fifth Flotilla and the submarines were preparing for sea. On 25 December 1912, he asked whether there were special preparations for war going on in the ports. Soon afterward, on 23 January 1913, he offered £400 for the 1911 *Torpedo School Report*, and requested a sketch and precise details of the new fire-director and details of the fire-control fitted on HMS *Thunderer,* which was described as 'an invention of Commander F.C. Dreyer, commanding the new small cruiser *Amphion*'.

On 17 February 1913, Schroeder was sent a long questionnaire, and this would correspond, in every respect, with the list sent to Lina Heine on 19 August 1914:

I. What departments the Admiralty have to deal with regarding:

(a) The coaling of the fleet

(b) Provision, enlistment of auxiliary vessels and merchant cruisers

II. How are the destroyer flotillas divided after the reduction of the number of their boats from 24 to 20. How many boats go to:

(a) A Squadron (formerly 12)

(b) A Division (formerly 8)

(c) A Sub-division (formerly 2)

III. What is the bearing of the submarine tubes of the *St Vincent*, *Colossus*, *Orion* and *St. George* class (if possible in degrees above beam).

IV. Are the torpedoes of the ships and submarines adapted for changing their course at a certain angle after having left the tube?

V. Weight and kind of explosive charge of torpedoes:

| | |
|---|---|
| 18" prime marks IIIx | ) at what distance and speeds |
| 18" prime marks IIIx(4) | ) are these generallyfixed (a) |
| 18" prime marks IIIxx | ) at night (b) by day (1) in |
| 18" prime marks IIIxx(4) | ) general practice, (2) in |
| 19" later marks | ) battle. |
| 21" mark I | ) |
| 21" mark II | ) |

VI. At what distance and speeds are torpedoes adapted on board of destroyers in war?

(a) by day

(b) By night

(1) the later marks of 18"

(2) the later marks of 21" mark I

(3) the later marks of 21" mark II

VII. How many submarines of the D and E class 18" or 21" torpedo tubes?

VIII. How do the gyroscopes of the 21" torpedoes work when running at great distances (that is to say between 8,000 and 11,000 yards). Reliable or not satisfactory?

IX. Does the 21" Mark II really run 11,000 yards? What is the speed at this or the greatest possible distance?

X. Which ships are fitted out with 21" mark I, which with mark II? Which destroyers are fitted out with 21" mark I, which with mark II? Have the ships only one or different kinds of torpedoes on board? That is to say single torpedoes of any new kind (one for each tube) and the rest of an older kind?

XI. a) How great is the total number of torpedoes on board of Battleships and on board Battlecruisers? Is there any material reserve of torpedoes for ships or destroyers ashore?

b) How many torpedo tubes have:– *King George, Marlborough, Princess Royal, Queen Mary, Tiger*?

XII. a) Particulars about length, breadth and height of the broadside torpedo-rooms of the new big ships?

b) How many torpedoes can be fired per minute from each tube?

c) Details on the special arrangements for torpedo-quick loading?

XIII. Construction. Add in reply the names of the ships corresponding to the particulars.

XIV. Which place is purposed for the artillery fire controls (previous in the foretop) of *Lion* and *Orion*.

XV. Which news can be procured about the type: 'light armoured cruiser 1,' as mentioned in the estimates 1912–13.

XVI. a) Particulars about the fire-control of *Lion* according to the reconstruction newly finished.

b) What place is the main fire-control station for *Lion, Orion* and newer ships? In the conning-tower or aloft?

XVII. a) Particulars about the 'firing-director' as on board of the *Neptune* and *Thunderer*?

b) Which ships are at present fitted with the firing-director and which will be equipped with it?

c) Where will the firing-director be placed in the very latest ships?

d) Details about the new fire-control system (of Commander F.C. Dreyer), which is designed to work in harmony with the fire-director and is fitted in the *Thunderer*.

XVIII. a) Which big calibres are manufactured at present? Which length?

XIX. Which is the highest and lowest speed for wheeling the big turrets?

XX. Description of the latest construction of sights and firing gears.

XXI. Are there combined firing gears for several big guns? On board which ships?

XXII. Particulars about the passing of the command of the guns:–
a) to the big guns
b) to the secondary armament
c) for firing torpedo-boats

XXIII. Particulars about the passing of the command of the guns:–
a) to the big guns
b) to the secondary armament
c) for firing torpedo-boats

XXIV. Which are the greatest firing distances of big guns?

XXV. Particulars about the anti-airship guns in the Navy.

XXVI. Particulars for fighting submarines.

XXVII. Drawings and sketches of the different shells for the 13.5" and 15" guns.

XXVIII. Particulars about the method of fighting torpedo-boats.

XXIX. Which range-finders are in the Navy? Which systems?

XXX. How many range-finders are on board a modern battle-ship?

XXXI. Where are these range-finders mounted?

XXXII. Particulars about the trial torpedoes (already stated) running 4,000 yards with 90 kn? By which means are they working without propellors?

Submarines.

XXXIII. a) Particulars about the D and E Class.

b) How many torpedo tubes have the boats of the D. and S. Class?

c) Have the new submarines 21" torpedoes (which boats)?

d) Are the submarines fitted out with submarine signalling apparatus?

e) If fitted out, how do they work?

f) In which way will the submarines be used in war?

g) Will submarines be sent near the enemy's coast? Which class? From which ports?

h) How do submarines manage their attacks? Are they spread over separated areas or do several boats work together?

Mines.

XXXIV. a) What kind of mines are used? Method of detonation, construction of sinker, depth of water up to which they can be used.

b) Which kind of mines and what number have the mine-layers (*Apollo* class) on board?

c) What is the charge of the mines composed of, and what is the weight of the charge?

d) Particulars about the hydrostatic gear.

e) Are the destroyers fitted out with arrangements for storing and throwing mines?

f) Is it possible to 'feel' the mines with the mine-sweeping gear of the mine-sweeping gun boats or trawlers, even when the mines do not explode or get loose, i.e. when a mine or its anchor cable fouls the sweeping cable, but gets clear by slipping?

g) By what method will mines only touched in this manner be noticed?

h) How is the sweeping-gear refitted for immediate further use when interrupted by explosion?

i) How do the sweeping gunboats or trawlers get clear from a caught mine?

k) Did they practise in carrying off and tearing off the mines, and with what result?

l) What is the maximum speed of:–

a) the gunboats.

b) the trawlers.

With sweeping gear out?

m) For which English ports at home and abroad is mining defence still provided for?

n) Are there any accommodations or designs to render mines unsharp after a given time or under certain circumstances?

o) Which technical experiments and changes have been made with mines during the last three years?

Outfit for the Fleet, etc.

XXXV. Are there oil fuel stores of the Admiralty in the following places:– (how is the oil stored in tanks or lighters)? (add to the reply the names of the places corresponding to the particulars).

Scapa Flow Great Yarmouth

Granton Lowestoft

Grangemouth Cromarty (Invergordon)

Dundee Harwich

The Clyde Falmouth

Coastal Defence

XXXVI. Is there a Battery planned or in course of construction on the entrance of the Cromarty Firth? What calibre of guns?

XXXVII. Are any experiments being made to provide airships with guns or instruments for dropping explosives? Does the War Office intend to order more airships in France?

General

XXXVIII. a) Directions and regulations about the scouting and searching of the armoured and the smaller cruisers.

b) Regulations about employment of submarines, their tactics, and exercises.

c) Weekly memoranda of the Admiralty concerning all subjects of interest, general orders, changements, etc.

d) Books about description of the offensive blockade, spherical mines. Instruction for the use of these mines.

On 21 February 1913, Schroeder was sent a further questionnaire, together with a request that he should procure the current Fleet Signal Manual and the current Fighting Instructions.

One of the last questionnaires recovered during the war was acquired in Bergen from a member of a Norwegian liner's crew. He produced a document that reflected continuing German interest in the Royal Navy, specifically requesting information about new warships, and details of submarines, anti-submarine tactics and coastal defences. Curiously, a particular officer, Commander Gordon Campbell, was singled out for enquiries to be made for an explanation for his rapid promotion. Other topics covered included political issues and the presence of British services in Norway.

Eight convicted PIRA terrorists, including Danny Morrison, were paid compensation of up to £200,000 in 2015 after it was revealed that the police had withheld evidence given by an agent, Freddie Scappaticci, code-named STAKE KNIFE. Morrison had been arrested in January 1990 for his involvement in the abduction in West Belfast of an alleged informer, Sandy Lynch, but his conviction had been quashed as unsafe when it emerged that details of Scappaticci's true role had been suppressed. Scappaticci has fled to Italy, and Lynch, reputedly a former INLA gunman, has been resettled abroad. Five other PIRA men had been convicted of keeping Lynch imprisoned for forty hours while he was interrogated, as had the owner of the house in Carrigart Avenue, his wife and their son.

# R

## RADICALISATION

From a counter-terrorism perspective, radicalisation is a process through which principally young Muslim men, often of stable backgrounds and good education, change into violent extremists. The catalyst may be influence from the internet or a radical imam, but the actual conversion is often marked by very distinct stages, being a change in mosque; a refusal to worship with the rest of the family; borrowing radical literature and videos from the mosque; participation in white-water rafting and other bonding, outdoor experiences with other Muslim youths; travel to Pakistan to attend one of the *madrassas*; abandoning use of a home computer or email account;

prolonged use of cyber cafés; browsing of dangerous websites; and finally, visits to airline schedules or other websites. Such behaviour is likely to result in surveillance, and maybe a clandestine search of premises to find traces of weapons and explosives or even a martyrdom video. Discovery of any such incriminating material that could be forensically connected to a suspect would then result in interdiction.

## RAFTER
The discovery that even radio receivers with no transmitting capacity emit a weak signal provided signals intelligence technicians with the opportunity to identify the locations of receiving equipment tuned to specific wavelengths. This technique, code-named RAFTER, meant that monitoring personnel searching the airwaves for illicit broadcasts could not only pinpoint receivers, but even trace the frequency to which they were tuned. A technical breakthrough with profound implications for clandestine communications, RAFTER was deployed by MI5 in an aircraft to patrol over south London in the hope of finding a location where a Soviet **illegal** might be listening to a **numbers station** or other source of suspicious broadcasts, such as an orbiting satellite. Although RAFTER was considered a major triumph, and was tested in Canada and the United States, no Soviet spy was ever traced with the apparatus.

## RATS
The acronym for remote administration tools, RATS provide the capability to take covert control of a remote electronic device, such as a mobile phone or laptop. Depending upon the make and model of a mobile phone, software can be downloaded to transform the instrument into an active microphone and record conversations, even when ostensibly switched off.

## RECOGNITION PROTOCOLS
When a newly assigned **case officer** is scheduled to meet an existing agent for the first time, each will be given details of the other's appearance. Gervase Cowell, the SIS **station commander** in Moscow in 1962 recalled that he had been instructed to conduct a fleeting **brush contact** with a woman in the GUM department store who would be wearing a red raincoat, but as he approached the site at the appointed time he encountered two such women, so he aborted the *Treff*.

Under interrogation in June 1950 David Greenglass revealed to the FBI that in 1944 he had been shown a V-shaped piece of cardboard, cut from a Jell-O box, which, he was told by his brother-in-law, Julius Rosenberg, would identify his new contact. When Harry Gold subsequently called at Greenglass's home in Albuquerque in June 1945, he produced the cardboard from his wallet, which matched the corresponding piece Greenglass had retained.

## RED BOOK

The weekly summary of the British Joint Intelligence Committee assessments, officially known as the *Weekly Survey of Intelligence*, was until 2008 circulated to a limited number of Cabinet members. It was also known as the Red Book, after its distinctive cover. It was distributed on Friday mornings, and the first recipient was the Queen, who read every edition from the time when she succeeded to the throne in February 1952. The document was approved by the full JIC which met in 70 Whitehall on Thursday mornings, at exactly the time when the Cabinet was gathering in 10 Downing Street.

The JIC consists of the four heads of the security and intelligence services (MI5, SIS, GCHQ and the Defence Intelligence Staff); the permanent under-secretaries of the Foreign Office, Home Office, Ministry of Defence and Treasury; the CIA London station chief, and the representatives of the Australian SIS and New Zealand Security Intelligence Service. The JIC structure is managed by a small secretariat and built on a series of Current Intelligence Groups (CIG), small sub-committees drawn from Whitehall which monitor events, draft reports and make recommendations on requirements. There are usually about half a dozen geographical sub-committees, the points where resources and requirements meet, and priorities are assessed. Some CIGs, such as that dealing with Eastern Europe, are permanent fixtures, while others will be created or dissolved as the needs arise. The Assessment Staff, all seconded from other government departments, may provide one individual to chair several CIGs simultaneously.

A CIG will read all relevant Foreign Office telegrams, study foreign newspapers and monitor reports from the CIG's component agencies. The pressure on the Assessment Staff is considerable, with Whitehall demanding instant responses and guidance on events around the world. There are around two dozen members of the assessment staff attached to the JIC, drawn almost equally from the Ministry of Defence and the Foreign Office. Of those on secondment from the MoD, about half are from the armed forces, the remainder being civil servants. Individual desk officers are assigned to particular geographical areas, and they are responsible for preparing the very first draft of a JIC report, which is then submitted to the CIG chairman who distributes it among the CIG's membership. Typically a CIG will consist of desk officers from SIS, GCHQ, SIS, the Defence Intelligence Staff (representing the MoD), the Foreign Office and the CIA and perhaps MI5 or the Home Office. Once a CIG has agreed the text of a report it is submitted to the Head of the Assessment Staff who, having approved the document, will pass it to the full JIC through the secretariat. When the JIC meets, the head of the Assessment Staff will be accompanied by the chairman of whichever CIG has a report under consideration. Having been accepted by the full JIC, the paper will be circulated as an official JIC assessment.

The speed with which this process works is remarkable, the first stage in the weekly cycle being a meeting held on Monday morning at which the Head of the Assessment Staff and the appropriate CIG chairman choose the topics to be discussed by the individual CIGs, and an agenda will be prepared by the same evening with a warning notice distributed to the CIG members. Typically a CIG will meet early on a Tuesday morning and will have a report drafted by the afternoon, when it is passed to the Head of the Assessment Staff. By 3 p.m. the following day the paper will be on the desk of the chairman of the JIC, who will hold a briefing the same evening in preparation for the full JIC the following morning. Having received JIC approval, the final document will be included in the Red Book, ready for distribution to ministers on Friday morning.

The advantage of the JIC, compared to its foreign counterparts, lies in its anonymity. Whereas in the United States the equivalent system is handicapped by the sponsoring agency's determination to emphasise its own role, and indulge in the kind of interdepartmental politicking that is so prevalent when rival organisations compete for limited resources, the British model depends upon consensus. Every report is unsigned, thus giving no clue to the origin of its author, and allowing the full CIG to endorse it without losing ground in the bureaucratic turf-war fought by aspiring mandarins anxious to enhance the budgetary interests of their favoured body. The disadvantage of the arrangement is that by the time the CIG chairman and the head of the Assessment Staff have amended a paper, and rubbed off most of the sharp edges, it will have become quite a bland product. A further weakness, later highlighted by the Franks Committee in the aftermath of the 1982 Falklands conflict, was the JIC's constitutional inability to take the initiative by drawing attention to specific concerns without first having been asked to do so by another branch of government.

## REDEFECTION

An individual who defects to an adversary and then undergoes a change of heart, for whatever reason, and returns home, is known as a redefector. In July 1985 the KGB officer Vitali Yurchenko, an unexpected **walk-in** to the CIA in Rome changed his mind three months later, evaded his CIA escort and went to the Soviet embassy in Washington, DC, where he held a press conference to assert that he had been the victim of an **abduction** and had been drugged.

Other redefectors include Anatoli Cheboratev, a GRU officer who defected in Brussels in October 1971; Anton Sabotka, a KGB **illegal** in Canada in 1972; Nikolai Petrov, a GRU officer in Jakarta in June 1972, Lieutenant Artush Hovasenian of the KGB, in Turkey in July 1972; and Evgenni Sorokin in Vientiane in September 1972.

Redefections are usually accompanied by claims of maltreatment, as happened in September 1983 when the Soviet journalist and former deputy editor of the *Literary Gazette*, Oleg Bitov, defected in Italy, only to redefect to Moscow from London the following August. He claimed at a press conference that he had been abducted by the British Security Service but the reality was that he had succumbed to depression and had been unable to complete a contract for the publication of his memoirs, *Tales I Could Not Tell*. Bitov had been a KGB **cooptee** and the enquiry held upon his return found it expedient to accept his version of events. One of the officials sitting on the investigation panel was Yurchenko, whose subsequent behaviour was doubtless influenced by the decision.

In July 2010 an Iranian physicist, Shahram Amiri, claimed that he had been kidnapped by the CIA in June the previous year while on a pilgrimage to Mecca, and he returned to Tehran where he had been engaged on atomic weapons research at the Malik-Ashtar Industrial University. At a press conference held in the Iranian Interests Section of the Pakistani embassy, Amiri asserted that he had resisted the CIA's torture and bribery.

## REFERENTURA

The physical office space devoted in diplomatic premises to a *rezident* and his staff is known as the *referentura* and will be manned twenty-four hours a day and closely guarded. The first account of the security precautions surrounding a GRU *referentura* was given by Igor Gouzenko, a GRU cipher clerk who defected from the Soviet embassy in Ottawa in September 1945.

Once the local counterintelligence apparatus has identified the area occupied by the *referentura* it will become the target for surveillance, so invariably it will be located on an upper floor, with the windows barred and shuttered to nullify laser eavesdropping. Access will be restricted and the rooms will be subject to regular sweeps to detect any electronic listening devices.

Whenever new diplomatic premises are constructed much effort is applied to the identification of the likely location of the *referentura* so measures can be taken to assist in the task of monitoring the conversation of members of the *rezidentura*.

## REMOTE SENSOR

An electronic device deployed to detect certain activity, such as movement or heat, a remote sensor has many intelligence and security applications. In an Northern Ireland context such equipment proved invaluable in support of surveillance operations conducted in remote rural environments where physical observation was difficult or impossible. The Provisional IRA routinely chose farm buildings in which to hide its arms caches because they were difficult to monitor by conventional surveillance techniques.

# REMOTE VIEWING

In 1984 the Washington journalist Jack Anderson reported that the Defense Intelligence Agency had sponsored research into paranormal powers, including the ability to participate in astral travelling and report on observations made at long distance. The US intelligence community terminated funding the project in 1995 after the CIA concluded that the project offered no intelligence advantage.

# RENDITION

Introduced during President Ronald Reagan's administration, rendition was a method adopted by the CIA to transfer prisoners from foreign to US jurisdiction, usually on chartered US-registered private jets. Subsequently confirmed in June 1995 by President Bill Clinton in his Presidential Decision Directive 39 (PDD-39) and his successors, the procedure was extended in 2011 to move terrorist suspects to different jurisdictions, including Egypt, Jordan, Morocco, and Libya, and to **black** sites in Poland, Thailand, and Afghanistan for interrogation.

Rendition has its origins in the 1984 Comprehensive Crime Control Act, which extended the authority of the FBI to crimes committed overseas against American citizens, thus allowing the Bureau to investigate incidents of air piracy, including the hijackings of TWA Flight 847 and Royal Jordanian Flight 402 in June 1985.

Rendition became controversial on 2 November 2005, when *Washington Post* journalist Dana Priest published a story in which she revealed the existence of CIA black sites. Consequently, Mary O. McCarthy, a CIA officer on the inspector general's staff, was dismissed for leaking classified information to Priest. That these facilities existed was confirmed by President George W. Bush ten months later, on 6 September 2006.

In February 2003 a suspected Egyptian terrorist, Hassan Mustafa Osama Nasr, was seized in Milan and flown from the US air base at Aviano to Cairo for interrogation at Tura prison. The former cleric later alleged that he had been tortured by the Egyptian Mukhabarat while detained for fourteen months. He has been granted political asylum by Italy, and in 2009, twenty-three of the CIA personnel involved in the operation, including Robert S. Lady, the local CIA chief of base, were indicted on criminal charges of **abduction**.

In February 2004, the European Parliament debated a motion relating to a total of 1,245 flights thought to have been rendition-related, and in January 2012, the Polish government announced an investigation of proceedings against Zbigniew Siemiątkowski, formerly the chief of the Foreign Intelligence Service, who was accused of having collaborated with the CIA by providing facilities at Szczytno-Szymany airport and at a former Soviet Red Army base at Stare Kiejkuty.

## RENEGADE

A distinction should be made between renegade intelligence officers, such as Philip Agree and Edward Lee Howard from the CIA who become **defectors**, and those who become hostile to their former employers and disclose information intending to damage the organisation. More recently Edward Snowden, a former NSA contractor, has crossed the line from being the source of leaks, to an asylum seeker in Russia.

In the United States the group of former CIA personnel who have actively campaigned against the organisation, and are regarded as holding inimical views, includes Frank Snepp (*Decent Interval*), John Stockwell (*In Search of Enemies*), Victor Marchetti (*The CIA and the Cult of Intelligence*), Melvin Beck (*Secret Contenders*) and Ralph McGehee (*Deadly Deceits*). The NSA is also wary of some of its former staff, such as the authors Jim Bamford (*The Puzzle Palace*) and Matthew Aid (*The Secret Sentry*).

Into a rather different category fall two former CIA officers who have been indicted or convicted of crimes. Edwin P. Wilson was arrested in 1982 and sentenced to fifty-seven years' imprisonment for supplying arms and matériel to Colonel Muammar Qaddafi's regime in Libya, but his conviction was quashed in 2004 and he died in September 2012. His business associate Frank E. Terpil, who had been dismissed from the CIA in 1971 after just six years, was also indicted, and fled in September 1980 to Havana, where he remains. In his absence he was sentenced the following year by a New York State court to fifty-three years' imprisonment for conspiring to smuggle 10,000 guns to South American revolutionaries.

In a British context the term renegade was applied at the end of the Second World War to soldiers, usually disaffected PoWs, who had joined the enemy and committed treason. A few, such as Sergeant

Harold Cole, had been deployed by the Germans to collect intelligence, in his case as an *agent provocateur* to expose MI9 escape lines in German occupied France. Some of the renegades joined the Legion of St George and wore SS uniforms, but were never deployed as intended on the Russian Front. All were prosecuted at the end of the war and received terms of imprisonment.

SIS and MI5 have regarded a small group of officers, including Henry Landau (*Secrets of the White Lady*), Leslie Nicholson (*British Agent*), Peter Wright (*SpyCatcher*), David Shayler (*Defending the Realm*), Annie Machon (*Spies, Lies and Whistleblowers*) and Richard Tomlinson (*The Big Breach*), as renegades for publishing unauthorised disclosures about their respective organisations, but only Tomlinson, who was dismissed from SIS in 1995, and Shayler who left MI5 in 1997, have been prosecuted and imprisoned. A much larger group of retirees who have made unauthorised disclosures, but for ostensibly noble motives, have been looked on more benignly. These include Anthony Cavendish (*Inside Intelligence*), Brian Crozier (*Free Agent*), Desmond Bristow (*A Game of Moles*) and Cathy Massiter. Unique among intelligence staff is Katharine Gun, a GCHQ linguist who was charged with breaches of the Official Secrets Act in 2003; her prosecution was abandoned in February 2004.

## REPORTS OFFICER
Within the CIA Directorate of Operations a Reports Officer is the intelligence professional responsible for drafting the reporting for headquarters summarising the information received from agents managed by their colleagues, the **case officers**.

## RESEAU
During the Second World War clandestine networks operating in German-occupied France were known as *reseau*, a generic term that did not imply control by a particular Allied organisation, whereas a **circuit** was generally regarded as being in radio contact with London.

## RESETTLEMENT
Following defection, an **asset** may be resettled, a lengthy process not unlike a conventional witness protection programme in which an individual is given a new identity and found a job in a different region or country so as to be hard to trace if there is a danger of retribution.

Intelligence agencies in receipt of **defectors** manage resettlement personnel who specialise in this narrow field and act as intermediaries between the client, who must be acclimatised in an unfamiliar environment, and the appropriate authorities. Defectors, by their nature, are notoriously difficult to handle and may suffer from **post-usefulness syndrome**. They may also be entirely self-deluded in their assessment of the threat to their safety. In Northern Ireland, for example, there have been several cases of defectors who have judged it safe either to re-establish contact with their families, or even accept assurances concerning their safety.

In 1999 a long-term RUC Special Branch informant, Martin McGartland, code-named CAROL, was resettled in Whitley Bay as 'Martin Ashe' but in 1999, two years after his new identity had been compromised during a prosecution for driving offences, he was attacked by two gunmen who shot him six times. McGartland survived the experience and wrote *Fifty Dead Men Walking* in 1997 and *Dead Man Running* in 1999.

In April 2006 Denis Donaldson was killed by two blasts of a shotgun into his chest at his family's holiday cottage at Glenties, in remote Donegal, after he had publicly acknowledged in December 2005 having acted as a spy for the RUC Special Branch and MI5 inside Sinn Féin for the past twenty years. Originally from West Belfast, and a well-known republican with a conviction in 1971 for possession of explosives, he claimed that he had been recruited at a vulnerable moment in his life. As a senior Sinn Féin official, who had travelled to the Lebanon and to the United States to promote the republican cause, he would have been regarded as an exceptionally valuable asset, yet he declined removal and resettlement.

Resettlement for Provisional IRA informants has usually meant a period of readjustment in a safe, controlled area, such as the Sovereign Base Areas of Akrotiri and Dhekilia in Cyprus, followed by a new occupation, either in Great Britain or in Canada or Australia.

There is some evidence that the KGB has pursued defectors, and Nikolai Khokhlov, who sought political asylum in February 1953, later survived a cup of tea laced with radioactive thallium in Frankfurt in September 1957. In November 2006 Aleksandr Litvinenko, a former KGB and FSB officer, died after he was administered polonium-210. It is also known that the KGB discovered the whereabouts and resettlement details of Vladimir Petrov in Australia and Igor Gouzenko in Canada, but Yuri Andropov decided against assassinating them.

The resettlement of defectors is a fraught business, not least because the individuals may find the process of readjustment hard, and be unused to the management of money. Complaints occur, and Vladimir Suvorov actually brought a legal suit against the CIA, alleging breach of contract.

## REZIDENT

The senior intelligence officer in a Soviet or Russian *rezidentura* is known as the *rezident,* and is the equivalent of a chief of a CIA station, or a British SIS **station commander**, or a French *chef de poste*. Additionally, there may be a parallel **illegal** *rezident* in a particular country.

Much is known about the status, behaviour, duties and responsibilities of a *rezident*, usually from their subordinates who defected during the Cold War. *Rezidents* are usually undeclared and work under diplomatic cover. During the entire period of the Cold War, from 1945 to 1989, only a single Soviet *rezident* defected, Vladimir Petrov who was granted political asylum in Australia in 1954. Petrov and his wife Evdokia were career NKVD officers who previously had served in Stockholm.

During the Cold War the FBI arrested the KGB's illegal *rezident* in the United States, Willie Fisher, **alias** Rudolf Abel, but he refused to cooperate with his captors before he was exchanged in a **spy swap**. Similarly, the KGB illegal *rezident* in London, Konon Molody, was arrested in January 1961, but he also exercised rigid discipline and refused to acknowledge his true role or identity until he was released in April 1964 in return for Greville Wynne.

A *rezident* may not hold the senior diplomatic rank that befits their status, which may be higher than the ambassador's, but the deference shown by their colleagues may be revealing. FBI surveillance on the Soviet consulate in New York revealed that a lowly attaché received far more attention from the doorman than the consul general himself, and ultimately that person was positively identified as the NKVD *rezident*.

# REZIDENTURA

In the Soviet and Russian overseas foreign intelligence collection model the *rezidentura* is the focus of all clandestine operations. The legal *rezident*'s staff will be accommodated in a **referentura** within diplomatic premises, while his **illegal** counterpart will not enjoy diplomatic protection and will be under some other commercial or **non-official cover**.

Within the *rezidentura* the various branches of the organisation will be represented, reflecting the relative interests of the Kolony (SK Line), Illegals (Line N); Counterintelligence (Line CI); Scientific (Line X) and political (Line PR). The Western equivalent of a *rezidentura* is, for the CIA, a station, headed by a station chief, maybe with subordinate bases in the same country. The British also use the term station, although originally SIS established bureaux overseas, but changed the word upon the interwar introduction of the organisation's independent radio communications net. The French DGSE refer to their representatives' offices as a *poste*.

# RIP

The acronym for reinvestigation **polygraph**, a RIP was required by all CIA personnel every five years, but as a result of the **damage assessment** following the arrest of Aldrich Ames in February 1994 the procedure was changed, and random examinations were introduced at unpredictable intervals.

# ROLL-BACK

During the Cold War the West's strategy of aggressively confronting Soviet hegemony was encapsulated in the term roll-back, and was at the heart of operations conducted in Albania, Poland and the Baltic States to force the Warsaw Pact onto the defensive. Roll-back was the justification for a policy that was intended to challenge the basis of the Red Army's occupation of Eastern Europe and undermine satellite regimes. Apart from the success of CIA operations to prevent Italy from electing a Communist government in April 1948, roll-back achieved little until Tadeusz Mazowiecki was appointed Poland's first non-Communist prime minister since the end of the Second World War.

# ROLLING CAR MEET

A **case officer's** rendezvous with an agent, where the **asset**, often in a **denied territory**, is picked up in a car at an agreed location at a particular time, is known as a rolling car meet. The vehicle's interior light may have been disabled to avoid showing that a door has been opened, and a previously deployed **JIB**, intended to demonstrate to any hostile surveillance that the passenger seat is already occupied, will be dismantled for the period of the meeting.

# ROLL-OVER AGENT

A network prepared in anticipation of an invasion, where the agent or organisation will remain passive until an enemy occupation has been established, is known as a roll-over. A roll-over agent is distinct from a **stay-behind** as the latter is more likely to engage in sabotage and other paramilitary activity.

During the liberation of Europe in 1944 Allied intelligence agencies were well informed about the enemy's plans to embed agent networks which would only become active after the area had been occupied. In preparation MI5, SIS and OSS created dedicated teams, known as Special Counterintelligence (SCI) units, to identify and take control of personalities who appeared in the ISK and ISOS radio traffic. The first SCI landed on OMAHA Beach on D+3, and a second was delivered to St Tropez two months later. As the invasion forces gained ground in the north, a further SCI unit, designated the 62nd SCI, was sent in early July 1944. The first agent to be located was a Portuguese dockyard clerk living in Cherbourg. When the 31st SCI unit arrested him, he wasted no time in volunteering a confession. Apparently, he had worked for the NordDeutscher Lloyd shipping line before the war and had agreed to spy in a stay-behind network when the Germans abandoned Cherbourg. According to ISOS he was known as EIKENS, and his radio messages were to be received by the Abwehr in Wiesbaden and Stuttgart. The SCI **case officers** recruited EIKENS and code-named him DRAGOMAN, which fitted his new occupation. He was given notional employment as an interpreter in the US Army's Port Office.

DRAGOMAN's case officers began meeting his radio schedules on 13 July, but it was not for a further twelve days that they made contact with his Abwehr controllers. DRAGOMAN was accepted as completely genuine by the Abwehr and continued to contact until the end of the war. In all, he transmitted more than 200 separate messages.

On 25 August 1944 the first SCI units entered Paris and began mopping up the networks identified by ISOS. One of the SCI's principal targets was the Abwehr headquarters in the Hotel Lutetia, but many of the records had been removed or destroyed before Paris was liberated. Fortunately, an Abwehr NCO, who was later code-named JIGGER, volunteered his services to the SCI and described many of the Abwehr's stay-behind sabotage networks. He also accompanied SCI officers to various arms caches, which had been left to equip these networks, and supplied several batches of files missing from the Hotel Lutetia. His help was so valuable that the Abwehr later tried to launch a mission to assassinate him.

Another important volunteer was KEEL, a French Sicherheitsdienst agent who had a long history of collaboration. He gave himself up on 28 August, but just a month later he was lynched by a French revenge squad. However, instead of terminating KEEL, the SCI unit concerned pretended that he had hurt his wrist in an accident (to explain the change in his Morse technique) and maintained contact with the Abwehr for a further seven months.

By the end of September 1944 the SCI units based in Paris were running six Abwehr radio sets and were doing so with the benefit of knowledge acquired from ISOS, captured enemy documents and the statements of captured Abwehr officials who had been shipped back to England for interrogation at MI5's Camp 020.

At about the same time that the SCIs were being organised in Paris, DRAGOMAN was contacted by another German agent, code-named DESIRE. He was promptly arrested, but he proved too unreliable to **turn**. Nevertheless, he unwittingly compromised a third agent, Jean Senouque, code-named SKULL, who was arrested on 26 August and transferred to Camp 020. SKULL was to prove one of the most important **double agents** of the war, and one of seven agents run from Le Havre by an energetic Abwehr officer, Friedrich Kaulen. He was well known to ISOS, but as soon as SKULL was placed in custody his other agents began to be arrested and turned. By mid-December only two remained at liberty, the others having agreed to supply their case officer with information specially prepared by the SCIs.

SKULL himself resumed contact with the Abwehr on 27 November and was appointed Kaulen's paymaster in northern France. Ironically, one of the first of SKULL's payments was to DRAGOMAN in Cherbourg, an act that served to convince his 31st SCI masters that the Germans had accepted him completely. Kaulen was so highly regarded by the Abwehr that an elaborate operation, TRIPOD, was planned by the SCI to trap him. The idea was to lure the German controller to Bordeaux, which was still in enemy hands, and then ambush him at a prearranged rendezvous. If the operation was successful, the 31st SCI would spread the news of the deaths of both Kaulen and SKULL. Kaulen agreed to attend the *Treff* with SKULL on the banks of the Gironde and, on 6 April 1945, accompanied his agent into a nearby field which was filled with French and American soldiers. Unfortunately, a torch was lit at the wrong moment and an American NCO panicked. In the ensuing chaos Kaulen was shot dead and SKULL was half-strangled. The only consolation that could be obtained from TRIPOD was the fact that every one of the agents referred to in the documents found on Kaulen's body was already operating under Allied control.

## ROLL-OVER CAMERA

A device perfected by KGB technicians, a roll-over camera was a photographic apparatus capable of copying documents simply by running it over the paper. The image was stored on a film which could then be processed and developed. Such a camera, with the appearance of a leather wallet or cigarette case, was acquired by MI5 in September 1968 when an RAF chief technician, Douglas Britten, was arrested as he attempted to deliver classified documents to the Soviet consulate in London, his contact Aleksandr Borisenko having failed to show up for a rendezvous. Previously they had met on a park bench in Harlow. Under interrogation Britten, who worked at 399 Signals Unit at RAF Digby in Lincolnshire when he was detained, confessed that he had spied for the KGB since his recruitment in 1962 by Aleksandr Kulakov. The RAF investigation into Britten, a father of four children who had served in Cyprus between 1962 and 1966, was headed by Air Commodore George Innes and Wing Commander Gerry McMahon of the RAF Provost Police. Meanwhile Kulakov, who had returned to Moscow after four meetings with Britten in 1962, was posted to Copenhagen in 1966, where he remained for four years. He later visited France and the United States before he was granted a visa to stay in Canberra for ten days in November 1975, ostensibly as head of the International Department of the Soviet Academy of Science, but then failed to leave Moscow after some adverse publicity in Australia.

Another example of a Soviet roll-over camera was acquired in August 1987 when 31-year-old Staff Sergeant Leonard Safford of the Army Strategic Communications Command at Suitland, Maryland, was arrested after he had delivered classified information to two diplomats, Nikolai F. Popov, at the Soviet embassy in Washington, and Anatoli Koreyev of the Soviet mission to the United Nations. They had paid him $1,000 and given him a roll-over camera for photographing documents. Safford, with twelve years' military service, was court-martialled in December 1967 and was sentenced to twenty-five years' imprisonment.

## ROLL-UP
The decision to exploit a single source of intelligence and detain all members of a particular spy ring simultaneously is known as a roll-up. Such an intervention effectively precludes any plan to manipulate a network, either by passing it **chicken-feed** or persuading some of the components to become **double agents.**

In 1983, following the arrest of Vladimir Vetrov in Moscow on a murder charge, the French and US authorities proceeded to arrest KGB Line X sources which he had previously compromised. They included William Bell, a helicopter engineer in California, and his UB contact Marian Zacharsky; a South African naval officer, Dieter Gerhardt, who was detained at a hotel in New York; and Pierre Bourdiol, whom Vetrov himself had recruited in 1973. Code-named FAREWELL by the French Direction de la Surveillance du Territoire, Vetrov was duly convicted of murder in Moscow in 1982 and sentenced to fifteen years' imprisonment. Later the KGB would discover his espionage, following which he was executed.

Bourdiol was a highly regarded 56-year-old Thomson-CSF engineer who had worked for Aérospatiale on sensitive projects that included five years on the Ariane European launcher between 1974 and 1979, and on the development of intercontinental ballistic missiles. Arrested in France in November 1983, he was sentenced to five years' imprisonment in June 1987.

Also arrested on a tip from Vetrov was Manfred Rotsch, then head of the Messershmitt-Bölkow-Blohm planning department who had supplied the KGB with details of the Tornado fighter. Rotsch was detained in September 1984, just a week before his scheduled retirement, and in July 1986 he was sentenced to eight and a half years' imprisonment. According to his confession, Rotsch had left East Germany in 1954, having agreed to spy for the KGB, to work for Junkers and then had joined MBB in Munich. In August 1987, just a year into his sentence, Rotsch was exchanged in a spy **swap** for an East German doctor, but then returned with his wife to their home in Munich.

Another dramatic roll-up was the arrest in June 2010 of a group of Russian SVR **illegals** in the United States, and their controller, Pavel Kapustin (travelling as Christopher Matsos) in Larnaca, Cyprus. The eleven detained by the FBI were Anna Chapman in New York; Andrey Bezrikoy (**alias** Donald Heathfield) in Cambridge, Massachusetts; Lydia and Vladimir Guryev (alias Cynthia and Richard Murphy) in Montclair, New Jersey; Alexei Karetnikov in Redmond, Seattle; Mikhail Vasenkovin (alias Juan Lazaro) in Yonkers, New York; Natalia Pereverzeva (alias Patricia Mills) in Arlington, Virginia; Vicky Pelaez in Yonkers, New York; Mikhail Semenko in Arlington, Virginia; Elena Vavilova (alias Tracey Foley) in Cambridge, Massachusetts; and Michael Zottoli (alias Mikhail Kutzik).

Roll-ups on this scale are rare, because of the likelihood that such action would jeopardise the individual responsible for supplying the information, although sometimes such intervention is hard to avoid. When George Blake betrayed the details of SIS's network in East Germany in 1959 many arrests followed, although on that occasion it was not immediately apparent that a single **mole** had been responsible. Those SIS assets known to have been caught and interrogated at the Hohenschöenhausen Stasi prison included Hans Möhring, a 42-year-old state planning commission employee, who was released from to the Federal Republic in 1976 upon payment of a ransom; Colonel Robert Hofmann of the National People's Army (NVA); a member of the Potsdam building committee who was arrested in 1961, sentenced to five years' hard labour, and released in August

1964; Otto Georgi, aged 64 when he was arrested in March 1958, was a stenographer who had worked for German governments since 1918. He was sentenced in February 1959 to life imprisonment, but was released in September 1964 and remained in East Berlin until his death in the 1970s; Hans Schiller, a 40-year-old planner in the Ministry for Mechanical Engineering who was arrested in March 1960, sentenced to fifteen years' imprisonment and released in October 1966; Wolfgang Rabinstein, a 38-year-old staff member of the Foreign Trade Ministry who was arrested in November 1959 and sentenced to life imprisonment in December 1960. He was released from the Frankfurt (Oder) prison in 1969 and remained in the GDR.

There is no firm evidence that any of the agents were executed, although the fate of a Colonel Hofmann appears to be uncertain as there is no official record of his conviction.

In 1985 the CIA became aware of the KGB's recent arrest of more than a dozen CIA and FBI sources in the Soviet Union, including Sergei Vorontsov, code-named GT/COWL, who had spied since late 1984, and his CIA contact, Michael Sellers, who was detained while on his way to a rendezvous in Moscow and expelled. Also, in March, GT/VILLAGE was recalled from the Soviet consulate in Surabaya, Indonesia, and vanished. Two months later, on 7 May, another member of the Moscow station, Erik Sites, was ambushed while attempting to meet GT/EASTBOUND. On 1 July Vladimir V. Potashov (GT/MEDIAN), an arms control negotiator at the Soviet Institute for USA and Canada Studies, who had spied since 1981, was taken into custody, and three days later Dmitri Polyakov was summoned unexpectedly to the Lubyanka and arrested. Soon afterward Colonel Vladimir M. Piguzov (GT/JOGGER) who had been recruited in Djakarta and had been assigned to the KGB's Andropov Institute training academy, dropped from sight. This was an especially mysterious and sinister loss for Piguzov had not been in contact with the CIA since 1979 when he returned to Moscow. He had proved himself to be an exceptionally useful source by identifying David H. Barnett, a CIA retiree working on a training programme on contract, who was arrested in April 1980 and sentenced to eighteen years' imprisonment. It was almost as if, having exhausted the current hot cases, someone was rifling the DO's dormant files to find less valuable spies to betray. Practically as confirmation, Boris Yuzhin (GT/TWINE), who had been the TASS correspondent in San Francisco in the 1970s and had returned to Moscow in 1982, was arrested on 23 December 1986. Almost simultaneously, Colonel Vladimir M. Vasilev (GT/ACCORD), a GRU officer recruited in Budapest in 1983, who had identified a GRU network in which a US Army sergeant, Clyde L. Conrad, had been active in West Germany, was also caught. Vasilev's loss was significant, for he had also enabled the Swedish security police to arrest Conrad's controllers, Dr Sandor Kercsik and Kercsik's younger brother Imre, and roll up a large Hungarian military intelligence network headed by retired warrant officer Zoltan Szabo.

This roll-up was so widespread that it strongly suggested the existence of two, if not three, moles. The subsequent investigation concentrated on CIA officers Aldrich Ames and then Brian Kelley before acquiring proof that the FBI's Robert Hanssen had been haemorrhaging secrets since November 1979.

## ROMEO

The intelligence officer or agent who deliberately sets out to seduce a vulnerable woman for the purpose of espionage, to obtain her cooperation or access to information, is known generically as a **Romeo** (sometimes Raven), a technique perfected by Markus Wolf's Hauptverwaltung Aufklärung (HVA). In 1960 Karl-Heinz Schneider romanced a 31-year-old divorcée, Marianne Lenzkow, while posing as a Danish intelligence officer, and recruited an East German actor, Roland Gandt, to play a supporting role. Gandt soon became engaged to Marianne's younger sister, Margarethe Lubig. Both women were employed as secretaries in sensitive positions in the Federal German government, and agreed to provide classified information to their lovers, whom they believed to be Danes.

In 1968, Schneider turned his attention to a future Bundesnachrichtendienst (BND) **analyst**, Gabrielle Gast, while she was completing her doctorate in Karl-Marx-Stadt. She later applied for a job with the BND at its headquarters in Pullach and by 1987 was deputy chief of the BND's Soviet Bloc political branch, and a dedicated convert to Communism. Three years later, Gast was betrayed by an HVA **defector**, Colonel Heinz Busch, who revealed that Gandt, code-named VENSKE, had been ordered by Schneider to seduce and run an agent and had done so for more than twenty-five years. Furthermore, the agent's sister, code-named ROSE, had fallen for Gandt, and both women had been run under a **false flag**. BND **molehunters** quickly identified ROSE as Margarethe Lubig, who confessed and implicated her sister, who died before she could be brought to trial in Düsseldorf.

Another of Markus Wolf's Romeo spies was an HVA officer, Herbert Schöter, who started an affair with Gerda Osterreider, a slender 19-year-old student who was studying languages at the Alliance Française in Paris. When she returned to Bonn in 1966 she found a job as a cipher clerk in the Foreign Office and gave her lover the original teletype tape on which incoming diplomatic telegrams were printed. Five years later she was posted to Warsaw where, in Schöter's absence, she had an affair with a German journalist to whom she confessed her espionage, and when he reported her she was sentenced to three years' imprisonment.

The HVA's strategy was to exploit the relative shortage of men in West Germany, and prey on vulnerable young women who might not hold particularly senior posts in the federal government, but nevertheless enjoyed access to very sensitive information.

Within the Allied air intelligence community raven is the term applied to intercept operators and other technical personnel flying on airborne signals intelligence collection flights.

## RUMSFELD DICTUM

When he was the US Secretary of Defense, for the second time, in 2002, Donald Rumsfeld made an observation about the value of intelligence, relating to the search for Iraqi weapons of mass destruction. This comment has endured: 'There are known knowns. These are things we know that we know. There are known unknowns. That is to say, there are things that we know we don't know. But there are also unknown unknowns. These are things we don't know we don't know.'

## RYAN

The Russian acronym for *Raketno Yadernoye Napadenie*, Russian for 'nuclear missile attack'. In the three years leading up to NATO's annual exercise ABLE ARCHER, held in November 1983, Soviet **analysts** became increasingly concerned about the threat of a surprise nuclear attack and in May 1981 the KGB compiled a list of 292 indicators, in the five areas, categorised as political, military, intelligence services, civil defence and economic, that might be interpreted as being precursors to just such an offensive. Relevant *rezidenturas* were instructed to assign personnel to watch certain designated indicators which, according to Oleg Gordievsky, a Line PR KGB officer in London, included observation on certain identified buildings to monitor unusual activity. In February 1983 Gordievsky passed his SIS **case officer** a circular distributed by Moscow setting out the procedures to be adopted. Altogether 300 KGB officers in cities deemed likely to be engaged in first-strike planning were earmarked for the task.

In July 1984 the KGB's Chairman, Viktor Chebrikov, directed the First Department of the First Chief Directorate to take the unusual step of establishing a group of fifty analysts to direct the collection programme and provide round-the-clock early warning of an impending first-strike intended to decapitate the Soviet air defence command and control organisation.

Perpetrated by double agents, the broadcast of false military wireless traffic and the imaginative creation of an entirely bogus Allied order of battle, Operation FORTITUDE reinforced the Axis assessment that orthodox doctrine would dictate an Allied landing across the shortest stretch of the English Channel during the summer of 1944, thus allowing the maximum time for aircraft to support the ground troops. Luftwaffe reconnaissance flights over East Anglia were duped by apparent concentrations of armour, as betrayed by tell-tale tank tracks, and the assembly of poorly camouflaged landing craft in river estuaries. Unimaginative Wehrmacht analysts could not contemplate any large-scale amphibious undertaking without the requirement to capture at least two major ports intact, so as to ensure the logistical resupply. In reality, of course, the Allies towed two huge, prefabricated harbours, code-named MULBERRY, across to the Normandy beaches, thereby taking the defenders entirely by surprise.

# S

## SAFE-HOUSE
Any apartment or house earmarked for a clandestine purpose may be regarded as a safe-house provided it has not attracted the attention of an adversary. For maximum security, a safe-house will not be used on a regular basis, and probably will provide overnight accommodation for an **asset**, or provide an environment in which a **case officer** can meet an **agent** in relative safety.

## SAMSON SYNDROME
Behaviour characterised by the commission of a more serious crime when earlier misconduct has likely compromised security is sometimes known as Samson syndrome. Typically an individual is motivated to commit a much greater offence, convinced that their career will be terminated as soon as their record is revealed during their next scheduled background security check. The rationale is that since the likely penalty if caught will be much the same, an offender might as well maximise the benefit.

This happened in 1983 when an MI5 officer, Michael Bettaney, was caught travelling without a ticket on a train from his home in Coulsdon, Surrey, to his office at headquarters in Gower Street. He was convicted of fare-dodging, but he was conscious that this was the third time he had been convicted of a crime, and he was already on his final warning. He had previously appeared in court for the same offence, and for being drunk in the street.

Realising that his latest, undeclared police arrest would show up when he underwent his next security **clearance**, Bettaney knew he had only a limited period left in his trusted position in the Soviet counter-espionage section. Accordingly, he approached the KGB *rezident* in London, Arkadi Gouk, supplied him with a sample of MI5 reports to prove his bona-fides, and offered to provide much more.

This was a classic example of Samson Syndrome, but in this case Bettaney's **pitch** was compromised from the start because Gouk had consulted his deputy, Oleg Gordievsky, and concluded on his advice that his anonymous donor was actually a provocation, unaware that Gordievsky had been an SIS **asset** since 1974. Gordievsky had reported the episode to his SIS **handler**, prompting an urgent **molehunt** within MI5 that resulted in Bettaney's arrest and a twenty-three-year prison sentence.

Statistics are hard to discern, but it is likely that involvement in espionage may escalate once the initial, apparently limited transaction has taken place. Testimony from Aldrich Ames and Robert Hanssen suggests that both men had not intended to become long-term sources for the Soviets, but had renewed contact to repeat their offence when they had exhausted their illicit proceeds. In Hanssen's case the FBI officer had first sold classified material to a Soviet trade delegation official, actually a GRU officer, in New York in November 1979 for $20,000, and allegedly had intended to make this a one-time event, taking the precaution to retain his anonymity. However, short of money five years later, he re-established contact with the Soviets in Washington, DC, in 1984, and began to make further sales to the KGB until his arrest in February 2001.

## SAYANIM

The people of the global Jewish diaspora are known within Mossad as the *sayanim* and regarded as a potential resource for operational support. The issue is regarded as politically sensitive because it raises the age-old controversy of dual or divided loyalties, and understandably Israeli governments prefer the pretence of maintaining a distance between the state and potentially vulnerable Jewish communities abroad. Individual *sayan* may be requested occasionally to assist in acquiring an apartment, car or medical assistance or providing some other logistical or documentary help for an operations officer known as a *katsa*. Mossad headquarters maintains a comprehensive register of the *sayanim* and identifies the particular background and skill of those listed, divided into those who are currently active, and those who are held in reserve but have given an indication of their willingness to cooperate should the need arise.

## SEALS AND FLAPS

The techniques involved in the surreptitious inspection of private correspondence is known as 'seals and flaps', a term that was introduced by the US Office of Strategic Services during the Second World War to provide a shorthand term for a training programme which indoctrinated authorised personnel into methods of defeating the conventional ways of sealing envelopes, diplomatic pouches and other potentially sensitive communications.

The modern methods of opening the mail range from the application of steam to the insertion of a knitting needle to extract a letter.

## SECOND-STOREY MAN

The personnel responsible for making illicit entries into sensitive premises, often diplomatic or consular offices, are known in the vernacular as 'second-storey men'.

Between 1942 and July 1966 the FBI conducted such operations through a dedicated unit at the Special Investigative Division at the Washington, DC, headquarters headed by Special Agent Ed Tickell, who was responsible for developing a high-speed, portable photocopier, concealed in a small suitcase, which was used to copy documents on site.

Because of the illegal nature of the source, the resulting information could never be used in prosecutions, but was referred to generally within the Bureau as 'a highly reliable confidential source whose identity cannot be disclosed'.

In July 1968 the FBI's assistant director, Cartha ('Deke') DeLoach, asked Bill Sullivan, then head of the intelligence division, for an account of recent **black bag jobs**, and it was explained:

> We do not get authorisation for 'black bag' jobs from outside the Bureau. Such a technique involves trespass and is clearly illegal; therefore it would be impossible to obtain any legal sanction for it. Despite this, 'black bag' jobs have been used because they represent an invaluable technique in combatting subversive activities of a clandestine nature aimed directly at undermining and destroying our nation. The present procedure followed in the use of this technique calls for the Special Agent in Charge of a field office to make his request for the use of the technique to the appropriate Assistant Director. The Special Agent in Charge must completely justify the need for the use of the technique and at the same time assure that it can be safely used without any danger or embarrassment to the Bureau. The facts are incorporated in a memorandum which, in

accordance with the Director's instructions, is sent to Tolson or to the Director for approval. Subsequently this memorandum is filed in the Assistant Director's office under a 'Do Not File' procedure. In the field the Special Agent in Charge prepares an informal memorandum showing that he obtained Bureau authority and this memorandum is filed in his safe until the next inspection by Bureau Inspectors, at which time it is destroyed.

Also through the use of this technique we have on numerous occasions been able to obtain material held highly secret and closely guarded by subversive groups and organizations which consisted of membership lists and mailing lists of these organisations. This applies even to our investigation of the Ku Klux Klan. You may recall that recently through a 'black bag' job we obtained the records in the possession of three high-ranking officials of a klan organization in Louisiana. These records gave us the complete membership and financial information concerning the klan's operation which we have been using most effectively to disrupt the organisation and, in fact, to bring about its near disintegration. It was through information obtained through our black-bag operations that we obtained the basic information used to compromise and to bring about the expulsion of William Albertson, the former Executive Secretary of the Communist Party New York District organization.

In short it is a very valuable weapon which we have used to combat the highly clandestine efforts of subversive elements seeking to undermine our Nation.

The issue of the Bureau's surreptitious entries became public in July 1975 when *Newsweek* revealed that the FBI broke into an average of one embassy a month, and in recent years had conducted 1,500 burglaries of premises occupied by organised crime or extremist organisations such as the CPUSA and the Ku Klux Klan. The article also described the defection of a cipher clerk, Frantisek Tisler, from the Czech embassy in Washington in July 1959, an incident which had involved the theft of a cipher machine by FBI personnel dressed as garbage contractors, and revealed that most of the entries had been staged 'to get information that could help the National Security Agency break foreign codes'. It was claimed that the Polish, Yugoslav,

French and Japanese embassies had been targets, as had most of the Arab embassies, although it was said that 'the only problem was tripping over the Israelis already inside'.

Some **crypto** equipment burglaries are known as 'smoking-bolt' operations where an entire device, such as a cipher machine, is removed, leaving behind only the mechanisms designed to secure the hardware.

Some of the FBI's entries were to plant listening devices, and between January 1957 and March 1975 the attorney general approved 172 of these operations.

## SECRET WRITING (S/W)

The technique of concealing a message by writing it in invisible ink is known as secret writing and is an ancient practice in clandestine communications. There are various methods of completing the task, which is to convey hidden text to the intended recipient.

The chemical selected as ink is critical as circumstances may require it to be stored as an innocuous substance, such as perfume, or be impregnated into fabric. In an operational environment the solution may have to be a formula that will resist detection by conventional methods, such as an iodine test. Another expedient is the application of a special carbon sheet which leaves a virtually untraceable message on the chosen medium which may be an ostensibly innocent letter, or perhaps a newspaper or magazine.

The receiving correspondent simply has to apply the developer, which may be another chemical, or merely heat, to make the hidden message legible. During the First World War agents were taught to use urine, lemon juice, formalin and semen as secret ink, as these liquids were almost traceless but reacted to heat applied by an iron.

In wartime, when the regular mails are subjected to censorship inspection, the counter-espionage authorities routinely test suspect documents for alien substances and maintain laboratories to experiment with new reagents.

In the earliest cases of secret writing detected during the First World War, several German spies were discovered in possession of the necessary material. In February 1915 Carl Muller, arrested on his third arrival in Britain from Rotterdam, and a Deptford baker, John Hahn, were found to have used lemon juice, while Anton Küpferle, detained upon his arrival from New York, mixed lemon juice with formalin. After this trio had been exposed, the law was changed, and the Defence of the Realm Regulation 24A was introduced to prohibit all secret communications.

On one occasion a pair of German agents was overheard agreeing that interlinear writing in secret ink was the best way to defeat inspection by the postal censor. At the end of the conflict MI5 reported that:

> Reginald Rowland and Lizzie Wertheim used lemon juice and also probably colourless scent, such as Eau-de-Cologne, with talc powder to fix it. Willem Roos and Haicke Janssen used scent and wrote in a microscopic hand on the margins of newspapers and books. They despatched from six to ten newspapers or books daily and always sent a postcard to notify that a message was on the way. The frequent use of music for recording information should also be noted. Besides the mediums used by arrested spies others were discovered in the course of the summer. Medicines containing essential oils were sent to prisoners of war who used them together with code, such as a dot to indicate a place, or a corner slightly turned down or a tear in the margin. Preparations of powders, pomades, soap, hair-lotion, dentifrice, labelled with the genuine labels of Parisian firms, were also pressed into service. Soap and ferro-cyanide of potassium was another mixture used on slightly tinted paper.
>
> Agents in Switzerland used Oja-paste, a yellowish paste diluted with water and scented with rose on unglazed yellow paper. Ten parts of acetate of lead, to 50 of water; alum, milk, thin well-boiled starch water are also mentioned as mediums. When soap was used it required much dilution with water or a faint trace was noticeable on the paper.

Alfredo Roggen, arrested in Scotland in August 1915 and executed in September, used oil of peppermint and talc powder and Fernando Bushman, travelling on a Brazilian passport, used scent, writing minute figures on old bills, letters, pages of a Spanish newspaper, railway timetables, envelopes, censor's labels and music.

MI5's chemist advised that a message written in a perfume, such as eau de cologne when used with talcum powder, should last for three weeks to a month, and the post office in Rotterdam noted that secret writing had been found along the gummed edges of envelope flaps, and described how one such example envelope had been included with seals.

During and after the Second World War, when radio provided a faster means of clandestine communication, there was less use of secret writing, which was largely confined to the concealment of potentially incriminating material, such as ciphers and other non time-sensitive data. However, in 1942 an escaped British PoW named Hewson turned up at the British embassy in Berne and confessed that, because of his Irish parentage, he had been approached to spy for the Abwehr. He had been captured in Crete and, having been recruited, was sent to Brussels for training in secret writing, using a particular match as a pen. Hewson's disclosures were greeted with great interest at MI5 because a similar matchbook had been found recently in the possession of a pair of Dutch espionage suspects, the Erasmus brothers, who had posed as refugees. They too had been trained in Brussels.

There were a couple of other espionage cases in which secret writing played a role. In 1941 a Portuguese diplomat in London, Rogeiro de Menezes was found to be corresponding with his sister, sending her an enclosure to be readdressed to a man named Mendez, containing secret writing. As this mail was posted to Lisbon through the diplomatic pouch, and had been detected by XXX, MI5 was obliged to act cautiously, but it succeeded in bringing up the writing which became visible under a combination of ammonia fumes and ultraviolet light. After his arrest de Menezes confessed that he had been recruited by the Sicherheitsdienst.

In August 1942 a Portuguese, Ernesto Simoes, arrived in Poole on an espionage mission and was found to be carrying the ingredients for secret writing. He made a full confession.

A method of secret writing popular with the Germans was the use of Acqua Vitae which became visible with the application of methylene blue.

Another method of secret writing, employed by both the British and the Germans, was the aniline pencil, which was described in his diary by MI5's Guy Liddell:

The method is to rub an analine [sic] pencil all over a piece of paper, to place this facedown on the piece of paper to be used for secret writing and then to place another piece of paper on top. The message is written on the top piece and is impressed on the bottom piece in analine, which is not visible and will not react to any reagent. The only method of reproducing the message is by a sensitised paper, since the analine prevents the light from getting through. Specially selected letters are being submitted to a test with strips of sensitised paper.

In October 1943 Liddell recorded that MI5's scientific adviser, Professor Henry Briscoe, had completed a review of all the secret writing techniques employed by the enemy:

Censorship now had about thirty-five reagents or methods of throwing up secret writing. Seven of these were he thought highly secret but were more in the nature of technical processes which had thrown up one particular ink and might quite possibly throw up others about which we at present knew nothing. It seemed important to us all that these should be safeguarded at any rate until the Second Front opened. There were one of two which, either because they disclosed our own offensive inks or indicated our superior efficiency, it might well be wise never to disclose to anyone; those numbered twenty-eight. Twenty of these had already been handed to the French at the beginning of the war and were probably already in the hands of the Germans. We felt that as the Belgian Congo was perhaps of decreasing importance owing to the opening up of the Mediterranean, there was no particular point at this stage in giving them more than twenty reagents that we had already given the French. We thought, however, that there would be advantage in giving North Africa the full twenty-eight while retaining the seven. As soon as the Censorship on the continent got going we would consider what further assistance we could give. It was agreed that a note of this should be prepared and should be endorsed by all the parties concerned, namely ourselves, SIS, and SOE. We would then approach the Americans and obtain their approval.

In January 1944 the Allies acquired a huge advantage in the covert communications field when the Norwegian resistance obtained a copy of a German censorship manual which described all the tests applied by Axis postal inspectors, and detailed the formulae of their reagents.

In April 1944 MI5 arrested Pierre Neukermans, a Belgian pilot who had succeeded in smuggling S/W ingredients through the searches conducted at the London Reception Centre. He had been at liberty for six months, during which he had sent worthless information to the enemy. At his trial he pleaded insanity, but was convicted and hanged.

Later in 1944 MI5 identified a Norwegian refugee, Knut Brodersen, as a German spy carrying hidden instructions, written in S/W, in a tooth and under a toenail. Both items were recovered. He was followed by a Pole, Wladislaw Wellmann, who arrived from Gibraltar and promptly surrendered his S/W material.

During the Cold War MI5's scientific section invented a universal detection system which involved a weak radioactive isotope which proved very effective at identifying the chemical compounds employed for secret writing.

## SECURITY CHECK
Radio operators working under clandestine conditions are often trained to insert a confidential indicator in a message to demonstrate that they are not transmitting under duress, and in the control of an adversary. Such checks will most likely be a prearranged deliberate mistake so that a text entirely free of error is likely to signal hostile manipulation.

Scrutiny of a captured operator's past traffic may give a clue to the nature of the security check, so Allied agents transmitting from occupied territory during the Second World War were warned to destroy all copies of their messages as soon as practicable, together with any other redundant cipher material.

In June 1943 a Canadian SOE agent, John Macalister, code-named VALENTIN, was arrested by the Gestapo at a random vehicle checkpoint when driving to Paris five days after he had been dropped into France. Macalister's transmitter was then played back in a *Funkspiel* for ten months, and arranged fifteen arms drops, and the reception of seven more parachute agents until SOE realised the **deception**. Among the first victims was F Section's Noor Inayat Khan code-named MADELEINE, who had landed by Lysander on 16 June to operate a radio for the CINEMA **circuit**. Having been compromised by VALENTIN, Khan was placed under surveillance, and was eventually arrested on 13 October, but in the meantime she had held several meetings with undercover Gestapo agents and had unintentionally contaminated several other SOE personnel. After her arrest her radio was also used by the Sicherheitsdienst to communicate with London which, even at this late stage, appeared to be unsure of the situation in the field. This deception was possible because at the time of her capture Khan had ignored her instructions and retained copies of her past messages, thus allowing her German captors to identify her procedures and her unique security-check.

Partly because of compartmentalisation in London, the lessons of security-check failures were not circulated to other organisations engaged in clandestine operations, and ignorance of the enemy's skills in this field allowed further breaches. When SOE's RF Section had experienced an enemy **playback** on the OVERCLOUD circuit in December 1941, none of the lessons were learned by, or circulated to, N or F Sections. In that particular case the Comte de Kergolay, code-named JOEW, had been captured with his radio set in December 1941 and had operated it under enemy control until early in 1943. As soon as JOEW omitted his security check, which he never disclosed to the Abwehr, RF recognised the traffic as a playback *Spiel* and handled it accordingly, designating the double deception SEALING WAX. After the war the French authorities convicted de Kergolay of collaboration, but a fellow SOE officer, Forrest Yeo-Thomas, was able to clear him of the charges relating to OVERCLOUD and have his life sentence reduced. Nor was this an isolated incident. SOE's PHONO and BUTLER circuits came under enemy control, and the consequences were dire. In the PROSPER debacle, reckoned to be the worst of its kind, estimates of those involved in the wave of arrests that followed vary, but Professor M.R.D. Foot acknowledged that a figure of 400 would be 'conservative'. Others suggest 1,500, and certainly PROSPER boasted 144 fully accredited agents, and a total of 1,015 helpers, although exactly how many perished in the extermination camps is unknown.

## SELECTOR

Within the Allied signals intelligence community the term selector refers to an individual who had been identified as a target for collection and thus been the subject of telephone, mobile phone and email interception, initially to develop a pattern of behaviour and contacts and then, if justified, full-scale electronic surveillance.

## SEMTEX PILL

During 'the Troubles' in Northern Ireland one of the greatest challenges for the British security authorities was the problem of the very large quantities of the malleable, waterproof high explosive Semtex-H, manufactured by Synthesia Pardubice at Semtin (a suburb of Pardubice, ninety kilometres south-west of Prague), which had been smuggled into the Republic as donations from Libya, where the regime had purchased a total of 700 tons.

The Provisional Irish Republican Army generally entrusted the Semtex, which was a distinctive red colour and had a shelf life estimated at ten years, to reliable quartermasters who stored it in caches at secret locations that were difficult either to detect or keep under physical surveillance. Occasionally these sites would be identified, and the question arose as to appropriate response, the objective being to neutralise the material without compromising the source of the information.

Analysis of Semtex by scientists at the Royal Armament Research and Development Establishment (RARDE) at Fort Halstead in Kent revealed it to be composed of crystalline pentaerythritol tetranitrate (PETN), a very powerful high explosive somewhat similar to, but more stable than nitroglycerine. Semtex, packed into brick-sized blocks, was popular with terrorists because it did not give off a vapour and was hard to detect, even by sniffer dogs trained to find plastic explosives.

The solution devised by the RARDE laboratory was the development of a capsule containing a chemical compound which, when inserted into the putty-like explosive, reacted with the principal components in the Semtex and turned it inert. The result was that on many occasions PIRA terrorists planted and intended to detonate a Semtex bomb, only to experience a misfire. Without the opportunity to return to the scene to examine the device, the bombers would write off the experience as bad luck, or an unreliable batch of Semtex and explosive, thereby protecting the source of the information.

## SHOE

In the Russian espionage patois, a shoe is a passport. Famously Felix Dzerzhinsky remarked that 'men walk easily in their own shoes', thereby suggesting that an **alias** is never quite as effective as an authentic identity. One of the most successful of the NKVD's **illegal** *rezidents*, and immortalised in Moscow as 'a great **Chekist**', Arnold Deutsch, was unusual in that he travelled on his own authentic identity papers and in 1936 operated under authentic cover, as a graduate student at London University.

## SICK PILL

An expedient introduced in Northern Ireland to help agents avoid participation in acts of terrorism was the sick pill, a tablet that, within moments of being ingested, provoked a period of intense retching and vomiting, thus giving the **asset** the excuse to withdraw from the assigned role on grounds of obvious ill-health, to the point of being a hazard to his co-conspirators.

## SIGNAL SITE

Classic tradecraft to deliver a prearranged message is to leave a signal at a place which can be inspected regularly, at a distance, without requiring the close scrutiny that might alert hostile surveillance. Often this will be curtains drawn in a window, or a chalk mark or piece of adhesive on a roadsign, or even a vehicle parked in a designated location with the front wheels pointing in a specific direction. The objective is for both parties, the signaller and the recipient, to avoid doing anything unusual and thereby attracting attention. If a signal is on a route driven regularly by a **case officer**, a check for its appearance will be next to impossible to detect. The signal may be intended to initiate an emergency procedure, such as a meeting or an **exfiltration**, or merely to confirm that a **dead drop** has been filled and requires servicing. Once the intended recipient has spotted the signal, and interpreted its meaning, a second, quite different signal at another site may be left to confirm that the drop has been serviced.

## SILENT CALL

One method of clandestine communication between an agent and **handler** is the use of a silent call, involving the agent ringing a particular telephone number and then terminating the connection without the exchange of any words. The objective is to register the contact, on a particular number at an agreed time, an act which conveys a message, whereas there is no incriminating conversation to be recorded by interception.

Famously Oleg Penkovsky's plan in 1962 included provision for an almost silent call to be made to the apartment of the SIS **station commander** in Moscow, Gervase Cowell, to warn of an imminent surprise nuclear attack. Penkovsky made the call, but Cowell chose to ignore it, interpreting the event as either a mistake or, as was later suspected, a **Samson syndrome** scenario.

## SIXTH SENSE

**Case officers** and agents often develop a sixth sense about the dangers surrounding a *Treff*. In 1952, after the fifth member of the Cambridge ring, John Cairncross, had fallen under MI5's suspicion, a rendezvous was arranged with his KGB case officer, Yuri Modin, at a west London tube station. When Modin approached the agreed meeting place, a park bench opposite West Acton underground station, he sensed hostile surveillance and strolled past, returning to the *rezidentura* without making contact. Modin's *rezident* disciplined him for abandoning his agent, and Cairncross was mystified by the absence of his **handler**. MI5's **Watcher Service** had indeed kept the scene under observation but had failed to spot Modin. Their report, describing Cairncross's evident irritation, suggested that the Soviets had been tipped off to a trap, prompted a lengthy **molehunt** until Modin himself revealed that it had been nothing more than his instinct that had caused him to abort the meeting.

Modin's subsequent career suffered for what his *rezident* alleged was a breach of his duty to his agent, and he only served overseas again in India. In reality, Modin's sixth sense had prevented a disaster that would have compromised both men.

## SOURCES AND METHODS

At the heart of any intelligence collection agency lie the specialist techniques developed to support the mission of mounting clandestine operations. Disclosure of these procedures to an adversary, or even publication generally, may compromise an organisation's ability to undertake secret activities.

## SPECIAL POLITICAL ACTION (SPA)

The euphemism employed by SIS and Whitehall for a major clandestine intervention, perhaps with regime change as an objective, as was intended to happen with Operation WESTWARD HO, a guerrilla campaign conducted against the Soviet occupation of Latvia, Lithuania and Estonia after 1947. Similar operations were undertaken in Albania, code-named VALUABLE to undermine Enver Hoxha's regime in Tirana, and in the Caucasus, code-named CLIMBER, to establish networks in the southern republics of the Soviet Union, In 1953 Operation BOOT, the replacement of Mohammed Mossadeq as Iran's prime minister with General Fazlollah Zahedi, proved successful, but the failed attempt to seize the Suez Canal in October 1956 left the Foreign Office, and future foreign secretaries, highly risk averse to any large-scale activity with a significant **blowback** potential, leaving SPA somewhat discredited.

## SPECIAL RELATIONSHIP

The close cooperation between the United States and the United Kingdom in the atomic and intelligence fields has often been described as the 'special relationship' and is manifested by a unique degree of collaboration. In the intelligence field the relationship probably dates back to December 1940 when two senior FBI officers, Clarence Hince and Hugh Clegg, travelled to Britain to undertake a tour of the country's most secret establishments, including MI5's headquarters in St James's Street, where they were briefed by Guy Liddell; SIS's head office in Broadway to be seen by the Chief, Stewart Menzies; Bletchley Park, to be indoctrinated into the cryptographic work then under way, and to the Radio Security Service at Barnet where they learned about the GROUP V traffic exchanged between an Abwehr transmitter on Long Island, and Berlin. Before they returned to Washington Hince and Clegg were authorised by J. Edgar Hoover to reveal to MI5 that the GROUP V traffic was in fact supervised by an FBI **double agent**, and transmitted by an FBI officer.

The purpose of the tour was Winston Churchill's wish to prove that Great Britain could not just hold out against Nazi Germany, but actually possessed the means to prevail, given sufficient time. In the scientific field, the prime minister authorised the disclosure of three potentially war-winning technological breakthroughs: centimetric radar, proximity fuses, and degaussing, and he was equally determined to share the country's intelligence secrets, which resulted in March 1943 in a communications intelligence agreement to standardise signals intelligence procedures that was renewed in October 1944 and then formalised in March 1946 with the Britain–United States treaty, known as BRUSA. This was later updated by the UKUSA agreement of March 1953.

SIGINT collaboration, based on the sharing of the product derived from intercept facilities provided by Canada, New Zealand and Australia, known as the **Five Eyes**, gave access to collection sites to components of the US National Security Agency in return for an unrestricted sharing of the **finished intelligence**. The other British intelligence services also developed strong links with their counterparts, and MI5 encouraged the establishment of an FBI legal attaché at the embassy to act as an intermediary between the two organisations. In addition, both MI5 and SIS created a wartime foundation for mutual cooperation and trust by creating a War Room staffed jointly by British and American personnel, with the Office of Strategic Services X-2 branch assigning officers to MI5's headquarters to shadow their British allies in counterintelligence operations. Similarly, OSS officers were indoctrinated into ISK and ISOS (referred to as ICICLE and TRIANGLE) and participated in the three-man Special Counterintelligence units deployed to France to find and manage Abwehr **roll-over** spies.

MI5 in particular found the arrangement to its advantage, allowing Irish-American OSS officers to act as intermediaries with G-2, Dublin's intelligence service.

In the post-war era Anglo-American cooperation has widened and deepened, with the CIA station chief in London routinely invited to attend the weekly Joint Intelligence Committee as an *ex officio* member. The degree of connectivity was illustrated in detail in 2013 by the **renegade** contractor Edward Snowden who revealed the scale of the cooperation and the extent of the programmes and projects run jointly by GCHQ and the NSA.

In November 2009 a former State Department officer, Kendall Myers, claimed that the fraudulent nature of the special relationship, describing it as 'one-sided' and 'a myth', was part of his motivation for spying for the Cubans.

## SPECIAL SURVEILLANCE GROUP (SSG)

The equivalent of MI5's **Watcher Service**, upon which it is based, the Special Surveillance Group, known simply as 'the Gs', are surveillance experts who have completed the course at the FBI Academy in Quantico, Virginia. They do not carry the same credentials as FBI special agents and cannot make arrests, but are known as investigative specialists.

## SRAC

The Short-Range Agent Communication device was developed by the CIA's Office of Technical Services in 1973 in support of contact with an important GRU **asset**, Dmitri Polyakov, who had been recruited in New York and was posted to the Soviet embassy in New Delhi as military attaché. SRAC technology would become the foundation of what would later develop into text-messaging.

The objective was to supply the agent with a miniature low-power burst transmitter that could be used to communicate over short distances without fear of interception. The equipment, code-named BUSTER, was slightly larger than a pack of cigarettes, weighed just over half a pound, and boasted a small, single-digit display to show a Cyrillic letter, and a tiny keyboard less than an inch and a half square.

When he was given the device by his CIA case officer the agent also received instructions to employ his normal **one-time pad** to encipher his message, and entered the encrypted text into the device which had a memory of up to 1,000 characters. When he was within 1,000 feet of the receiving station he simply pressed the 'send' key and the signal was transmitted. A red flashing light confirmed a successful transmission.

Although ingenious and technically a breakthrough in covert communications, it was impossible to disguise and therefore highly incriminating if found. An improved version, code-named **DISCUS**, would later be supplied by the CIA to Colonel Ryszhard Kuklinski in Warsaw, and to Adolf Tolkachev in Moscow.

## STAND-IN

When a security or intelligence agency requires a substitute to impersonate someone, that individual is known as a stand-in. In 1946 when the atomic physicist Alan Nunn May had been identified as a Soviet spy and was scheduled to hold a *Treff* with his contact outside the British Museum, MI5's nominee Klop Ustinov adopted the role of the Russian. In that case May had been alerted to the trap, but based on information from Vasili Mitrokhin, who had defected in 1992, an FBI special agent undertook a similar operation in December 2003 and arrested Robert Lipka, a former NSA **analyst**. In June 2000 the FBI applied the same tactics to incriminate Colonel George Trofimoff, then in his retirement in Florida. The same technique was also used against Michael J. Smith, a CPGB member and technician employed by the Thorn-EMI defence contractor, who confided in an MI5 officer, believing him to be from the Russian SVR, in August 1992. Smith's past activities had been betrayed by his former **handler**, Victor Oshchenko, who had **defected** earlier in the year in Paris.

## STATIC OBSERVATION POST

The foundation of any successful counterintelligence operation is identification of an adversary's **order of battle**, and the starting-point is surveillance on sites known to accommodate hostile professional intelligence personnel, such as diplomatic premises, or diplomats' homes, in which activities will be routinely monitored. Famously, MI5's A4 section occupied premises above a tobacconists in High Street Kensington to record the movements of Soviet staff entering Kensington Palace Gardens. Similarly, the FBI operated cameras from the AFL-CIO headquarters in Washington, DC, directly opposite the entrance to the Soviet embassy.

On Easter Sunday 1983 Michael Bettaney took advantage of his knowledge of the surveillance rota on the Holland Park home of the KGB *rezident*, Arkadi Guk, to deliver his written **pitch**, confident that the MI5 watchers had gone home at midnight.

## STATION COMMANDER

Members of the Intelligence Branch of the British Secret Intelligence Service (a distinction with the non-operational General Service branch) who are posted overseas to represent the organisation and head an SIS station are known as station commanders. Very likely they will be declared to the appropriate counterpart of their host country and will act principally in a liaison capacity. Within SIS that individual will be known by an abbreviation which indicates their geographic location, such as H/PARIS, rather than their name. The actual size of the station will vary in size from one or two officers, supported by an SIS secretary who may occasionally undertake operational work, to the thirty employed at the height of the Cold War in Hong Kong.

In some countries the station will not be declared, which requires additional counterintelligence and counter-surveillance precautions to be taken to protect the true identity of the officer who will be known to the rest of his regular diplomatic colleagues in the embassy or consulate. In a few countries the presence of a declared station will be the subject of agreed restrictions. Prior to the fall of the Shah of Iran in 1979 SIS operated a station on the top floor of the embassy, headed by George Webb who, like his predecessors, had been declared to SAVAK but had agreed not to have any contact with the mullahs or the volatile Islamic religious community.

## STAY-BEHIND

A network which has been created solely for the contingency of conducting operations in the event of an enemy occupation is known as 'stay-behind'. The concept was developed in 1940 in Britain following the unanticipated *Blitzkrieg* occupation of Belgium, France, Denmark, the Netherlands and Norway where no preparations had been made for such an eventuality. Following the unsuccessful Norwegian campaign, in which so-called Independent Companies attempted to engage in unconventional warfare, Peter Fleming was tasked by the War Office to establish a stay-behind capability in southern England in territory likely to be the target of a German invasion. He opened a training school at Coleshill House, near Faringdon, and used the Home Guard Auxiliary Units as **cover** to recruit what was intended to become the foundation of an anti-Nazi resistance organisation that could operate from ingeniously constructed hides in woods, and be well stocked with weapons and supplies buried in local caches.

The same principles were adopted in the post-war era when many northern and central European countries, in fear of a Soviet occupation, made secret preparations to resist, supported by NATO. Norway, Belgium, Italy and the Netherlands developed stay-behind networks, as did the supposedly neutral states of Sweden, Austria and Switzerland.

## STEGANOGRAPHY

The skill of concealing information inside an otherwise innocuous message or image is steganography. In the post Cold War era terrorist organisations adopted the method of hiding images and instructions in ostensibly harmless websites on the internet. Those authorised to access the covert material were entrusted with the appropriate instructions, while others could visit a page, or scrutinise an image, without suspecting that it contained something illicit.

The vulnerability of steganography is that it consumes a significantly larger amount of data and therefore can be susceptible to detection by analytic programs which scan to identify such anomalies.

## STRATEGIC DECEPTION

The concept of deliberately misleading an enemy by providing false information is as old as warfare itself, often a manifestation of opportunism to achieve a tactical goal, but the employment of **double agents** to deliver a fabricated strategic plan is largely a product of the Second World War and, specifically, the success enjoyed in the Middle East by 'A' Force, a military intelligence unit established for the sole purpose of conveying the false impression to the Deutsche Afrika Korps that Allied forces in Egypt were significantly greater than they really were. This was accomplished by constructing, through a series of agent messages purporting to report sightings of military units, a wholly bogus Allied **order of battle**. The overall effect was enhanced by the Allies' ability to skew the enemy's false appreciations by monitoring Axis radio communications, and by the interrogation of prisoners and the study of captured maps and documents.

Deception during the North African campaign, conveyed primarily through the Security Intelligence Middle East double agent code-named CHEESE, proved so effective that a plan to divert Axis attention from the D-Day landings scheduled for the Normandy beaches in June 1944 was drawn up using techniques refined by 'A' Force. Code-named FORTITUDE, the objective was initially to promote potential landing-sites in southern France, Bordeaux and, in particular, the Pas-de-Calais region, and then to suggest that, even after the assault had begun, that it was nothing more than a diversion to be followed later by a major offensive across the shortest part of the English Channel. Central to the scheme was a non-existent First US Army Group which had supposedly been assembled in southeast England.

The British embraced strategic deception to such an extent that it was institutionalised within the Whitehall structure by the establishment in October 1942 of the London Controlling Section (LCS) to supervise and coordinate all Allied deception plans. In conditions of great secrecy, the LCS continued to exist into the Cold War.

The interrogation of senior German military staff after the conflict proved that strategic deception had played a major role in the successful prosecution of the war, and the capability was retained, although NATO had few opportunities to engage in such stratagems. However, according to the KGB **defector** Anatoli Golitsyn, the Kremlin had embraced the principles of strategic deception, known within Soviet doctrine as *maskirovka*, and was intent on presenting peaceful co-existence as a policy to conceal an unchanged, long-term commitment to international revolution and subversion.

Strategic deception is now acknowledged as an essential component of all military planning, and the 1991 liberation of Kuwait in DESERT STORM was accompanied by the promotion of rumours, intended to be believed at face value by the Iraqis, that the Coalition intended an amphibious assault on Kuwait City, whereas General Norman Schwartzkopf's real aim was a left-hook across the desert.

## SURVEILLANCE DETECTION ROUTE (SDR)

Often referred to as 'dry-cleaning', a surveillance detection route is a path through particular streets, shops, parks and **choke-points** taken by either a **case officer** or an agent, for the purpose of identifying any hostile surveillance. For a professional intelligence officer, perhaps working under a category of **cover** likely to attract the local security apparatus, or the attention of an adversarial intelligence agency, the objective is to identify any surveillance without indicating that the surveillance has been compromised, and to shake off the unwanted observation by a method that is itself not incriminating.

For case officers seeking to engage in an **operational act**, perhaps the servicing of a **dead drop**, privacy is essential, and the SDR procedure may take several hours. The agent, on the other hand, may not have the luxury of time, and therefore may be directed to take a particular route before engaging in a potentially compromising act, so that friendly watchers, either on the street or in a **static observation post**, may detect hostile surveillance in time to abort the operation.

## SWALLOW

In KGB parlance the women employed to seduce Western men in an effort to compromise them in a **honeytrap** were known as swallows, while their male counterparts were referred to as **ravens**. Among those known to have been victims in Moscow are the CIA officer Edward Ellis Smith; the French ambassador Maurice Dejean, and the British ambassador, Sir Geoffrey Harrison.

## SWAP

The exchange of intelligence **assets** was established in July 1941 when the NKVD's **illegal** *rezident* in New York, Gaik B. Ovakimian, who had been arrested for breaching the State Department rules about the registration of foreign agents, was deported to Vladivostok from San Francisco on the SS *Kim* in return for the simultaneous release of three men and three women from Soviet gaols, although none had actually been American spies. Indeed, the FBI would come to regard two of the women as espionage suspects.

The six were: Pelacgrya Habicht, wife of the United Press correspondent in Moscow, under arrest on undefined charges; Dr Michael Devenis, a naturalised citizen originally from Lithuania, detained in 1940 as a bourgeois capitalist; Wasyl Cisiecki, an American arrested in Poland in 1939, and sentenced to five years' for illegal possession of firearms; Neonila Shevko Magidoff, wife of an American citizen; Dr Witold Putkowski; and a 10-year-old American child Norman

Wagshal, whose Polish mother had not previously been allowed to travel. Despite the terms of the exchange, Cisiecki was not released; Dr Putkowski moved to Warsaw where he practised as a physician; and Dr Devenis was finally freed in May 1942.

Of the women, Mrs Habicht would come under suspicion after her arrival in the United States for her Communist associations, and her contact with Shura Lewis, known to be close to the NKVD *rezident* in New York, Vasili Zubilin, and his wife. Mrs Magidoff's husband was Robert Magidoff, a naturalised citizen of Russian birth, whom she married after he had been posted to Moscow as an NBC radio reporter. After her release Mrs Magidoff lectured for Russian War Relief and later for the National Council of American–Soviet Friendship. She, too, was known to the Zubilins and after the war, having acquired an US citizenship, travelled to the Soviet Union as an accredited correspondent for the *Courier-Journal* of Louisville, Kentucky. He husband, the author of *The Anger and the Pity*, would be appointed Professor of Russian Literature at New York University in 1961.

Also expelled with Ovakimian was Mikhail Gorin, an Intourist representative in Los Angeles who had been arrested with his wife Natasha after incriminating documents had been found in the pocket of a suit he had absent-mindedly sent to be cleaned. At their trial in March 1939 Natasha was acquitted but her husband had been sentenced to six years' imprisonment.

At the end of January 1961 an informal swap was negotiated when two American flyers, shot down earlier in the same month, were freed to travel to Czechoslovakia in return for Willie Hirsch, a German-born writer and medical illustrator employed by *Life* and *Soviet News Today* under the name John Gilmore. He had been arrested in Chicago in October 1960 after he had been seen in contact with Igor Melekh, an officer accredited to the United Nations. The airmen were the pilot and navigator Captain John B. McKone and Captain Freeman Bruce Olmstead, whose reconnaissance plane, an RB-47H on a flight from RAF Brize Norton, had been brought down over the Barents Sea by a MiG-19 flown by Vasili Polyakov, with the loss of four members of the crew: Major Willard G. Palm, and three **raven** intercept operators, Major Eugene Posa, and Captains Dean Phillips and Oscar Goforth, the last flying on his first operational mission.

It was not until February 1962 that swaps became institution-alised, when intermediaries, among them an East German lawyer, Wolfgang Vogel, negotiated the release of Willie Fisher, **alias** Rudolf Abel, in Berlin for U-2 pilot Francis Gary Powers. This was followed in April 1963 by the release of three CIA technicians, Wally Szuminski, David Christ and Thornton Anderson, who had been arrested in Havana in September 1960 in the act of installing listening devices in an apartment accommodating the New China News Agency. The trio were flown to Homestead Airforce Base, accompanied by a dozen Bay of Pigs veterans, in return for Francisco Molina, a Cuban gunman serving a prison sentence of twenty years to life for shooting a 9-year-old Venezuelan girl during an exchange of gunfire at a New York restaurant while Fidel Castro was visiting the United Nations in September 1960, together with three G-2 men convicted of conspiring to blow up oil refineries in New Jersey and department stores in Manhattan.

Later the same year, in October 1963, two GRU illegal support officers working at the Soviet mission to the UN, Ivan and Alexandra Egorov, were exchanged for two Americans imprisoned in the Soviet Union. They were a Jesuit priest, Walter Ciszek, who had been incarcerated in a labour camp between 1941 and 1955, and then released under restrictions to the city of Norilsk; and Marvin Makinen, a student sentenced in Kiev in 1961 to ten years' imprisonment for espionage. Although Egerov held the rank of First Secretary in the Soviet delegation to the United Nations, and had previously served in diplomatic posts in Ottawa and New Delhi, he did not enjoy diplomatic immunity.

In July 1969 eleven alleged Bundesnachrichtendienst agents, who were actually political prisoners, and three Heidelberg University students, Walter Naumann, Peter Sonntag and Volker Schaffhauser, convicted of espionage in the Soviet Union, were released by the East Germans at the Herleshausen border-crossing in return for the KGB illegal Yuri Loginov, who had been arrested two years earlier in Johannesburg, and Heinz Felfe, a KGB **mole** in the BND who had been arrested in November 1961 and sentenced to fourteen years' imprisonment.

Three months later, in October 1969, Vogel negotiated the release of the British academic Gerald Brooke, imprisoned in Moscow in

April 1965 for distributing subversive literature, in exchange for Konon Molody, alias Gordon Lonsdale, and Morris and Lona Cohen, alias Peter and Helen Kroger, who had been convicted of breaches of the Official Secrets Act in March 1961.

In April 1978 a Soviet spy and former US Air Force NCO, Robert Thompson, who had been sentenced to thirty years' imprisonment in May 1965, was swapped for Miron Mareus, an Israeli pilot captured in Mozambique, and Alan Van Norman, an American student who had been arrested in East Germany in August 1977 and convicted of arranging an escape to the West.

In October 1981 three HVA spies, Gunter and Christal Guillaume, who had been sentenced to fourteen and eight years' imprisonment respectively in December 1975, and a former Foreign Ministry secretary, Renate Lutze, sentenced in 1979 to six years, were handed over to the East German authorities at Herleshausen in exchange for 3,000 exit visas and the release of thirty convicts identified as political prisoners. Also included in the deal were three people serving life sentences, one of whom had already spent thirteen years in jail.

In February 1986 Vogel arranged the exchange at Berlin's Glienicke Bridge of the Russian dissident Anatoli Shcharansky and three prisoners, among them the Czech tennis player Jaroslav Javorský, sentenced in Prague to thirteen years' imprisonment in December 1978 for trying to smuggle his girlfriend to the West; Wolf-Georg Frohn who was alleged to have been a CIA **asset**, and Dietrich Nistroy, a BND agent and former Bundeswehr officer code-named HELWIG, sentenced to life imprisonment in October 1982.

In return for the four, the West freed twenty-four people, among them the StB spies Karl and Hana Koecher; the Polish SB officer Marian Zacharsky; the HVA spy Detlef Scharfenorth, an economist who had been arrested in Cologne in September 1984; Yevgenni Zemlyakov, a member of the Soviet trade delegation in Cologne arrested in April 1985 and sentenced in Düsseldorf to three years' imprisonment; Alfred Zehe, an East German physicist arrested in Boston in November 1983; Alice Michelson, a KGB courier arrested in New York in October 1984; Penyu Kostadinov, a Bulgarian DS officer arrested in Manhattan in an FBI sting in September 1983; and Jerzy Kazmarek, alias Lanusz Arnoldt, an SB illegal arrested in Bremen in March 1985.

In August 1989 there was another intra-German swap, this time involving an East German doctor categorised as a political prisoner, and Manfred Rotsch, an aeronautical engineer who had been sentenced in 1986 to eight and a half years' imprisonment after he had been betrayed by his former KGB **handler**, Vladimir Vetrov. In another exchange in the same year Elke Falk, formerly a secretary in the Federal Chancellor's office, was freed in a swap, months after she had been convicted in May 1989 in Düsseldorf of having spied for the HVA since 1975, and sentenced to six and a half years' imprisonment.

In July 2010 ten SVR illegals, among them Anna Chapman, were swapped for the release in Vienna of Colonel Alexander Zaphorovsky, formerly the head of the SVR's First Department, and KGB retiree Gennadi Vasilenko, and two SIS assets, Igor Sutyagin, and a GRU officer, Colonel Alexander Skrypal.

Most recently a CIA source, Rolando Sarraff Trujillo, was released from prison in Cuba in December 2014 in exchange for three Cuban DGI officers, Gerardo Hernández, Antonio Guerrero and Ramón Labañino, all arrested in Miami in 1998. Sarraff was a former DGI officer who had worked for the CIA for many years and had been responsible for compromising the RED WASP network, later arrested in Florida in September 1998, and the DIA analyst Ana Montes caught in 2001. He was arrested in December 1995 and sentenced to twenty-five years' imprisonment.

When Yuri Nosenko defected to the CIA in 1964 he claimed to have read the KGB's file on Lee Harvey Oswald, and thereby delivered the message, by assertion that the former US Marine was considered an unreliable psychiatric case, that the Kremlin had not been behind the assassination of John F. Kennedy. However, some counter-intelligence experts tripped up Nosenko in his lies and pointed out the inconsistencies in his narrative. The controversy over Nosenko's motives and authenticity became uniquely divisive within the organisation because of the implications. Although he was incarcerated at Camp Peary for twenty-three months, he would eventually be released, compensated and rehabilitated. Nevertheless, some considered the Agency management's *volte-face* to have been an act of expediency rather than professionalism.

**I**

## TAGGING

One method of maintaining discreet surveillance on a target, either an individual or a vehicle, is the use of a tag which allows the person to complete a lengthy counter-surveillance procedure and then, having created a false sense of security, be picked up once again. Cars can be monitored through the installation or attachment of a variety of **beacons**, while people can be sprayed with **spy-dust** or some other chemical that will discreetly attract attention when passing through a **choke-point**.

When John Vassall came under suspicion as a Soviet spy in London, prior to his arrest in September 1962, consideration was given to radiating classified documents and installing sensors at the admiralty's exit doors to detect the illicit removal of restricted material. The proposal was abandoned on health grounds when MI5 was advised that there was no healthy or safe level of exposure to radioactivity that could be measured on a Geiger counter.

In maintaining tight control over the movements of espionage suspects in Moscow, the KGB's Seventh Chief Directorate developed a technique of installing a tiny beacon transmitter in the heel of a suspect's shoes which had been sent to a cobbler for repair. The operational life of the equipment was dependent upon the battery, which required frequent replacement.

## TALENT SPOTTER

An agent who identifies and recommends a potential candidate for recruitment is known as a talent spotter, and if the individual is deemed suitable there is likely to be an encounter for an insider to make an assessment before the process culminates in a **pitch**, or an overt proposal. Generally a talent spotter remains in the background, exercising discretion about the contribution made, but in the post-war era in Britain numerous university dons with previous intelligence experience fulfilled the role and put forward the names of likely recruits.

In Great Britain the Secret Intelligence Service adopted the procedure of having the candidate receive an invitation to an interview with

Admiral Sir Charles Woodhouse at the Foreign Office Coordination Staff at 3 Carlton Gardens. At the meeting the retired naval officer, who had commanded HMS *Ajax* during the Battle of the River Plate in December 1939, would sound out the person about undertaking work 'of a secret nature that could not be disclosed to family or friends', avoiding any direct mention of SIS. Thereafter a further interview might take place before an offer of a place on the Intelligence Officers' New Entry Course (IONEC) was made.

The Security Service also relied on personal recommendations, often from retirees, before future staff were siphoned off during meetings of the Universities' Appointments Board.

## TERMINATION WITH EXTREME PREJUDICE

In August 1969 the *New York Times* alleged that the expression 'terminate with extreme prejudice' was a euphemism then current within the US military intelligence community in Vietnam for **assassination**. However, no supporting evidence has ever been produced, and the suggestion that the term was a variation on a standard employment contract, which refers to the legal expression 'termination with prejudice' remains unsubstantiated by any corresponding file entry. Certainly the Vietnam War, as in many conflicts, produced its own vocabulary, the '9mm retirement plan' being one such popular euphemism.

Another alleged CIA euphemism is 'executive action', as mentioned in a 1961 memorandum from Dick Bissell addressed to Bill Harvey and disclosed by the Church Committee. The organisation was also credited with possessing a 'Health Alteration Committee', which in February 1960 had recommended the assassination of Iraq's prime minister, Abd al-Karim Qasim, with a poisoned monogrammed handkerchief.

## THIRD COUNTRY AGREEMENT

The exchange of sensitive intelligence in a liaison relationship between two intelligence agencies may be on the basis of the restriction that the information may not be shared with a third country without the explicit approval of the originator. Breach of this fundamental condition is likely to lead to a suspension of any further cooperation.

Observance of a third country agreement can lead to difficulties, as happened in Canada in September 2002 when incriminating intelligence was supplied to the Canadian Security Intelligence Service about a terrorist suspect, Maher Arar who was arrested in New York and deported to Syria. Upon his release he returned to Canada in October 2003 to bring a legal action against the authorities, who were prevented by agreement from disclosing evidence originating with the CIA. Arar was later exonerated of any links to al-Qaida by a commission of enquiry, and was paid $10.5 million. The debacle led to the resignation of the RCMP Commissioner Giuliano Zaccardelli who had given conflicting versions of his organisation's involvement.

## THUMPER

In Northern Ireland remote covert seismic sensors designed to detect movement at sites under surveillance, such as arms caches in rural locations, were known as Thumpers, after the cartoon rabbit. The devices were intended to alert the authorities if the weapons and explosives hidden in farm buildings, on which it was difficult to maintain permanent physical observation, were approached or disturbed by terrorists.

## TOMBSTONING

The technique of developing an **alias** identity may begin with a procedure known as tombstoning, which is the acquisition of an authentic passport in a genuine name for an impersonator. The method, sometimes known as a dead-double, was first made public by Frederick Forsyth in his novel *The Day of the Jackal*, in which a professional hitman, planning to assassinate President Charles de Gaulle, prepares a false identity.

Tombstoning requires a survey of graveyards in the required country to obtain the death dates of infants who died so young that they probably did not travel abroad and have a passport application made in their name. Having identified a candidate with a birth date roughly matching the age of the impersonator, a request is made for the relevant birth certificate. Once obtained, a passport application is made in the name of the dead child, but with the current photo of the impersonator. The trick is to find, or forge the signature of, a suitable referee, and arrange a delivery address that will not compromise the recipient.

On the basis that issuing authorities do not reconcile birth and death records, tombstoning can only be detected if a check is made to verify the referee, a very rare, time-consuming and expensive procedure. Once equipped with a genuine passport in a false name, the impersonator can then develop a **legend** and acquire a driving licence, open a bank account and even enhance legitimacy by paying tax.

A good example of tomb-stoning was the Canadian passport held by Konon Molody, the KGB **illegal *rezident*** in London who posed as 'Gordon Lonsdale'. After his arrest in January 1961 Lonsdale's passport was traced and an interview with the doctor who delivered him in Cobalt, Ontario, confirmed that he had been circumcised as a baby, whereas Molody had not.

In 1938 a German spy, Gunther Rumrich, was arrested after he had plotted to steal a batch of passport blanks from the US State Department. In 1954 a corrupt New Zealand diplomat, Paddy Costello, based at the consulate in Paris, supplied authentic passports to a pair of Soviet illegals who posed as a couple, Peter and Helen Kroger, from Gisborne, New Zealand. A search of their home in the London suburb of Ruislip revealed two British passport blanks, a pair of New Zealand passports concealed behind a bookcase and two Canadian passports, issued in June 1956 to James T. Wilson and Jane M. Smith.

Alternatives to tomb-stoning are reliance on stolen passports, which can only be employed as a short-term expedient; 'turn-over' passports donated illegally by the legitimate holder; and an outright forgery, where a counterfeit or altered document is acquired, or the production of a genuine passport by the appropriate authority, but under alias. Fabricating a passport may involve tampering with a stolen blank, or altering the photo or details in the pages of the real item. Neither expedient is entirely satisfactory as the data on the document will not correspond with the record held by the issuing authority. During the Spanish Civil War volunteers fighting in the International Brigade were required to surrender their passports, and often these were not returned. Some later showed up in the possession of Soviet espionage suspects. Similarly, during the 1973 Yom Kippur War, Jews who had travelled to Israel to replace reservists mobilised for military service were invited to donate their passports so they could be exploited by Mossad during **exfiltration** operations.

Some governments have been known to donate genuine passports in false names, and in 1980 the Canadian administration obtained parliamentary approval to participate in an attempt to rescue American diplomats trapped in Tehran.

The imprisonment for six months of Elia Cara and Uriel Zoshe Kelman in Auckland, New Zealand, in July 2004, after they had pleaded guilty to passport fraud, was a demonstration of Mossad's need to acquire third-country documentation, in this case for a third Mossad agent, Zev Barkan, to travel to target countries. Mossad is a large consumer of all types of passports because of the travel restrictions, especially in the Middle East, on all holders of Israeli passports. In those circumstances Mossad *katsas* will routinely possess several passports, although only the best will be used for crossing international frontiers, the others being delivered to an operational area by pouch carried by a diplomatic courier. According to the former *katsa* Victor Ostrovsky, the basement of Mossad's headquarters accommodates a large vault where thousands of stolen passport blanks are stored, together with donated and other real passports, next to a security printing facility equipped with samples of the paper used by various countries for the manufacture of travel documents.

## TRACKER

An electronic device which emits a signal to allow surveillance from a distance, battery-powered trackers may be attached magnetically to a target vehicle so its movements may be monitored by a receiving apparatus, or, with sufficient access and time, more sophisticated equipment may be fitted that may be concealed within the engine compartment or radio, and draw its power from the vehicle's own systems, thus making it more difficult to detect.

Detection of some tracking devices may be made more difficult if they are only activated remotely by an external signal, such as the equipment installed by the FBI during the Cold War at certain **choke-points** in Washington, DC, which meant that a target vehicle, perhaps driven by Eastern Bloc intelligence professionals, could be driven a certain distance before the tracker began transmitting.

Another surveillance technique, for aerial surveillance, was to paint the target car's roof with a transparent solution that reflected under infrared or ultraviolet light, thus making the vehicle easy to identify from an aircraft.

In October 1998 Sinn Féin leader Gerry Adams discovered a tracking device in the wing mirror of a vehicle in which he was driven. In 1999 MI5 fitted integral tracking equipment which transmitted a linear digital satellite signal from the roof, and recorded all conversations held inside a target vehicle, a Ford Mondeo registered to the wife of Martin 'Duckster' Lynch, a convicted terrorist who had been imprisoned in 1982 after the RUC recovered weapons from a car he was driving. Lynch was suspected of having been the intelligence officer of PIRA's Belfast Brigade before he was appointed PIRA's adjutan general.

Conventional trackers were difficult to install because of the time required by technicians to conceal the equipment, which prompted an effort to recruit agents who could provide access to the vehicles. PIRA routinely protected its pool of cars, and employed a notorious enforcer, Paul 'Chico' Hamilton, to supervise security among the bodyguards and drivers, who included Roy McShane, who was recruited as a source by MI5, and Terence 'Cleeky' Clarke.

Hamilton, who acted as Adams's bodyguard for eight years, had been sentenced to twelve years' imprisonment for the attempted murder of a major in the Gordon Highlanders in 1977. Fifty-eight-year-old McShane, formerly the PIRA commander in the Turf Lodge area of West Belfast, and living in the Divis Tower until he was withdrawn by MI5 in 2008, was a divorced father of four.

A total of eighty cars were adapted at the factory, fitted with their own individual rechargeable energy sources and then introduced into the market in Northern Ireland in the expectation that some would fall into the hands of paramilitaries. In the example used by Gerry Adams, the Provisional IRA took four days to dismantle the Mondeo, in which a compromised discussion had been held, for the voice-activated equipment to be discovered.

## TRAIN-WATCHING

During the First World War the British SIS developed an extensive network of agents in German-occupied Belgium, Luxemburg and France, who were employed to observe the movement of trains carrying enemy troops, and to report on railway cars carrying cavalry, infantry and artillery. These expert observations were taken across the Dutch frontier by professional *passeurs* who ensured that the messages were delivered to their SIS **handlers** within thirty-six hours. Details of one of the most successful organisations, LA DAME BLANCHE, were disclosed by Henry Landau in his 1935 account, *Secrets of the White Lady*.

## TRASH COVER

A useful source of information, especially when constructing a suspect's **pattern of life**, is the removal and examination of the household rubbish, also known as 'dumpster-diving', 'trash-trawling' and 'trash archeology'. The procedure involves a swift collection followed by a leisurely combing of the detritus. Even paper that has been shredded can be reconstructed, and the source can provide valuable insights into an individual's home life. However, the act of taking someone's rubbish amounts to theft in many jurisdictions, as ownership is not transferred until the waste material has been collected by the legitimate contractor, so the technique is not without legal hazards. In 1988 a French DGSE officer under consular **cover** was caught in Seattle as he attempted to place the contents of a Boeing executive's trash bin into his car, and there was a similar incident in the Houston suburb of River Oaks in May 1991 when a van registered to the local French consulate was photographed by the FBI as the consul, Bernard Guillet and a well-dressed companion, removed the trash from the home of a defence contractor.

## TREE SHAKER

In FBI parlance a tree shaker is an **asset** who is infiltrated into a target organisation with the purpose of stimulating the membership into action so as to identify activists, extremists and likely criminals, thus allowing limited resources to be concentrated on worthwhile individuals.

The distinction in role between an *agent provocateur* and a tree shaker is a fine one, but generally the latter has no single person to entrap, whereas the former has a more disruptive mission.

## TREFF

The German word for rendezvous, *Treff* has been adopted by the international intelligence community to mean a personal, clandestine meeting held between a **case officer** and agent.

## TRIPLE AGENT

A **double agent** is said to have become a triple agent in two circumstances: either an agent is despatched originally with the purpose of becoming a double agent for an adversary, yet retaining the original loyalty; or a double agent finds a means of alerting their original employer to the fact that they are now operating under the enemy's control. The purpose of the **security check** given to radio operators is so they may alert their correspondent to their true status.

The fact that an agent may work for the intelligence agencies of more than two countries does not mean they have become a double agent. In 1939 Renato Levi reported to the British Secret Intelligence Service that he had been approached by Clemens Rossetti of the Abwehr. His instructions from SIS were to accept whatever role the Germans gave him, and they in turn consulted their Italian counterpart and Axis partner, Count Carlo Sircombo of the Servizio di Informazione Militare. When Levi was sent on an Abwehr mission to France, he reported to the SIS station in Paris which passed control of him to their French allies, the Service des Renseignements. When in 1941 Levi turned up in Cairo, code-named ROBERTO, he was handled by Security Intelligence Middle East and assigned the **code name** CHEESE by his case officer, Evan Simpson. Although Levi worked for five different intelligence services and four different countries, this did not make him a triple agent.

During the Second World War, a conflict in which experience necessarily was gained quickly, all external encrypted communications from London were required to be controlled by one of the two British agencies, MI5 or SIS, and the rule was enforced by the Radio Security Service which monitored the airwaves. The French, Belgian, Dutch, Polish, Greek, Norwegian, Danish and Yugoslav governments-in-exile complied with the demand, and were also required to declare any suspicion of a controlled **asset** to the appropriate British authority. This prohibition on running independent double agents also extended to other British organisations, such as Special Operations Executive, where hostile **penetration** was an occupational hazard.

## TRUTH SERUM

During and after the Second World War much research was undertaken by various intelligence agencies to find a drug that would reduce inhibition in subjects undergoing interrogation to the point that they would instinctively give truthful answers to questions. Much clinical work concentrated on sodium pentothal and another hypnotic, scopalomine, both of which sometimes achieved a state of sedation, drowsiness, confusion and disorientation in volunteer patients, but neither ever proved sufficiently reliable to be termed a truth serum.

During the Second World War MI5's chief psychiatrist, Dr Harold Dearden, who participated in many interrogations conducted at Camp 020, where enemy spies were detained and questioned, recommended a psychological approach to the treatment of prisoners. This proved very effective, although his successor, the noted narcoanalyst Dr William Sargant, advocated the administration of barbiturates to create an atmosphere of euphoria in which an over-confident patient would become uncharacteristically talkative.

Reports during the Cold War that the Soviets had invested heavily in psychotropic drugs, and had synthesised a compound designated SP-117 led the CIA to sponsor scientific experiments in the field. There were also reports that some show-trial defendants, who had made demonstrably exaggerated public confessions, appeared to have been heavily medicated. Then, in 1985, Oleg Gordievsky described how he had been drugged by KGB interrogators at Yasenevo when he had fallen under suspicion as a **mole**. Finally, in 1992 another KGB **defector**, Aleksandr Kouzminov, who had spent the previous ten years in Department 12 of the KGB's Directorate S, supplied further details about SP-117, describing it as odourless, colourless and tasteless.

From 1953 CIA-sponsored experiments with minute doses of the hallucinogen LSD-25 were conducted under a project code-named MK/ULTRA, later MK/SEARCH, until 1973 when the programme, which had involved up to eighty institutions and an estimated 183 independent researchers, was terminated. The operation was acknowledged publicly during the 1975 Church Congressional hearings, and many of the surviving files were declassified and became the subject of a Senate report in 1977.

# TURN

The process of persuading an agent to abandon their controller and adopt the role of a **double agent** is known as **turning**. Credit for pioneering the pre-war management of double agents usually has been given to the French Service des Renseignements, as outlined by J.C. Masterman in *The Double Cross System in the War of 1939 to 1945*, but the psychological techniques for persuading enemy agents to come under control were developed at Camp 020, at Ham Common, by MI5's resident psychiatrist, Dr Harold Dearden, who believed that gentle persuasion, exploiting an innate sense of self-preservation, would achieve better results than threats and coercion, pressure that would engender resentment and lead inevitably to betrayal. Accordingly, although Camp 020's monocled commandant, Colonel Robin Stephens, enjoyed a fearsome reputation and imposed a strictly disciplined regime, he would not allow any mistreatment of prisoners and reacted with anger when Colonel Alexander Scotland was seen to assault an inmate in his cell. Scotland was promptly banned from the entire Latchmere House establishment and reported to a higher authority.

Dearden, who had served as medical officer for the 3rd Battalion, Grenadier Guards, during the First World War, was a distinguished physician and celebrated author, but is probably best known in the intelligence community for developing some of the sensory deprivation techniques later commonly used. These included restricting a prisoner's food, water, light and conversation, to break the will to resist. Decisions regarding the survival or prosecution (and likely execution under the 1940 Treachery Act) of a detainee were not made by Dearden, but he did identify candidates suitable for turning, among the first of whom was Wulf Schmidt, a Nazi spy who was arrested in September 1940 soon after he had landed by parachute in Cambridgeshire. Schmidt later explained that it had been Dearden, who had sat at the end of his bed and offered him a swig from a bottle of whisky, that had convinced him to work against the Abwehr. Thereafter code-named TATE by MI5, Schmidt continued to live under his **alias**, Harry Williamson, until his death in October 1992 at the age of 80. Originally from the most southern province of Denmark, Schmidt became very attached to his MI5 **case officers** and even voted for Winston Churchill in the 1945 general election. Simply put, Schmidt was persuaded that he had been duped by his Abwehr **handlers**, who had shown a ruthless and reckless disregard for his survival, and that the best way to save his own life was to cooperate fully and enthusiastically. His captors also demonstrated to him that his predecessor, Goesta Caroli, was in MI5's hands, and that the organisation already knew a great deal about Schmidt. This information had come from the cryptographic sources ISK and ISOS, although TATE was obviously never indoctrinated into that material.

Turning agents is a complex business and requires an interrogator to win the trust of the interviewee, but almost all the double agents managed by MI5 during the war were willing volunteers, including the most successful of the conflict, GARBO, CHEESE, BRUTUS and TRICYCLE. There was only an element of reticence with the very first, SNOW, but even he initiated the arrangement by volunteering to contact the enemy with a hitherto unknown transmitter.

Arrested at his home on Long Island, New York, and imprisoned in May 1965, Robert G. Thompson was released in a spy swap in April 1978, the only American ever to have been exchanged to the Eastern Bloc. In return, an Israeli pilot captured by guerrillas in Mozambique was repatriated. Although he claimed to be a Soviet illegal, Thompson's FBI interrogators were satisfied that he really was an American citizen born in Detroit who had been serving in the US Air Force in Berlin when he offered himself for recruitment to the KGB. Resettled as 'Gregor Best' just outside East Berlin, Thompson operated as a Stasi agent and engaged in false flag operations against the local US embassy staff by pretending to be a CIA officer.

# U

## UNBILLABLE CALL
A telephone call that goes deliberately unanswered, and is followed immediately by a second call that is terminated after a predetermined number of rings, and does not result in a completed connection, is known as an unbillable call. Such signals will have a pre-agreed meaning, such as 'meet at the arranged rendezvous at midday' but theoretically leave no trace of the contact. However, there is an electronic record of both calls, even if they did not result in a billable connection, the details of which can be recovered from the service provider's metadata.

## UNCONSCIOUS AGENT
Where a source is unaware that they have been recruited by an intelligence agency, they are known as unconscious agents. This is a different concept to the **false flag** where the agent is unaware of the true loyalty or nationality of the organisation which employs them. In 2004 a Russian arms control expert, Oleg Sutyagin, was convicted of espionage, having accepted an invitation to contribute to what appeared to be a legitimate academic journal. He was unaware that the entire enterprise was a commercial front for SIS. A member of the United States of America and Canada Institute in Moscow, Sutyagin was charged with passing information on nuclear submarines and weapons to a British company that the prosecution claimed was a **cover** for the US Defense Intelligence Agency.

While attending an academic conference in King's Norton, near Birmingham in 1998, Sutyagin had been approached by Sean Kidd and Nadia Locke who commissioned him, on behalf of an entity named Alternative Futures, to participate in a consultancy agreement. However, after his arrest by the Federal Security Service (FSB) in Kaluga in October 1999 Sutyagin was accused of having supplied classified information to the DIA in return for a regular retainer of £1,000 a month, from an organisation that consisted of a small **front company** equipped with a fax and telephone answering machine, operated from a suite of rented offices in the City of London. On the occasions Sutyagin visited the offices, a staff of four or five people were visible.

In his defence Sutyagin insisted that his contributions had been drawn from open sources, and never contained classified information. By the time his case had come to trial Kidd, Locke, their colleague Christopher Martin, and the company had disappeared.

In December 2005 Sutyagin was transferred to a penal colony at Kholomogory, but he was not informed in July 2010 of his inclusion in the exchange for ten SVR **illegals** recently arrested in the United States.

## UNDECLARED DEFECTOR

While some **defectors** have been willing to acknowledge their role publicly, others have deliberately concealed their disappearance, either to protect vulnerable members of the family, or to delay the imposition of any counter-measures. When the KGB officer Victor Sheymov was **exfiltrated** from the Soviet Union in 1980 his departure was disguised so maximum intelligence advantage could be extracted from the situation, and went unacknowledged until 1992. When Standa Kaplan defected from the Czech StB in 1973, no public comment was made, although he was used as a lure to encourage Oleg Gordievsky to develop a relationship with SIS in Copenhagen a year later.

## UNDERGROUND MEMBERSHIP

During the Cold War when background security screening and vetting procedures were introduced to identify Communist Party members and prevent them from gaining access to classified information, some parties adopted the expedient of underground membership, setting up secret branches where the membership adopted **aliases**, and their membership records were kept separately from the rest of the party.

## UNDERGROUND RAILROAD

Though not literally a railway, the route taken by evaders in German-occupied Europe during the Second World War was often referred to as an underground railroad. It was actually a series of **safe-houses** through which evaders passed, usually into the relative safety of Vichy territory, or to be guided by *passeurs* across the Pyrenees into neutral Spain. Those managing the routes took considerable risks as there was a permanent danger of **penetration** by the enemy which frequently attempted to insert *agents provocateurs* into the system.

# UNMANNED AERIAL VEHICLE (UAV)

First deployed in the Vietnam War, UAVs, often referred to in the media as drones, offer an aerial intelligence-collection platform. The first generation was the RQ-1A Predator, built by General Atomics Aeronautical Systems in San Diego to fly reconnaissance missions and transmit tactical intelligence in real time to a pair of controllers operating the aircraft remotely. It was flown operationally for the first time over Kosovo in 1999, is 27 feet long and has a wingspan of 49 feet. Since 2001 each Predator aircraft has been armed with two air-to-ground Hellfire missiles, and have been deployed to attack terrorist targets. In November 2001 al-Qaida's military commander in Afghanistan, Mohammed Atef, was killed by a missile fired from a Predator. The missile hit his home outside Kabul and also killed his bodyguard, Abu Ali al-Yafi'i and six others. The Hellfire missile, developed at the US Army's Aviation Center at Fort Ruckner, weighs 101 pounds and is a laser-guided precision weapon.

Operating a UAV in a ground-attack role is infinitely preferable to the alternative, a jet requiring airborne refuelling, perhaps flown from a distant aircraft carrier, with minimum loiter capability over the target area. UAVs, flown remotely from comfortable, stress-free, custom-built booths thousands of miles away, offer many more options and plenty of time to check coordinates, rules of engagement and other requirements before seeking permission to release a weapon. With improved accuracy, the risk of collateral damage is minimised, and the potential for **blowback**, in the form of pilot capture, eliminated entirely.

Another Predator, in the Yemen, destroyed a vehicle in November 2002 in which seven al-Qaida high-value targets were travelling a hundred miles east of the capital Sana'a. Among them was Qued Salim Sinan al-Haethi, known as 'Abu Ali', who had planned the attack on the USS *Cole* and the French oil supertanker *Limburg* in October 2000. In this case the Predator had been launched from Djibouti, and to be quite certain of accurate identification Abu Ali was on his mobile phone in conversation with another al-Qaida terrorist who was in American custody.

Pushed by a propeller, the Predator flies relatively low and slow, typically at 10,000 feet at a speed of 90mph, which makes it vulnerable to anti-aircraft fire, and it is unable to fly in poor weather conditions.

However, it has a long flight duration and can supply a live video link to its controllers, who will have undergone specialist training at Eglin Air Force Base. Each Predator is priced at $3.7million, with a complete system, including four aircraft, costing $25 million.

In May 2005 two more senior AQ terrorists were targeted. Haitham Yemeni was killed by a Predator in Pakistan, and in December Abu Hamza Rabia was killed with five others in their hiding place in north Waziristan.

On 13 January 2006 a Predator fired Hellfire missiles at a house owned by Bakhtpu Khan in Damadola, north-eastern Pakistan, killing eighteen people. The intended target had been the al-Qaida leader Ayman al-Zawahiri, but he was not among the casualties, although five senior terrorists were killed, including al-Zawahiri's son-in-law Abd al-Rahman al-Maghrebi, Midhat Mursi al-Sayid Umar, Abu Abayda al-Misri and Abu Khabab, who had formerly commanded the notorious Darrunta training camp.

The second generation UVA was the Lockheed-Martin RQ-3 DarkStar, a stealth aircraft first flown in March 1996, but the project was terminated in January 1999.

The third-generation UAV is the Global Hawk, manufactured by Northrop Grumman in San Diego, a high altitude reconnaissance platform the size of an executive jet with a wingspan of 116 feet. With a very long range of 10,000 miles and an endurance of up to forty hours at 65,000 feet, each aircraft costs $40 million. Equipped with a variety of sensors, the aircraft's operations are controlled from Beale Air Force Base in southern California, with the imagery processed at the National Guard's 152nd Intelligence Squadron at Reno, Nevada. The Global Hawk proved highly effective during Operation IRAQI FREEDOM when it flew on eighteen consecutive days, controlled by personnel of the 11th Reconnaissance Squadron, based at Indian Springs Auxiliary Airfield. Missions in Iraq have been controlled by the Combined Operations Center at the Prince Sultan Air Force Base in Saudi Arabia.

## UNOFFICIAL ASSISTANCE (UA)

The Secret Intelligence Service can often rely on support from expatriates and others well disposed towards British interests, and this deniable aid is known simply as UA. In October 1956 the CIA station in London, headed by Dan Debardeleben, Cleveland Cram and Chester Cooper, continued to supply U-2 aerial reconnaissance imagery of Egyptian airfields to their British counterparts long after the State Department had issued an ultimatum and withdrawn the US ambassador in protest at the Anglo-French invasion of Egypt during the Suez crisis.

Similarly, in April 1982 Chile's Anglophile director of air intelligence, General Frederico Mattei, authorised the clandestine installation of a Marconi S-259 mobile radar at Balmaceda, complete with an RAF crew, on top of the Andes overlooking the Argentine airfield at Comodoro Rivadavia with range to track aircraft over Rio Grande, the base for Exocet-armed Super Etendards. The apparatus was flown in conditions of great secrecy from the Shetlands to RAF Brize Norton, and then to Santiago, in a successful operation intended to give the Royal Navy's task force advance warning of air raids.

## UNSUB

The abbreviation for 'unidentified subject', the term was coined by the FBI to indicate that a particular individual has not been identified by a true name. Similarly, the NSA adopted the acronym UCN for unidentified **cover** name, followed by a numeric designation, to describe espionage suspects whose Soviet cryptonym could not be established. In such circumstances the counterintelligence staff is likely to look for collateral, as happened with UCN/9 who appeared in seven VENONA texts in 1943. The culprit was a British journalist, Cedric Belfrage, who had been denounced by Elizabeth Bentley as one of her lover Jacob Golos's agents. Based in New York, Belfrage had joined British Security Coordination in December 1941, and his departure to London on 27 May 1943 neatly coincided with a message from the NKVD *rezident*, Nikolai Zubilin, who had referred to UCN/9's return to Britain two days later. Furthermore, UCN/9's **parole** or recognition signal in London, concerned 'Molly', which happened to be the Christian name of Belfrage's wife, herself the author of a cookery book.

According to Bentley, Belfrage's espionage had come to an abrupt conclusion in the autumn of 1943 when he was compromised inadvertently by Earl Browder. Apparently Golos had shown some of Belfrage's material to Browder who had used some of it as the basis of an article in *The Protestant*, a CPUSA-controlled publication. Terrified that SIS might trace the source of the leak, Belfrage had broken off contact with Golos. Significantly, VENONA contained no further references to a source code-named UCN/9 after September 1943.

The money belts containing British gold sovereigns routinely issued to SIS personnel in the Balkans during the Second World War became a source of danger as word spread. One victim was 28-year-old David Russell, a Scots Guards officer and recipient of the Military Cross who had fought at Tobruk with the 1st SAS Brigade. He is thought to be have been murdered by Romanian bandits during a robbery in September 1943 in the village of Varciarove near the Danube, just weeks after he had been parachuted into Yugoslavia on a mission code-named RANJI. His last signal was received on 13 August, but his assignment to make contact with the local resistance was completed in Bucharest by his wireless operator Nicolae Turcpanu, a former signalman from the Goeland Shipping Company. Russell is one of only two SIS officers ever to have been killed while on a mission. The other was Bill Stuart who was mortally wounded during a Luftwaffe air raid on Tito's headquarters in May 1943 while participating in Operation TYPICAL, having been parachuted into Montenegro.

# V

## V-MANN

An abbreviation of *Vertrauensmann*, the German word for confidential source, the term was applied to Abwehr agents before and during the Second World War. *V-manner* were also assigned a **code name** and a four-digit number to identify their individual dossier in the files. Thus the celebrated spy Renato Levi, code-named ROBERTO, was designated V-7501.

## VEIL

In 1982 President Ronald Reagan authorised the CIA, then headed by William Casey, who was also a member of his Cabinet, to develop several **deception** strategies, code-named VEIL and VECTOR, designed to mislead the Soviet leadership about White House foreign policy goals. These **codewords** appeared on documents relating to the project which promoted the belief that the administration had abandoned conventional peaceful co-existence and detente in preference for a more aggressive stance with heavy investment in sophisticated weapons technology.

## VENLO

The **abduction** in November 1939 of two SIS officers, Richard Stevens and Sigismund Payne Best, on the Dutch frontier by the Sicherheitsdienst proved a major embarrassment for the British and created considerable political **blowback** in the Netherlands. The pair had intended to meet a German officer purporting to be part of a well-organised anti-Nazi movement in the Luftwaffe, but were entrapped and remained in enemy hands until the end of the war. Thereafter, anyone purporting to represent opponents of the regime was treated with great circumspection by SIS, and considerable care was taken in arranging *Treffs*. Later described in detail by Best in his memoir *The Venlo Incident*, the episode became notorious as an illustration of the hazards of maintaining contact with shadowy groups that make extravagant but tantalising claims.

# VIGILANCE OF COLLEAGUES

After the arrest of a particularly damaging **mole** a **damage assessment** will likely be initiated to identify what lessons might be learned from the breach of security. At the heart of such a review is bound to be an account of the precise circumstances in which the culprit was caught, but candour in this instance can compromise **sources and methods,** so a euphemism, 'the vigilance of colleagues' is often cited as the reason for opening an investigation. However, it is rare for other intelligence personnel to submit reports describing suspicious behaviour or sudden unexplained wealth, and in reality most **molehunts** are precipitated by a **defector** who, as part of their **meal-ticket,** will offer snippets of information that, when supported by additional research, will narrow the field in the search for a traitor. The defector's contribution will be deliberately concealed, partly in an effort to protect that person's safety by not advertising their value, but also to encourage security awareness and deter others contemplating treachery.

Following the conviction of MI5 officer Michael Bettaney in 1983, the Security Commission reported that he had been identified as a spy by his colleagues, whereas in fact SIS had been tipped off by their **asset** Oleg Gordievsky that the KGB's London *rezident* had received a **pitch** from an anonymous source who had demonstrated access to Security Service files.

When he was Home Secretary in 1910 Winston Churchill signed the very first letter interception warrant for a specified individual, and wrote to all the chief constables urging them to cooperate with Vernon Kell, the newly appointed head of the Secret Service Bureau's Home Department. The procedure introduced by Churchill, allowing each warrant to last just six months unless renewed, would survive largely unchanged until 1986 when Parliament legislated on the issue for the first time. Between 1911 and the outbreak of war MI5 intercepted 1,189 letters to those believed to be involved in German espionage. Suitably impressed, Churchill retained a lifelong interest in, and understanding of, secret intelligence.

# W

## WALK-IN

An intelligence source who makes direct contact with a diplomatic mission to deliver a **pitch** is known as a walk-in, and is generally considered especially valuable as someone who has already self-recruited. The disadvantage is that, depending on the venue, the putative **agent** may have compromised themselves by having been photographed by the local security apparatus which might be expected to maintain surveillance on the premises. To avoid the imposition of an immediate **damage control** exercise, designed to take the appropriate counter-measures to mitigate the loss, some effort may be made to persuade the walk-in to return to their normal duties, at least for a short period, so as to maximise the advantage and **meal-ticket**.

Perhaps the most famous walk-in was Anatoli Golitsyn, from the Helsinki KGB *rezidentura*, who turned up unexpectedly, accompanied by his wife and baby daughter, on the doorstep of the local CIA station chief Frank Friberg in December 1962. He carried with him a selection of recent KGB circulars, and a scrap of paper with details of ten KGB **illegals** he had handled, among them Yuri Loginov. Having served in the KGB's department dealing with information from spies inside NATO he was able to give sufficient information for George Paques and Hugh Hambleton to be identified eventually as **moles**. He also suggested leads to a spy in the British Admiralty who turned out to be John Vassall. However, he insisted that several Western intelligence agencies had been **penetrated**, and revealed that the KGB had adopted a strategy of global **deception** to conceal its true objectives.

According to the **defector** Vitali Yurchenko, when the NSA **analyst** Ronald Pelton visited the Soviet embassy in Washington, DC, in January 1980 to deliver his **pitch** he was smuggled out of the rear entrance, hidden in an embassy vehicle, because the KGB *rezidentura* sought to avoid the FBI surveillance on the building. Aldrich Ames was confident that he could explain the FBI reports of his visits to the embassy as being part of his duties to cultivate Viktor Cherkashin. Some of the Soviets' most important agents, including John Walker in

December 1967 and Ames in April 1985, have been walk-ins. Thus, to deter such people, an adversary's diplomatic premises will be subjected to **wiretaps** and measures taken to interdict those seeking to seeking to make contact by telephone to make an appointment to sell classified material.

Other significant walk-ins include SIS's best agent during the First World War, German marine engineer Karl Krueger who volunteered in Rotterdam; Hans Bernd Gisevius and Fritz Kolbe, both valuable German sources who contacted Allen Dulles, the Office of Strategic Services representative in Berne in January and August 1943 respectively; Gilles Brunet, a senior Royal Canadian Mounted Police (RCMP) Security Service officer in Montreal; Aleksei Chisov, a GRU **illegal** who turned up at the CIA station in Paris in 1955 and was code-named UN/ACUTE; and Commander Dieter Gerhard of the South African Navy who visited the Soviet embassy in London in 1960.

## WATCHER SERVICE

Established by MI5 in 1910, the surveillance specialists who maintain observation on suspects work for a section now designated A4 and work in teams on foot, in unmarked vehicles and from **static observation posts**. Although they are regarded as among the most proficient of their kind anywhere in the world, members of the KGB *rezidentura* in London became familiar with them and reached an unspoken understanding as a professional courtesy, that a certain signal would be given in any pub to indicate an imminent departure, so as to all the A4 staff to finish their pints of bitter. One celebrated KGB case officer, Yuti Modin, claimed that he would always breakfast in the same café to rendezvous with his watchers in London, but would elude them if he had an important *Treff* by simply failing to show up on time.

## WET JOB

The term originated with the Soviets who institutionalised the concept of eliminating opponents with the establishment in April 1943 of Smersh, an NKVD unit created to identify and liquidate people suspected of having collaborated with the Nazis. Smersh, an abbreviation of *smert spionnen* ('death to spies'), was wound up in March 1946 but the NKVD retained the capability in a unit designated

Department 13. However, long before the existence of Smersh, the NKVD had demonstrated its willingness to act as an instrument of the Kremlin by organising the **abduction** and murder of various émigrés, among them the Ukrainian General Simon Petlura, murdered in Paris in May 1926; White Russian General Aleksandr P. Kutepov, grabbed off a Paris street in January 1930; and General Eugene Miller who disappeared in September 1937.

The **assassination** of Leon Trotsky in August 1940 by Ramón Mercader amounted to further proof, is any was needed, that the Soviet state was perfectly willing to sponsors assassination overseas. When Mercader was finally released from prison in Mexico in August 1960 he was feted as a hero in Moscow and decorated.

The Israeli government has also sanctioned assassination as a policy, and Mossad contains an operational branch, Komemiute, which includes a *kidon* ('bayonet' in Hebrew) section staffed by three teams of twelve well-trained killers, usually with Israeli Special Forces experience. Following the massacre at the Munich Olympic Games in 1972 the Israeli cabinet established a secret sub-committee, known as Committee X, which ordered the extra-judicial killing of about thirty-five members of Black September, the breakaway Palestinian group responsible for the atrocity. The operation, code-named WRATH OF GOD, continued for some years. In December 1972 the PLO representative Mahmoud Hamshari was killed in Paris by an ingenious bomb that detonated inside his telephone. In January 1973 al-Fatah's Abad al-Chir died in an explosion under his bed in his room at the Olympic Hotel in Nicosia. In April Basil al-Kubaissi was shot in a Paris street; Three days later Kamal Nasser, Mahmoud Yussuf Najjer and Kemal Adwan were assassinated separately in their three Beirut apartments by thirty commandos that had slipped ashore from six darkened Zodiac inflatables. Three days after that raid Zaid Muchassi was killed by a bomb in his Athens hotel room.

Finally, in July 1974, a Mossad team was arrested in Norway after a Moroccan waiter, Ahmed Bouchiki, had been shot dead in Lillehammer in front of his pregnant wife. Until this last, disastrous shooting, when an entirely innocent man had been gunned down in a quiet residential street in the off-season ski resort, nobody publicly had linked the killings, but the .22 Beretta used to kill with Bouchiki with fourteen bullets was linked by ballistics to the bullets that had killed Wael Zwaiter in Paris and al-Kubaissi in Rome. Although the Norwegian Overaaksingstejeste estimated that at least eleven Israeli agents had participated in the surveillance on Bouchiki, which had incorrectly identified him as Ali Hassan Salameh, only seven were arrested. One, Yigal Eyal, listed at the embassy as a security guard, claimed diplomatic immunity and was expelled; Michael Dorf, the comms expert, was acquitted and the other five (Zwi Steinberg, Marianne Gladnikoff, Sylvia Rafael, Dan Aerbel and Abraham Geimer) were convicted of murder and imprisoned.

Mossad's last victim was Ali Hassan Salameh in January 1979 who was killed in a massive car bomb in Beirut. Salameh had been Black September's chief planner, and was thought to have masterminded the Munich attack.

Other known *kidon* interventions include the attempt on the life of Sheikh Khaled Mashal in Jordan in September 1997, and the murder of Mahmoud al-Mabhouh, a senior Hamas military commander, in his hotel room at the Al Bustan Rotani in Dubai in January 2010. Mashal was attacked as he approached his office in Amman by a *kidon* who sprayed a synthetic opiate, fentaryl, onto his neck. Later in the day the toxin plunged him into a coma but by then a chase had ensued in which a pair of *kidon*, both carrying Canadian passports, had been detained. Two others had fled the InterContinental Hotel to take refuge in the Israeli embassy where four more were in hiding. An infuriated King Hussein then intervened to negotiate a deal which Mossad's chief, Danny Yatom, personally flew into Amman and had a subordinate, Miska Ben David, deliver the antidote, naloxone, to save Mashal's life and secure the release and safe passage home of all six Israelis.

Al-Mabhouth's post-mortem showed that he had been immobilised with an injection between his toes of succinylcholine, a muscle relaxant and anaesthetic also known as suxamethonium, and then he had been asphyxiated.

Not all such Mossad assassinations have been quite so sophisticated. Another murder attributed to *kidon* is that of Dr Gerald Bull, the Canadian ballistics engineer who was found with five bullets in his back outside his Brussels apartment in March 1990. He had designed a huge weapon, with an estimated range of 600 kilometres and a projectile weighing two tons, for Iraq, for intended deployment against Israel, but the project, code-named Operation BABYLON, collapsed after Bull's death.

## WIRETAP

The American term for a telephone intercept, the technique of tapping a landline was illegal until 1934 when Congress passed the Federal Communications Act which made the exploitation of information gained through a wiretap unlawful, but did not actually outlaw the wiretap itself, or regulate its use by federal authorities. Accordingly, the FBI interpreted the law as allowing wiretaps for the collection of intelligence on the basis that evidence derived from the source could not be adduced in court.

The FBI was forced to acknowledge a wiretap in an espionage case in 1946 when a Justice Department clerk, Judith Coplon, came under suspicion of passing classified information (details of the FBI's wiretap targets and current investigations) to her NKVD contact. Coplon, code-named SIMA, had been mentioned in eight VENONA texts, and was placed under discreet surveillance which revealed that she was having an illicit affair with Harold Shapiro, a Justice Department attorney, and that she made two trips a month to New York to visit her parents. When she was followed to Manhattan on 14 January 1949 she was seen to meet a man for dinner who was subsequently identified as Valentin A. Gubitchev, an employee of the United Nations secretariat, and they were watched at two further meetings, on 18 February and 4 March. At this last rendezvous both were arrested, and Gubitchev was found to be carrying an envelope containing $125, while Coplon's handbag revealed a wealth of classified data, including some documents that had been prepared by the FBI as a **barium meal** to test whether Coplon gave them to her Soviet contacts.

At her trial the FBI concealed the exact nature of the 'confidential informant' that had led the investigation of Coplon and she deployed the defence that her relationship with Gubitchev was entirely romantic, and that the information she was carrying was nothing more than notes she had prepared while writing a novel. The prosecution neatly destroyed the 'innocent liaison' ploy by disclosing details of her affair with Harold Shapiro, and she was convicted and received a sentence of between forty months and ten years' imprisonment for conspiring to pass classified secrets to Gubitchev, who was also convicted.

Coplon's conviction was later overturned on appeal, on the technicality that the FBI's telephone intercept had been unlawful, and as the clear impression had been left that the FBI had begun its investigation as a consequence of a wiretap on Coplon's office line, all the evidence that flowed from that source was deemed inadmissable. The alternative was to reveal that the FBI had been led to Coplon by VENONA, but that expedient was considered too high a price to pay, so she was freed to marry one of her lawyers, Albert H. Socolov, and settle in Brooklyn where she opened several restaurants.

The legal status of wiretapping remained unregulated until 1968 when the Omnibus Crime Control and Safe Streets Act gave courts the authority to allow the procedure, noting the president's constitutional power to do the same 'to protect the United States against the overthrow of the Government by force or other unlawful means, or against any other clear and present danger to the structure or existence of the Government'. However, in 1974 the House Judiciary Committee heard testimony that during his re-election campaign in 1972 President Richard Nixon had ordered seventeen political opponents to be wiretapped. This led in 1978 to the Foreign Intelligence Surveillance Act which created a special court to consider applications for wiretaps based on certain declared criteria.

## WOMEN'S INTUITION

Some women are credited with a highly attuned sense of self-preservation, and it is believed they can detect unseen danger. Scientific evidence of this attribute has emerged during the CIA's Pipeliner counter-surveillance exercises when women who had not spotted any hostile watchers had been asked if they had felt they had come under observation. The response of the trainees was such that so many had accurately reported the time they had come under surveillance that it suggests such a **sixth sense** does exist.

When Helen Kroger was arrested in London in January 1961 she was identified by her fingerprints as an American, Leontina Cohen, a KGB spy originally from New York who had appeared in the 1945 VENONA traffic under the code name LESLEY. The FBI learned that she had worked in Manhattan as a governess for the Harry Winston jewellery family, and had used this role as cover, taking her charges, Ronald and Bruce, for afternoon walks, to be in regular contact in Central Park with the NKVD illegal *rezident*, Willie Fisher, alias Rudolf Abel. While Abel painted at his easel, Cohen admired his art and received her instructions concerning the agents she ran, who included the nuclear physicist Ted Hall. The FBI came to suspect, but could never prove, that Harry Winston, who died in December 1978, allowed his family business to launder Russian gems confiscated by the Bolsheviks, and thereby finance Soviet operations in the United States.

# X

## XX

In January 1941 a sub-committee of the Radio Board was established under the chairmanship of an MI5 officer, J.C. Masterman, to manage the information being passed through a growing stable of **double agents**. The Twenty Committee's objective was to request, acquire and authorise potentially valuable items of intelligence which could be delivered to the enemy with the approval of the relevant authorities. The committee met weekly at MI5's St James's Street headquarters on Thursday afternoons, and included representatives of MI5's controlled enemy agents section, designated B1(a) (Tommy Robertson, P.E.S. Finney, Cyril Mills, Ian Wilson); the Secret Intelligence Service (Frank Foley, Martin Lloyd, Desmond Bristow, Harold Blyth, Felix Cowgill, D.H. Ferguson, Stephen Hill-Dillon); London Controlling Section (John Bevan, Harold Petaval, Derrick Morley); the War Office Directorate of Intelligence (Paddy Beaumont-Nesbitt), MI 11 (E.P. Combe, E. Goudie, S.D. Graham, F. Thornton); Home Forces (I.B. Greig, D.W.B. Hogg, J.M. Kirman, Eric Mockler-Ferryman, Brian

Mountain; A.G. Proudlock); the Home Defence Security Executive (John Drew, Sir Findlater Stewart); the Naval Intelligence Division (Ewen Montagu, N.H. Clackson, J. Fenley Halahan, Edward Hastings, Ted Merrett. E.J. Passant, C.N. Shawcross, Peter Peer-Groves); Combined Operations (J.K. Arthur, Geoffrey Wildman-Lushington); Joint Intelligence Committee (Bill Cavendish-Bentinck); SHAEF Ops B (Sam Hood, Noel Wild, Ronald Wingate, Roger Hesketh, Frederic W. Barnes); Combined Operations (E. Neville, G.G. Rice) Air Intelligence (Air Commodore Buss, C. Byron, V. Chappell, Flight Lieutenant Curtis, A.F. Dick, P.L. Plant, G.E. Tennant); with John Marriott, Charles Cholmondeley, Christopher Harmer or Bill Luke from MI5 acting as secretary. The committee met for the 227th and last time on 19 May 1945. Altogether only sixty-five officers ever attended the gatherings, which averaged around a dozen members. MI5's Guy Liddell and Sir David Petrie, the NID's Edward Rushbrooke and SIS's Valentine Vivian visited occasionally. Other officers attending were R.F. Campbell, Major T. Cohen, and Captain the Hon. Leonard Cohen of the Ministry of Economic Warfare.

Although MI5's enemy double agent section, B1(a) was wound up at the end of the war, the XX Committee was re-established in September 1946 and renamed the Inter-Services Combined Intelligence Centre (ICIC) to run channels in the British zone of occupation in Germany and Austria.

## XXX

Also known as TRIPLEX, this source was a joint MI5/SIS enterprise managed during the Second World War by Anthony Blunt (for the Security Service) and David Boyle (for SIS) to acquire the contents of communications recovered from the diplomatic pouches of neutral missions in London. The method adopted clandestine access to the pouches when the courier was distracted by British agents, often male and female prostitutes and volunteers. The resulting intelligence was circulated to a very limited group of indoctrinated personnel in Whitehall, but the operation was betrayed to the Soviets by Blunt, himself an NKVD **mole.**

In the absence of any reliable information from the Royal Ulster Constabulary's Special Branch, the British Army developed its own clandestine methods to identify terrorist suspects. An undercover unit of volunteers established the Four Square Laundry in Belfast in 1971 offering a heavily discounted, twice weekly, domestic laundry service in nationalist neighbourhoods. This enabled covert surveillance to be conducted from the firm's familiar green delivery vans, and the clients' clothes and bed linen to undergo forensic examination for traces of weapons, blood and explosives. The operation was compromised, however. In October 1972 Provisional IRA gunmen ambushed one of the vans in the Dunmurry housing estate and murdered the driver, Sapper Ted Stuart. His companion, Lance Corporal Sarah Jane Warke of the Women's Royal Army Corps, narrowly escaped with her life and later was decorated with the Military Medal.

# Y

## YEZHOVSCHINA

The purge led by Nikolai Yezhov in 1936 became known as the *Yezhovschina*, and, as a manifestation of Stalin's paranoia, decimated the ranks of the foreign intelligence service.

## Y SERVICE

Radio interception is almost universally known by the single letter 'Y', although the term originated in the British Admiralty during the First World War. Thereafter the Directorate of Military Intelligence created the War Office Y Group which established a network of ground intercept sites across the empire.

## Z

**Z**

In 1937 the British Secret Intelligence Service authorised its former **station commander** in Rome, Claude Dansey, to create an **agent** network in Europe, targeted against Nazi Germany, but operating independently of the semi-transparent system of Passport Control Officers. Dansey favoured **journalist covers** and among his first agents were Frederick Voight, formerly the Berlin correspondent of the *Manchester Guardian*; Eric Gedye of *The Times*, his colleague John Evans in Prague and the *Daily Express* correspondent in Vienna, (Sir) Geoffrey Cox.

Dansey also specialised in exploiting commercial fronts, such as Sir Alexander Korda's London Films, a Highgate travel firm, Lammin Tours, and the General Steamship Trading Company.

## ZENIT

The GRU Soviet military intelligence term for a clandestine signals intelligence collection facility concealed inside a Soviet embassy overseas, the KGB equivalent being **IMPULSE**.

## ZEPHYR

According to Tony Mendez, CIA personnel who have undertaken the Pipeliner counter-surveillance course are known as ZEPHYRS and are considered sufficiently trained to be deployed to operations in **denied areas**.

Nigel West has written more than forty books on security and intelligence topics. His highly acclaimed works include *Double Cross in Cairo: M15 in the Great War* and *Operation GARBO: The Personal Story of the Most Successful Spy of World War II*. He has spent the past fifteen years at the Counterintelligence Center in Washington DC.

Reviews for other books by Nigel West:

*A Matter of Trust: MI5 1945–72*
'This fascinating book is so minutely documented that it could only have been written with the assistance of past or present members of the security services' – *The Sunday Times*

*Operation GARBO*
'A classic of espionage' – *Times Literary Supplement*

*GCHQ: The Secret Wireless War*
'West has done a brilliant job' – *Daily Mail*

*Double Cross in Cairo*
'A timely reminder to historians that the SIME archive, though scattered an incomplete, deserves more attention' – *The Spectator*

*At Her Majesty's Secret Service*
'A revelatory and refreshing work with significant new information about the fascinating history of MI6. West is a skilful and entertaining writer' – *Military Illustrated*

*MI5: British Security Service Operations 1909–45*
'The most accurate and informative history of the Security Service yet published' – *New Society*

*MI6: British Secret Intelligence Service Operations 1909–45*
'Authentic history more vivid than most fiction' – *Contemporary Review*

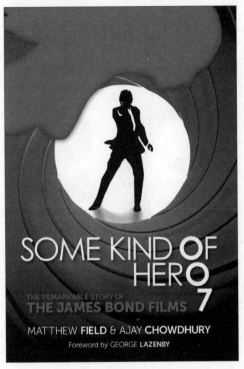

987 0 7509 6421 0

The first biography of the making of the
James Bond films, drawing on over a
hundred new interviews with the cast
and crew.

987 0 7509 6125 7

'Why make out to be something special? Everyone did their bit. I was just young and excited and willing to do anything, except go in the ATS!'